Avant-Garde to New Wave

Avant-Garde to New Wave

Czechoslovak Cinema, Surrealism and the Sixties

Jonathan L. Owen

berghahn
NEW YORK · OXFORD
www.berghahnbooks.com

First published in 2011 by
Berghahn Books
www.berghahnbooks.com

Library of Congress Cataloging-in-Publication Data

Owen, Jonathan L.
  Avant-garde to new wave : Czechoslovak cinema, surrealism and the sixties /
Jonathan L. Owen.
    p. cm.
  Includes bibliographical references and index.
  ISBN 978-0-85745-126-2 (hardback) -- ISBN: 978-0-85745-901-5
(paperback) -- ISBN: 978-0-85745-922-0 (retail ebook)
  1. Motion pictures--Czech Republic--History--20th century. 2. Surrealism
in motion pictures. I. Title.
  PN1993.5.C9O84 2011
  791.43'094371--dc22

                                                                2010052401

British Library Cataloguing in Publication Data

A catalogue record for this book is available from the British Library

Printed in the United States on acid-free paper

ISBN: 978-0-85745-901-5 paperback
ISBN: 978-0-85745-922-0 retail ebook

Contents

List of Illustrations

Acknowledgements

I would like to thank the following people for reading this work either in part or whole, in first or final stages, and for offering their helpful and considered feedback: Petra Hanáková, Jan Čulík, Samantha Lackey, Darren Waldron, Cathy Gelbin, Ricarda Schmidt, György Péteri and the students at the Program on East European Cultures and Societies at the University of Trondheim. Special thanks is due to my doctoral supervisors Lynne Attwood and Katya Young, to my thesis examiners Peter Hames and Chris Perriam, and to Ewa Mazierska, who provided insightful feedback, help in accessing films, texts and stills, and much general encouragement.

I wish to thank Mark Stanton at Berghahn Books for his sound editorial guidance. For the provision of study materials I express my gratitude to Dina Iordanova and the staffs of FAMU library, the John Rylands University Library of Manchester, UCL's School of Slavonic and East European Studies Library and the BFI. Stills have been provided by the Czech National Film Archive, the Slovak Film Institute, Second Run DVD, Bonton Film and Jakubisko Film, and in particular I would like to thank Iwona Łyko, Chris Barwick and Kathryn Havlová for helping me obtain these. All efforts have been made to obtain permission for the use of stills.

An early version of Chapter Seven has appeared in Polish in the journal *Panoptikum* (Vol. 14, No. 17, 2008), under the name 'Współczesny surrealizm czeski i odnowa języka: wczesne filmy Jana Švankmajera'; a truncated and significantly altered version of Chapter 5 has appeared in the Intellect journal *Studies in Eastern European Cinema* (Vol. 1, No. 1, March 2010), under the name 'Slovak Bohemians: Revolution, Counterculture and the End of the Sixties in Juraj Jakubisko's Films'; and parts of Chapter 3 have appeared in an article entitled 'Closely Observed Bodies: Corporeality, Totalitarianism and Subversion in Jiří Menzel's 1960s Adaptations of Bohumil Hrabal', published in *Canadian Slavonic Papers*, Vol. 51, No. 4, December 2009.

This book is dedicated to Helen and my family.

Surrealism In and Out of the Czechoslovak New Wave

Figure I.1 A poet's execution. *A Case for the Young Hangman* (*Případ pro začínajícího kata*, Pavel Juráček, 1969) ©Ateliéry Bonton Zlín, reproduced by courtesy of Bonton Film.

The abrupt, rebellious flowering of cinematic accomplishment in the Czechoslovakia of the 1960s was described at the time as the 'Czech film miracle'. If the term 'miracle' referred here to the very existence of that audacious new cinema, it could perhaps also be applied to much of its content: the miraculous and marvellous are integral to the revelations of Surrealism, a movement that claimed the attention of numerous 1960s filmmakers. As we shall see, Surrealism was by no means the only avant-garde tradition to make a significant impact on this cinema. But it did have the most pervasive influence. This is hardly surprising, as Surrealism has been the dominant mode of the Czech avant-garde during the twentieth century, even if at certain periods that avant-garde has not explicitly identified its work as Surrealist. Moreover, the very environment of the Czech capital of Prague has sometimes been considered one in which Surrealism was virtually predestined to take root. The official founder of the Surrealist movement, André Breton, lent his imprimatur to the founding of a Czech Surrealist group when he remarked on the sublimely conducive locality of the capital, which Breton describes as 'one of those cities that electively pin down poetic thought' and 'the magic capital of old Europe'.[1] Indeed, it would seem a given that Czech cinema should evince a strong Surrealist tendency, especially when we consider the Surrealists' own long-standing passion for this most oneiric of art forms.

However, the convergence between Surrealism and film in the Czech context was long thwarted by such factors as lack of commercial interest, Nazi occupation and, most enduringly of all, Communist cultural repression. In the interwar period members of the avant-garde occasionally realized film projects of their own: the poet Vítězslav Nezval collaborated on screenplays for several feature films, including Gustav Machatý's *From Saturday to Sunday* (*Ze soboty na neděli*, 1931), and the filmmaker Alexandr Hackenschmied even made commercial shorts. Surrealist elements 'escaped' in the 1930s films of the comedy duo Voskovec and Werich, and later in the magical animated films of the 1950s. Even Socialist Realism, with its tendentious idealizations of reality, can exhibit a certain involuntary Surrealism. Yet generally speaking, Surrealism, as a form that had been reviled and suppressed during the Stalinist years, had to wait for the cultural liberalization of the Sixties, ushered in with the reform politics that would culminate in the 1968 'Prague Spring', before it could make its mark on cinema. Surrealism's erstwhile absence from the screen was richly compensated for by the emergence of the Czechoslovak New Wave, one of the most intensely experimental film movements in an era of

---

1. André Breton, *Manifestoes of Surrealism*, translated by Richard Seaver and Helen R. Lane (Ann Arbor: University of Michigan Press, 1969), p. 255.

experimental film movements.[2] If one strand of New Wave experimentation headed in the direction of an ever-greater verisimilitude, the other tended towards fantasy, formal play and the exploration of the inner life. The Sixties climate of innovation and investigation meant that aesthetic practices and ideas that had traditionally been the preserve of the cultural margins could now be transposed to the mainstream. Liberated from the aesthetic constraints of the previous decade, filmmakers were eager to engage with the suppressed cultural heritage of the interwar years, as well as with contemporary negotiations of the avant-garde legacy.

It might be helpful at this point to clarify what we mean by 'Surrealism'. The term itself is a capacious and ambiguous one, having accrued many meanings since this faux-dictionary-entry definition from Breton's original *Manifesto of Surrealism* of 1924: 'Pure psychic automatism by which it is intended to express, either verbally or in writing, the true function of thought. Thought dictated in the absence of all control exerted by reason.'[3] Surrealism has gone through numerous shifts of orientation within the Czech context alone. Indeed with this study I hope to illuminate the diverse and sometimes contradictory ways in which Surrealism impacted on these films. Least controversially perhaps, Surrealism is a movement preoccupied with dreams and other imaginative products, and one that upholds the basic Freudian conception of a subjectivity divided against itself, haunted by the repressed impulses of a seething unconscious. It has long been conventional to consider Surrealism as Breton himself did, as the voice of Eros, a movement embodying and portending 'love and liberation'.[4] The influential critic Hal Foster has challenged or qualified this critical commonplace, suggesting how classic Surrealist art dredges up not only erotic desire but also such troubling phenomena as the compulsive repetition of trauma, considered by Freud a manifestation of the death drive. The attribution of a darker, morbid side to Surrealism is especially relevant when we turn to those variants of the movement outside the Bretonian norm, namely Bataille's 'heretical' counter-tradition and Vratislav Effenberger's postwar Czech grouping, whose

---

2. The national entity within which the 1960s films were made was, of course, Czechoslovakia. Hence, the nationality of these films is, technically, 'Czechoslovak'. There is a case for defining the New Wave, and Surrealism itself, as genuinely Czechoslovak phenomena, in so far as these developments impacted on both the Czech and Slovak regions. The focus of this study is generally limited to Czech cinema and culture, a 'bias' that ensues partly from the greater number of relevant Czech texts, and partly from practical necessities (availability of resources, personal expertise). The one chapter dealing with Slovak cinema focuses on a filmmaker, Juraj Jakubisko, whose work seems both closely connected to, and fascinatingly different from, that of the Czech filmmakers covered here.

3. Breton, *Manifestoes of Surrealism*, p. 29.

4. Hal Foster, *Compulsive Beauty* (Cambridge, MA: M.I.T. Press, 1993), p. xi.

abandoning of the noble, ideal and 'liberatory' was a matter of programme and principle.

What also requires qualification is the stereotype (perhaps more a popular than a critical one) of 'the Surreal' as a condition of airy transcendence or confinement to a world of make-believe. Surrealism asserts the interplay of the imaginary and the real, and ultimately problematizes the very distinction between the two: a dialectically-minded Breton pledged his faith in a mental 'point' where that opposition, along with the other apparent antitheses of 'life and death ..., past and future, the communicable and the incommunicable, high and low, cease to be perceived as contradictions'.[5] Surrealist 'discoveries' are derived from the concrete and everyday, a constant since those original fleeting visitations of what Breton calls the 'marvellous' amidst the quotidian world of boulevards and flea-markets. Supposedly revelatory of a secret order and necessity in reality, marvellous encounters (such as the fortuitous finds of 'objective chance') explode our commonsensical, rationalist apprehensions of that reality.[6] Foster, it should be noted, portrays the marvellous as the projection of 'unconscious and repressed material' toward the outside world.[7] Whatever the case, the 'real' remains a vital inspiration or reference point for the Surreal, and this is true above all of postwar Czech Surrealism, where the material and social worlds become grist to a much more disenchanted poetic mill and a sense of underlying chaos replaces intimations of immanent order.

If this general summary has not involved identifying a uniquely 'Surrealist' aesthetic, then this is in the spirit of practising Surrealists themselves, who scorn the association of Surrealism with particular artistic styles and even deny that 'true' Surrealism constitutes art at all. Filmmaker and animator Jan Švankmajer insists that Surrealism is everything *but* art: 'world views, philosophy, ideology, psychology, magic'.[8] Švankmajer is right to redress such popular reductivism, and indeed there is little artistic uniformity amongst the various manifestations of literary and plastic Surrealism, even considered as a single, long closed chapter of art history: it arguably makes more sense to speak of a shared politics of Surrealism, grounded in steadfast hostility to an essentially ever same 'status quo', than a shared aesthetics. Yet we should not neglect the aesthetic dimension: the Surrealist commitment to authentic self-expression has often mobilised formal innovation, and resulted in works of striking elegance and virtuosity, from the poetry of Nezval and Éluard to the paintings of Toyen and Istler.

---

5. Breton, *Manifestoes of Surrealism*, p. 123.
6. Michael E. Gardiner, *Critiques of Everyday Life* (London; New York: Routledge, 2000), p. 36.
7. Foster, *Compulsive Beauty*, p. 20.
8. Jan Švankmajer, 'Interview with Jan Švankmajer', in Peter Hames (ed.), *Dark Alchemy: The Films of Jan Švankmajer* (Westport: Praeger, 1995), p. 104.

The precise delimitation of what is and is not Surrealist is further problematized by those pre- and post-Surrealist avant-garde movements that share important characteristics with Surrealism. In the Czech context, the phenomenon of Poetism, a native movement that according to its founder Karel Teige anticipated Breton's Surrealism in many ways, exacerbates these problems of identification. Wrong as it is to regard Poetism as merely a forerunner or local variant of Surrealism – the former is distinguished by, among other things, its infatuation with modernity and technological progress, its resistance to Freudian psychoanalysis and its greater formal experimentalism – both movements are also bound by certain qualities, notably their commitment to cultivating the inner life and their foundation of a poetics of irrationality and surprising, 'illogical' juxtapositions. It might, to take another case, seem slightly easier to distinguish Surrealism from the Theatre of the Absurd, despite some overt similarities and the philosophical implications common to both movements from the outset (as discussed in Chapter 2). Yet Czech Surrealism itself grew even closer to the Absurd during the postwar period, at least through such conspicuous characteristics as a propensity towards the mordant and satirical. Surrealism shades into and interacts with its antecedents, contemporaries and descendants, and that interaction takes concrete form in the 1960s Czechoslovak cinema, where the Surrealist presence is often far from 'uncontaminated' by other movements. Determining where one influence ends and another begins can be an arduous task; a single cultural echo may easily be attributable to multiple voices. Nonetheless this study tries, at the risk of overly contentious judgement, to be as specific as possible in invoking avant-garde tradition.

Did the mark of the avant-garde make for a superficial graze or a searing wound? The central aim here is to show that the latter was the case, that the bond forged by 1960s Czechoslovak cinema with the avant-garde, and especially Surrealism, was a profound and fundamental one. That is true not only of the 'organically' Surrealist works of Jan Švankmajer but also of many of the New Wave films, despite Švankmajer's attempts to distance himself from what he clearly sees as the New Wave's ersatz, false or compromised Surrealism.[9] The body of this work comprises a close analysis of the films that exemplify the Czechoslovak cinema's avant-garde tendency at its most interesting, complex and fully developed: Pavel Juráček's *Josef Kilián* (*Postava k podpírání*, 1963) and *A Case for the Young Hangman* (*Případ pro začínajícího kata*, 1969), Jiří Menzel's *Closely Observed Trains* (*Ostře sledované vlaky*, 1966), Věra Chytilová's *Daisies* (*Sedmikrásky*, 1966), Juraj Jakubisko's *The Deserter and the Nomads* (*Zbehovia a pútnici*, 1968) and *Birds, Orphans and Fools* (*Vtáčkovia, siroty a blázni*, 1969), Jaromil Jireš's *Valerie and Her Week of*

---

9. Ibid.

Wonders (*Valerie a týden divů*, 1970) and Švankmajer's short films (the discussion here is largely restricted to Švankmajer's 1960s and 1970s films, with occasional references to later works).

Throughout the analysis use has been made of the insights of psychoanalytic and poststructuralist theory. The application of such critical tools can court accusations of imposing ill-suited and anachronistic theories on 'innocent' texts. To be sure, the ideas of, say, Jacques Lacan were hardly common currency even in the intellectually rich Czechoslovakia of the 1960s. Yet such theoretical frameworks in many ways represent the development of ideas and themes already implicit in the historical avant-gardes. Of course, Freud's psychoanalysis was itself of foundational importance for Surrealism; Lacan and Georges Bataille came to intellectual maturity within the broader milieu of the French Surrealist movement, and Julia Kristeva developed her conception of 'poetic language' in relation to avant-garde literature. In the Czech context specifically, the structuralist movement and the artistic avant-garde were closely connected with one another from the beginning. Psychoanalysis and poststructuralism are important here because they provide a vocabulary with which to discuss the aesthetics, concerns and 'discoveries' of Surrealism or Poetism, and help to identify theoretically what the avant-garde artists, and New Wave filmmakers, grasped intuitively. This approach best illuminates the transgressive (then and now) ideas at the heart of these films, focused as the latter are around desire, subjectivity, childhood, social or political authority, the imagination and, in its broadest sense, language.

Regrettably, most of those ideas or themes have seldom been explored in critical studies of the Czechoslovak New Wave, at least not in any sustained way. In part the present study grew out of a frustration with the existing critical literature, or lack thereof, on Czech and Slovak cinema (and indeed on East and Central European cinema more generally). To this day there are only a handful of book-length studies of the Czech New Wave in English, the best-known and most significant of which are Josef Škvorecký's *All the Bright Young Men and Women: A Personal History of the Czech Cinema* (1971) and Peter Hames' *The Czechoslovak New Wave* (1985; second edition 2005).[10] Škvorecký's book is, as its subtitle suggests, a personal account of those friends and collaborators that comprised the New Wave. It is an anecdotal work,

---

10. Škvorecký, *All the Bright Young Men and Women: A Personal History of the Czech Cinema*, translated by Michael Schonberg (Toronto: Peter Martin Associates, 1971); Hames, *The Czechoslovak New Wave* (London: Wallflower, 2005). The other texts are Jaroslav Boček's *Modern Czechoslovak Film* (Brno: Artia, 1965, translated by Alice Denešová) and *Looking Back on the New Wave* (Prague: Československý Filmexport, 1967), Jan Žalman's *Films and Filmmakers in Czechoslovakia* (Prague: Orbis, 1968) and Langdon Dewey's *Outline of Czechoslovakian Cinema* (London: Informatics, 1971), though these works are less studies than cursory guides.

entertaining and informative, yet it scarcely offers in-depth criticism. Moreover, its date of publication denies it the benefits of hindsight, as is the case with most of the other studies. Peter Hames' book amply fulfils its aim of providing a comprehensive, well-informed and clear overview of the New Wave, and Hames' critical judgements are always sound and perceptive. Yet, important as Hames' work is, a space still exists for intensive, focused studies of New Wave films. The dearth of sustained criticism is really no less grave in Czech scholarship. The fourth volume of the series *The Czech Feature Film* (*Český hraný film*, 2004) deals with the 1960s, yet these books are documentary in nature. A recent critical work co-authored by Zdena Škapová, Stanislava Přádná and Jiří Cieslar, *Diamonds of the Everyday* (*Démanty všednosti*, 2002), might claim the function of a definitive volume on the Czechoslovak New Wave.[11] Yet, in addition to being much less informative and exhaustive than Hames' book, this work's critical approach is somewhat pedestrian, with the authors settling for an essentially descriptive analysis of the various technical, narrative and thematic innovations of the New Wave. Disappointingly, in view of its recent date of publication, the book makes no use of contemporary theoretical perspectives.

Another problem that has afflicted writing on Eastern bloc cinema, English-language writing at least, is an excessive tendency to treat films as an adjunct of politics. In such studies as Daniel Goulding's *Liberated Cinema: The Yugoslav Experience* (1985) and the anthology volume *The Red Screen: Politics, Society, Art in Soviet Cinema* (1992, edited by Anna Lawton), films are regarded either as a conduit of official discourse, or as a forum for critique and dissent. This tendency can also be seen in studies of other artistic media, such as Alfred French's *Czech Writers and Politics: 1945–1969* (1982). Such an approach is particularly ill-suited to the Czech culture of the Sixties, which to a large extent was concerned precisely with breaking free of politics in its narrowest sense by asserting the importance of other aspects of existence. The Polish filmmaker Kazimierz Kutz once complained about Western attitudes towards Polish cinema during the Cold War, arguing that Polish films 'never had to compete intellectually': 'we were allowed to enter salons in dirty boots to describe communism, which the public wished a quick death'.[12] A similar attitude has long pertained to the other national cinemas of Eastern and Central Europe. This is not to deny the value and validity of the previously cited works, but rather to assert that there is a place for studies that look beyond the films' immediate socio-political context. Film scholarship is

---

11. Stanislava *Přádná, Zdena Škapová and Jiří Cieslar, Démanty všednosti: Český a slovenský film 60. let: Kapitoly o nové vlně* (Prague: Pražská scéna, 2002).
12. Kazimierz Kutz, quoted in Marek Haltof, *Polish National Cinema* (New York; Oxford: Berghahn Books, 2002), p. xii.

accustomed to dealing with such subjects as desire, sexual politics and radical aesthetic practices in relation to US or French cinema; where, then, are the books dealing with Czech (or Polish, or Hungarian) films in the same terms? Individual essays are to be found here and there that adopt such an approach: in the case of the Czech New Wave, Herbert Eagle has written sophisticated pieces on *Daisies* and *Closely Observed Trains*, the former essay dealing with the influence of Dada and Structuralism on Chytilová's film; Tanya Krzywińska has written a psychoanalytically oriented essay on *Valerie and Her Week of Wonders* for the (sadly now apparently defunct) online journal *Kinoeye*, where a number of interesting and original studies of Central and East European cinema have appeared; and Bliss Cua Lim and Petra Hanáková have both published excellent, theoretically informed appreciations of *Daisies*. Švankmajer's work, as always, constitutes something of an exception here, as in recent years there has been a relatively large amount of high quality criticism dealing with Švankmajer's aesthetic and philosophical concerns: most notably Peter Hames' admirably varied anthology *Dark Alchemy: The Films of Jan Švankmajer* (1995), but also individual pieces by Michael O'Pray, Paul Wells, Michael Richardson and David Sorfa.[13]

Certainly there is some justification for treating Eastern bloc films as symptomatic of political realities. The politicization of East European art is something for which the East European regimes themselves are largely responsible in the first place. A totalizing political culture transforms all activities into political gestures, of assent or dissent, and it seems such an attitude is contagious. In *The Book of Laughter and Forgetting* (*Kniha smíchu a zapomnění*, 1979), Milan Kundera relates an anecdote from the time of the 1968 Warsaw Pact invasion of Czechoslovakia, ordered by a Soviet Politburo anxious to halt the Dubček government's ambitious reforms and reverse an unprecedented liberalization. One man sees another man vomiting, to which the first responds, 'I know just what you mean'.[14] Yet a narrowly political approach is more apposite to some periods and countries than to others: the

---

13. Michael O'Pray, 'Surrealism, Fantasy and the Grotesque: The Cinema of Jan Švankmajer', in James Donald (ed.), *Fantasy and the Cinema* (London: BFI Publishing, 1989); Paul Wells, 'Animated Anxiety: Jan Švankmajer, Surrealism and the "Agit-Scare"', *Kinoeye*, Vol. 2, Issue 16, 21 October 2002 (http://www.kinoeye.org/02/16/wells16.php) (retrieved 20 September 2008); Michael Richardson, *Surrealism and Cinema* (Oxford; New York: Berg, 2006) (see chapter 8: 'Jan Švankmajer and the Life of Objects'); David Sorfa, 'The Object of Film in Jan Švankmajer', *KinoKultura*, Special Issue 4, Czech Cinema (Nov. 2006); David Sorfa, 'Architorture: Jan Švankmajer and Surrealist Film', in Mark Shiel and Tony Fitzmaurice (eds), *Screening the City* (London: Verso, 2003).
14. Milan Kundera, *The Book of Laughter and Forgetting*, translated by Michael Henry Heim (Harmondsworth: Penguin, 1983), p. 7.

constraints pertaining to Czechoslovakia or Yugoslavia during the 1960s were hardly those pertaining to the Soviet Union in the 1930s. To focus overwhelmingly on overt politics in the case of the Czech New Wave would be to miss the point that the New Wave was frequently oppositional and subversive precisely for exploring themes and asserting ideas that were neglected and even rendered taboo during the previous decade. Moreover, the reduction of these films to 'Aesopian fables' concerning the immediate political situation means also reducing politics itself to the day-to-day misadventures of totalitarian bureaucracies. The Czech philosopher Karel Kosík argued that the 'political, critical, revolutionary essence' of Czech culture in the 1960s 'did not consist of subtle political allusions nor explicit criticism of the political situation nor of veiled attacks on government leaders': '[T]hose were superficial, ephemeral things. The real, fundamental polemic of our culture lay in the fact that against the official … concept of Man, it put forth an entirely different concept of its own'.[15] The Sixties culture 'began to emphasise such basic aspects of human existence as the grotesque, the tragic, the absurd, death, laughter, conscience, and moral responsibility', phenomena that 'the official ideology had simply refused to acknowledge'.[16] While challenging the suggestion that the Czech culture of the Sixties universally reinforced Kosík's own humanist philosophical formulations, the present study would concur that the New Wave's polemic with its own society went deeper than direct political critique.

Of course, the Czech and Slovak filmmakers were faced with an obstacle that their politically and aesthetically radical Western counterparts never encountered: the repressive cultural practices of the Communist state, still operative, if less restrictively so, in Czechoslovakia for much of the 1960s. To what extent did the various confrontations with officialdom reflect an accurate understanding of these films and their subversive content? The struggle between the authorities and artistic dissidents was far from an even match intellectually speaking. In the case of films that were banned, suppressed or denounced, we must account for a large degree of stupidity, arbitrariness, literal-mindedness and plain wrong-headedness. In a 1966 diary entry, the director and screenwriter Pavel Juráček, pondering the fate of his latest project, lists the paranoid and foolish accusations made by various Party and industry authorities against the New Wave:

When they see in Ivan Vyskočil's moustache an allegory of Lenin, when they assert that *Slavnost* [Jan Němec's *The Party and the Guests* (*O slavnosti*

---

15. Karel Kosík, in Antonín J. Liehm (ed.), *The Politics of Culture*, translated by Peter Kussi (New York: Grove Press, 1971), p. 398.
16. Ibid., p. 399.

a hostech, 1966)] is a film about the hunt for Evald Schorm,[17] when in *Mučednici* [Němec's *Martyrs of Love* (*Mučednici lásky*, 1966)] they see Catholic mysticism and in *Sedmikrásky* [*Daisies*] 'a work foreign to our ideology' and when they consider all of us the agents of Kennedy's cultural offensive, then it's simple enough to figure out what is going to happen.[18]

No doubt there is some comfort in knowing that one's work has been suppressed for *aesthetic* reasons, yet this frequently seems not to have been the case. As in other *forms* of the state socialist system, entropy often reigned. The reason why many films were disliked seems to have been simply the fact that they were difficult to understand: *Daisies, Martyrs of Love, Valerie and Her Week of Wonders* and various films by Švankmajer were all denounced at one time or another as incomprehensible. This conflicted with the Socialist Realist precept that art should always be easy to understand: as goes the Czech joke made famous by Philip Roth, 'socialist realism consists in writing the praise of the government and the party in such a way that even the government and the party will understand it'.[19]

Of course, to some extent the objection to 'difficult' works derived from the fear that filmmakers might be smuggling in dissident messages safely wrapped up in impenetrable aesthetic forms. Yet, at the same time, this objection does reflect a degree of perverse appreciation. That very resistance to easily comprehensible and unambiguous meaning by many of these filmmakers should be seen as a significant and subversive quality, suggesting that reality is itself never fully comprehensible and legible, but always opaque, ambiguous and multifaceted. Perhaps behind that disapproval of 'difficult' aesthetics there lay a more substantial intellectual disagreement than is usually assumed. One might even suggest that the authorities were sometimes intuitively correct in their denunciation of certain films as subversive and 'foreign to our spirit', even if their objections could not be fully articulated. Yet one must also reckon with the fact that cultural censorship in Czechoslovakia, especially after the onset of Normalisation in 1969, frequently had more to do with the artist and his or her political sympathies, real or supposed, than with anything in the work itself. Censorship was more often a phenomenon dominated by the ad hominem, contingent and haphazard than a form of punitive critical exegesis. Thus it would be unwise to get too closely involved with tracing why this or that film was suppressed or criticized. In any case it ill-serves these complex and sometimes demanding texts to put them at the mercy of official interpretation.

---

17. A prominent, and controversial, New Wave director who plays the role of a dissident in *The Party and the Guests*.
18. Pavel Juráček, *Deník 1959–1974*, edited by Jan Lukeš (Prague: Národní Filmový Archiv, 2003), p. 456.
19. Carlos Fuentes, *Myself With Others: Selected Essays* (London: Picador, 1989), p. 167.

Appropriation or Recuperation? From the Underground to the Mainstream

The New Wave's experiments formed part of a wider engagement with the avant-garde by the mainstream Czech culture of the 1960s. This absorption of underground into 'overground' was a source of displeasure not only for neo-Stalinists and cultural conservatives but also, strange as it may seem, for the Czech Surrealists themselves, who considered such acceptance as yet another threat from a nebulous and pervasive 'establishment'. In a 1968 lecture, the Surrealist writer Zbyněk Havlíček warned against the 'old-new principle of modishness' that had ensued from the 'bankruptcy of the market of values'.[20] Quoting from another Surrealist, Jean Schuster, Havlíček suggested that Surrealism and the avant-garde had themselves fallen victim to this principle: 'the unusual applies as a recipe for painting, shock, the dream-like or provocation are the ingredients of the new literature, political pseudo-radicalism supports careers'.[21] The leader of the postwar Czech Surrealists, Vratislav Effenberger, saw the new taste for the avant-garde among artists and critics as indicative of a facile 'eclecticism' that was nothing but the reverse-side of the Stalinist hyper-uniformity that it had replaced. In other words, the Surrealists saw the popular appropriation of their movement as shallow, recuperative, another tactic of the cultural 'market' whose existence impinged on all authentic moral and spiritual values. Undeniably, Effenberger and Havlíček were prescient in attacking the commodification of Surrealism: from today's perspective, when the most hackneyed visual tropes of Surrealism, Dada and the Sixties counterculture are present in everything from television advertisements to music videos, such observations seem ever more relevant. This process of commodification is one in which the mannerisms and stock images of Surrealism, or its sibling movements, are severed from the qualities that made these movements original and subversive: psychic insight, socio-political critique, the perception of the marvellous within the everyday, intensive formal experimentation. In a sense this process illustrates the distance between 'Surrealist', a precise critical category, and 'surreal', the now ubiquitous synonym for weird, bizarre, funny-peculiar. Does the Czechoslovak New Wave represent another instance of such commodification? Does a film such as *Valerie and Her Week of Wonders* or *Josef Kilián* qualify as Surrealist, or merely surreal?

The larger issue here is whether avant-garde aesthetics or ideas can ever be incorporated into a commercial mass medium without some sort of compromise. In one obvious sense, the notion of 'commercialisation' seems

---

20. Zbyněk Havlíček, *Skutečnost snu*, edited by Stanislav Dvorský (Prague: Torst, 2003), p.218.
21. Jean Schuster, quoted in Havlíček, *Skutečnost snu*, p. 219.

inappropriate in regard to the New Wave: were not these films produced within an entirely state-controlled film industry that protected filmmakers from the vulgarising pressures of the marketplace? It is worth noting that members of the Czech avant-garde itself, including Karel Teige and Vladislav Vančura, promoted the creation of a nationalised film industry in the 1930s and 1940s, clearly in the hope that state funding would enable the creation of a cinematic avant-garde that would approximate modern developments in literature and painting. Of course, the nationalised industries of Communist states brought their own complications: even in the more liberal era of the 1960s, Czechoslovak filmmakers were at the mercy of political concerns, as well as the intelligence of often unsophisticated and culturally conservative bureaucrats. Additionally, Communist bureaucrats were not always averse to measuring a film's worth in terms of its commercial success, something that may be attributed both to the official precept that culture always be accessible for the masses and to straightforward economic interests. Ironically, the success that the more experimental Czechoslovak films enjoyed with international audiences was no doubt partly what made them tolerable to the authorities: in his autobiography Miloš Forman amply attests to the change that took place in official attitudes once a film had scooped some prestigious foreign prize.[22] Such recognition also meant plaudits for the regime. Michal Bregant describes the New Wave as an 'official' version of the avant-garde, fostered as a means of gaining a good image for Czechoslovak Communism abroad: 'The state needed positive representation on the outside and the so-called young cinema of the Sixties, which got an exceptionally positive reception around the world, was used as evidence of the liberal basis of communist cultural politics'.[23] Without disputing the 'artistic value' of the New Wave films, Bregant argues that the New Wave was implicated in the system from which it ostensibly stood apart: '[t]he films of the new wave were in essence not an alternative to the dominant stream, but a part of it, situated within the confines of what was permitted'.[24] Thus, totalising Communist power at once created and contained its own artistic opposition: for Bregant, the New Wave's conditions of production mean that it cannot attain the status of an authentic cultural 'alternative'.

Yet the strict opposition between the commercialised mainstream and a 'pure' underground sits oddly with the enthusiasm that many Surrealists and avant-gardists have held for the products of industrial cinema. The Parisian Surrealists were famously enthusiastic moviegoers, and far from baulking at

22. Miloš Forman and Jan Novák, *Turnaround: A Memoir* (London: Faber, 1994).
23. Michal Bregant, 'Skutečnější než realita: Alternativy v českém filmu', in Josef Alan (ed.), *Alternativní kultura: Příběh české společnosti 1945–1989* (Prague: Nakladatelství Lidové noviny, 2001), p. 423.
24. Ibid.

the more populist manifestations of cinema they seemed to find their own concerns and aesthetic principles manifested precisely in the most unrespectable and artistically suspect genres. A Surrealist pantheon of cinema would include Charlie Chaplin, Harry Langdon, the Marx Brothers, Mack Sennett, and such popular films as Cooper and Schoedsack's *King Kong* (1933) and Henry Hathaway's romantic melodrama *Peter Ibbetson* (1935). In his Devětsil period Karel Teige lauded Chaplin as one of the two great heroes (with Lenin) of the modern world, and the Czech Surrealist Petr Král has written a passionate, book-length exegesis of silent film comedy. Effenberger and Švankmajer have even praised the work of several New Wave filmmakers. However, they have favoured precisely those filmmakers whom one might associate with the 'realist' or '*vérité*' tendency of the New Wave: Forman, the documentarist Karel Vachek, and the early Chytilová. According to Effenberger, Forman's films cruelly satirise the worst aspects of the 'petty Czech citizen' and thereby strike 'exactly those centres of spiritual wretchedness, from which spring essentially all kinds of Fascisms and Stalinisms'. Effenberger further posits that, 'in [his] active understanding of reality, in this feeling for contemporary forms of aggressive humour, and for the critical functions of absurdity', 'Forman's work meets the most advanced functions of modern art'.[25] The praise for such films as Forman's suggests not only that 'the most advanced functions of modern art' can manifest themselves within the mainstream but also that a film can exhibit Surrealist qualities even if its maker was not consciously influenced by Surrealism at all. Conversely, however, a film that *is* consciously intended as a Surrealist film might turn out to be anything other than Surrealist – especially, as Švankmajer might suggest, when a filmmaker simply equates Surrealism with a particular artistic style.

Further examples of unwitting Surrealism can be found in Czechoslovak cinema. The great animator Jiří Trnka, despite having developed a very different animated technique from that of Švankmajer, might lay claim to a Surrealist sensibility, whether with the oneiric concerns of *A Midsummer Night's Dream* (*Sen noci svatojánské*, 1959) or the imaginative anti-Stalinist allegory of *The Hand* (*Ruka*, 1965). One might even assert that a film like Václav Vorlíček's critically neglected comic fantasy *Who Wants to Kill Jessie* (*Kdo chce zabít Jessii*, 1966) has Surrealist qualities. In Vorlíček's film, a trio of American-style comic-book characters escape from the dreams of the film's protagonist into real life, courtesy of a bizarre invention designed to eliminate bad dreams. While overtly light-hearted and having little to do with the New Wave, various aspects of the film – the grotesque parody of the utopian aspirations of science and of state attempts to regulate human activity, the disruption of 'bourgeois' order by the three superheroes, and of course the superheroes' repeated declaration 'freedom

---

25. Vratislav Effenberger, 'Obraz člověka v českém filmu', *Film a doba*, No. 7, 1968, p. 351.

for dreams!' – can conceivably be described as Surrealist. Furthermore, as a tribute to popular culture *Who Wants to Kill Jessie* is more successful than Jan Němec's New Wave *Martyrs of Love*, in which the various trappings of popular genres are worked through a portentous cinematic style.[26] Němec's film is generally reckoned to be a film in the Poetist tradition, yet it is Vorlíček who best approximates Devětsil's celebration of all that is most vital, modern and indeed subversive in popular culture. *Martyrs of Love*, a film that pays tribute to silent film comedy while seldom being funny itself, presents popular culture not in its vitality and modernity but as a quaint object of nostalgia, ghostly in the half-life of retrospect.

Yet the best of the avant-garde-inspired New Wave films avoid either making excessive compromises to mainstream tastes or reducing their avant-garde flavour to a few clichéd motifs and stylistic tics.[27] In a number of New Wave films the inspiration in question is most obviously that of a literary source: *Closely Observed Trains*, *The Miraculous Virgin*, *Marketa Lazarová*, *The Cremator*, *Larks on a String* and *Valerie and Her Week of Wonders* are all adaptations of avant-garde or at least modernist fictional works. However, that does not necessarily mean that the avant-garde credentials of these films are merely secondhand: most of these films use their source works as a pretext for forging an original and sometimes highly experimental visual language and as a means to comment critically on the present. Furthermore, the disapproval of, or lack of interest in, the New Wave expressed by the Czech Surrealists should not prejudice us *a priori* against these films. It could be suggested that Effenberger's preference for Forman over other New Wave directors springs from the affinities between Forman's sensibility and that of Effenberger's own group, committed as the latter was to the 'critical functions' of the imagination and an emphatic concreteness. As we shall see, the Czech avant-garde encompassed many different styles and viewpoints. The hazy lyricism and fluid stylistic refinement of a film such as *Valerie and Her Week of Wonders* could not be more anathema to Effenberger and his associates, but does that disqualify this film as a work of Surrealism? It will even be contended in the

---

26 Jim Knox, 'A Report on the 13th Brisbane International Film Festival', *Senses of Cinema*, September 2004 (http://www.sensesofcinema.com/contents/festivals/04/33/biff2004. html) (retrieved 10 November 2007).

27 In addition to the works analysed in this study are such films as Němec's *Diamonds of the Night* (*Démanty noci*, 1964) and *The Party and the Guests* (1966), František Vláčil's *Marketa Lazarová* (1967), Menzel's *Larks on a String* (*Skřivánci na niti*, 1969) and Chytilová's *The Fruit of Paradise* (*Ovoce stromů rajských jíme*, 1969). Juraj Herz did not class himself among the New Wave, but his extraordinary historical grotesque *The Cremator* (*Spalovač mrtvol*, 1968) deserves consideration in this context. Slovak New Wave cinema offers Štefan Uher's *The Miraculous Virgin* (*Panna zázračnica*, 1966), Jakubisko's *See You in Hell, My Friends!* (*Dovidenia v pekle, priatelia*, 1970–1990), and Dušan Hanák's *322* (1969) and *Pictures of an Old World* (*Obrazy starého sveta*, 1972).

discussion of Chytilová's *Daisies* that Effenberger has essentially failed to appreciate the subversive aesthetic practices of that film. Whether all of the films studied here are 'authentic', pure embodiments of Surrealism or the avant-garde is perhaps something best left to the individual viewer. That all of these films are in their own way complex, original and oppositional works is something that this volume will attempt to show.

The Politics of Irrationality:
Critical Aspects of Avant-Gardism

The most obvious connection between the avant-garde and the New Wave is to be found at the aesthetic level. This connection should be seen as the result both of the direct influence of the historical and contemporary avant-gardes, and of an intellectual environment that fostered the cultivation of avant-garde experiment: the Prague Structuralist movement was resurrected in the liberalised Czechoslovakia of the mid-1960s, and new critical approaches that were then circulating around Europe, including reader-response theory and French semiotics, penetrated Czechoslovak culture. That the experiments of the New Wave were a reaction against the norms of the previous decade should also be noted. Such postwar Czech Surrealists as Effenberger disdained any concern with the 'autonomous' role of aesthetics as frivolous and politically irresponsible; nonetheless, decisions regarding artistic form can have their own epistemological and philosophical (and therefore political) implications. Umberto Eco has even argued that '[t]he real content of a work is the vision of the world expressed in its way of forming'.[28] Of course, the more experimental New Wave films were subversive not only of Socialist Realism but of classical aesthetics more generally, and thus represent a break both with obviously propagandistic works such as Bořivoj Zeman's 'Mr. Anděl' films and with such excellent and undogmatic but conventional films as Jiří Weiss's *Romeo, Juliet and Dark* (*Romeo, Julie a tma*, 1960). While the incorporation of aesthetic codes into official dogma forces the issue of the political dimension of aesthetic form, it could be said, as Eco does, that this dimension is present anyway, even in the most enduring and apparently apolitical of artistic conventions.

One component of this aesthetic shift was the tendency towards a greater narrative and interpretative openness. This tendency is present even in the more realist or formally conservative films of the New Wave. It operates visually in Forman's work, for instance in the crowded images of *The Firemen's*

---

28. Umberto Eco, *The Open Work*, translated by Anna Cancogni (Cambridge, MA: Harvard University Press), p. 144.

Ball (*Hoří, má panenko*, 1968) that present us with multiple loci of action and thus compel or enable us to select our own objects of attention. In its most extreme form (in, say, *The Fruit of Paradise* or *Valerie and Her Week of Wonders*), this tendency manifests itself in that radical indeterminacy of meaning that, for Eco, makes a work of art an 'open work'. In certain cases the cultivation of such openness is, at least on one level, an attempt to approximate the radically ambiguous discourse of dreams, though it is also significant in itself. Ambiguity is nowhere so unwelcome as in Socialist Realism, where the desire to manipulate the spectator's thoughts and feelings in a particular way is reinforced by the para-aesthetic goal of ideological persuasion: Socialist Realism is not only normative but, ideally, transformative, as it aims, in the words of the notoriously orthodox critic Ladislav Štoll, to 'conquer that principle in man which ... gravitates to the past'.[29] According to Eco, the open work permits different discourses to intersect and coexist; it is, in Bakhtinian terms, 'dialogical', asserting the relativity of all viewpoints. Moreover, the open work changes the conventional, hierarchical relationship between author and consumer into a collaborative one: as Eco suggests, an open work is an unfinished work. No text is absolutely univocal, and even the most crudely propagandistic works cannot entirely delimit meaning to a single, coherent interpretation, yet avant-garde and modernist artists have sought to extend rather than restrict the scope for the participation of the spectator. (The concern for interpretive openness is of course even more prevalent and extreme in the postmodern, and the promotion of a multiplicity of meanings in these films is one of several things that connects the New Wave to a then barely incipient postmodernism.)

Another aspect of the shift in film style was a greater aesthetic self-consciousness. The assertion of language (or any other artistic medium) as self-sufficient entity was characteristic of the avant-garde even in the postwar period, and perhaps took its most extreme form in the 1960s writings of Věra Linhartová, where the process of narration is itself frequently seized on as a fictional subject. The avant-garde influence combines with that of re-emergent Prague Structuralism, a movement that was founded, like its French counterpart, on the notion of language as a system of signs and that dedicated itself to the close formal analysis of literary works. The then still active Jan Mukařovský, much of whose key work was reprinted in the mid-1960s, defined the single text as itself system or structure: for Mukařovský 'the meaning of [a text's] component units was determined much more by their place in the structure of the work than by their reference to individual realities'. In this sense the work of art could be considered 'an autonomous

---

29. Ladislav Štoll, 'Skutečnosti tváří v tvář', in Jiří Ševčík, Pavlína Morganová and Dagmar Dušová (eds), *České umění 1938–1989: programy, kritické texty, dokumenty* (Prague: Academia, 2001), p. 140.

sign'.[30] That emphasis on form, and the conception of the artwork as a specific structure, a reality unto itself, surely had an influence, however distant, on the formalist 'wing' of the New Wave (Chytilová, Němec, the Slovak New Wave filmmakers and, up to a point, Jireš). Perhaps more immediately important is the Prague Structuralists' principle, carried over from the Russian Formalists, of defamiliarization or estrangement: the principle that the specificity, indeed the value, of art consists in its emphasis on the materiality of 'language', its capacity to 'make strange' the medium of expression.[31] (The idea of estrangement will be discussed at length in relation to *Daisies*.) Once again, the emphasis on the plasticity of the medium can serve psychoanalytic concerns. The writings of Jacques Lacan were almost certainly unknown among the New Wave, and Kristeva's major work was unwritten when these films were being made (although books by the semiotician Roland Barthes and the Lacan-influenced Marxist theorist Louis Althusser were published in Czechoslovakia in the 1960s), yet such figures prove apposite here: in linking the materiality of expression to the prehistory of the subject, Lacan and Kristeva's theories have much to say concerning the poetics of Chytilová's and Švankmajer's films. Formalist aesthetics also have a more obviously political, Brechtian dimension, giving the lie to the idea that art can offer an objective, thus non-ideological, vision of the world.

That preoccupation with form did not mean that the New Wave neglected the representational practices of the avant-garde and their directly critical function. Once Socialist Realism stopped being enforced as the sole permissible aesthetic model, the question of how best to represent contemporary reality, indeed the very meaning of what constitutes 'realism', could freely be debated. In a 1960s interview, the critic Eduard Goldstücker pondered, apropos the modernism of Kafka, whether 'conventional literary means are capable of expressing the complex situation created by the history of our era'.[32] Goldstücker advocated the dynamic view of realism originally propounded by Brecht, suggesting that realism, 'as we have inherited it', is 'obsolete': nineteenth-century methods are inadequate for portraying twentieth-century realities, especially those of the postwar period.[33] A central insight of Effenberger's Surrealists is the idea that reality is itself no longer 'realistic', with recent history having surpassed the wildest imaginings of avant-garde art: 'what the Dadaists considered as the most powerful charge of provocative nonsense, is ... very tame and ... sweet in comparison with the absurdity of the horrors of Hitler's bloody machinery or with the mechanism of the

30. Jiří Veltruský, 'Jan Mukařovský's Structural Poetics and Esthetics', *Poetics Today*, Vol. 2, No. 1b, Winter, 1980–1981, p. 139.
31. Terry Eagleton, *Literary Theory: An Introduction* (Oxford: Blackwell, 1995), p. 99.
32. Eduard Goldstücker, in Liehm, *The Politics of Culture*, p. 284.
33. Ibid.

Stalinist epoch, which transformed the pages of the protocols of the Moscow trials into the libretto of a farce such as the Dadaists never dreamed of'.[34] Only fantastic and avant-garde forms can uncover that irrationality at the heart of the real. The role of imaginative art, if it is to resist becoming decoration or mere 'beautiful nonsense', consists in the 'concrete actualisation of the irrationality within the rational carapace of the contemporary world'.[35] Similarly, Zbyněk Havlíček defined his poetry as an 'absurd equivalent of an absurd world'.[36]

In Czech Surrealist terminology, the most penetrating representations are thus achieved by means of imaginative 'analogy' rather than through strictly literal depiction. Such a conception of imaginative art is not unique to Surrealism, and it is obviously also implicit in the Theatre of the Absurd, then much in vogue on Prague's theatrical fringe. The notion of fantasy as a means of social or political critique may evoke the now hackneyed idea of 'Aesopian' allegory, an idea frequently applied in discussions of East European cinema, yet this form of Surrealist or Absurdist critique offers something more profound: rather than representing reality in a disguised form, as in the Aesopian form, this method actually *reveals* reality in its authentic irrationality. Such critique adopts a logic similar to that of what Slavoj Žižek describes as a process of 'double reflection', where an apparently 'inverted', i.e. grotesque, topsy-turvy, image of reality acts to reveal the 'invertedness', the topsy-turviness, inherent in reality itself.[37] While a number of New Wave films (including Chytilová and Jireš's early work) comment on contemporary society through the techniques of Neo-Realism and *cinéma vérité*, practices themselves still radically new in the 1960s, many of the most successful films (*Josef Kilián, The Party and the Guests, Daisies, The Cremator, The Deserter and the Nomads, A Case for the Young Hangman, Valerie*, and *See You in Hell, My Friends!*) enact their critiques in the Surrealist or Absurdist terms described.

While all these innovations are important, arguably the most significant aspect of this engagement with the avant-garde, one that to a large extent underpins the other aspects, consists in the New Wave's approach to subjectivity. As previously noted, Karel Kosík argued that the Czech culture of the 1960s, including cinema, promoted a vision of human identity radically opposed to that of official ideology. In numerous films, this vision broadly approximates a Freudian or psychoanalytic model, embracing dreams,

---

34. Vratislav Effenberger, *Realita a poesie: k vývojové dialektice moderního umění* (Prague: Mladá Fronta, 1969), p. 55.

35. Ibid., p. 128.

36. Zbyněk Havlíček, quoted in Stanislav Dvorský, 'Z podzemí do podzemí: Český postsurrealismus čtřicátých let až šedesátých let', in Alan, *Alternativní kultura*, p. 127.

37. Slavoj Žižek, *For They Know Not What They Do: Enjoyment as a Political Factor* (London: Verso, 1991), p. 11.

fantasies and 'aberrant' desires. The imagination is ostentatiously present both through the literal representation of dreams and as a general cinematic property. Certain films, including *Valerie, Closely Observed Trains* and Švankmajer's *Jabberwocky*, even deal in explicitly Freudian 'language'. Whether or not all these films were directly influenced by the avant-garde (the three mentioned certainly are), that vision represents a fundamental reconnection of the 'mainstream' with the cultural underground, for psychoanalytic principles have always been at the centre of Surrealist thought. From the late 1920s onwards, Freudian psychoanalysis constituted one of the great taboos for orthodox Communism, the crude, disavowed appropriations of Soviet psychologist Aron Zalkind notwithstanding.[38] Freudian theory was attacked for its 'idealism' (with psychoanalysis compared unfavourably to the 'materialist' stance of Pavlov), its 'subjectivism' or lack of an empirical basis, and, not least, its preoccupation with sexuality (and 'deviant' sexuality at that). Moreover, Freudian conceptions of the self were completely incompatible with the Communists' task of creating the 'new man'. As Martin A. Miller writes, the Soviets demanded an individual 'who had transcended inner conflicts, who functioned in the external social world where the demons were visible'. 'In such a world,' this austere philosophy insisted, 'there could be no tolerance for Freud's psychic demons who carried out their devastation deep within the unconscious'.[39] Needless to say, in artistic terms this disapproval translated into a distaste for the representation of dreams and other imaginative forms, and for an immoderate concern with subjective experience or sexual life.

It is worth asking what the real implications were of this 'return' to Freud, psychoanalysis and their avant-garde representatives within Czech culture. The Marxist humanist philosophers considered this return something of a victory for their own ideas. According to Ivan Sviták, the avant-garde and modern art in general, in their preoccupation with 'chance, absurdity, madness, dream, sleep and the poetization [*sic*] of reality', uphold the

---

38. There were however Communists and Marxists who refused to share the Soviets' animosity to Freud, even before the advent of Marxist humanism and the New Left in the 1960s. As will be shown in the second chapter, the interwar Czech avant-garde was able to reconcile its Party allegiances with the psychic and libidinal concerns of its art. Another significant example in the Czech context is Záviš Kalandra, a critic, historian and Party member (until his expulsion in 1936) who had an avid interest in psychoanalysis (see Kalandra, 'The Reality of Dreams', *Slovo a smysl*, Vol. 2, No. 4, 2005, pp. 329–43). Kalandra's enthusiastic writings on Surrealism for the workers' press are quoted in a 1935 bulletin of the Czech Surrealist Group (Konstantin Biebl et al, 'Bulletin international du surréalisme', in Maurice Nadeau, *Histoire de Surréalisme* (Paris: Éditions du Seuil, 1964), pp. 400–12). Kalandra would ultimately be executed for conspiracy during the Stalinist-era political trials.

39. Martin A. Miller, *Freud and the Bolsheviks: Psychoanalysis in Imperial Russia and the Soviet Union* (New Haven; London: Yale University Press, 1998), p. 113.

'humanist aim'.[40] Kosík, as we have seen, aligned cultural developments with contemporaneous trends in philosophy, arguing that the Sixties culture, cinema included, presented an image of 'man' as an 'active' subject, indeed as a 'potential revolutionary'.[41] Yet is not the relation between a psychoanalytically inclined avant-garde and Marxist humanism, and specifically the relation between the unconscious and the key humanist principle of agency, more problematic than this? Sviták praises modern art for positing an authentic humanity that is being forgotten or eroded within the technology-obsessed present: avant-garde and imaginative art defend an integral selfhood against a modern world determined to render the individual a 'dull rationalist, ... deprived of his emotions and fantasy', and 'a willing cog in the machine of an almighty state'.[42] Yet the self proposed by psychoanalysis, and valorised by Surrealism, is a self dominated by unconscious instincts. Another Marxist philosopher committed to the notion of individual agency, Jean-Paul Sartre, rejected the Surrealist model of the self as incompatible with the idea of revolutionary praxis. Surrealism, with its psychoanalytic conception of the unconscious, postulated the existence of mysterious, in a sense alien, forces that moved 'through' the individual. How could a person 'haunted' in this way become a rational, determined and responsible agent of change? If the type of individual fostered by modern society is a cog in the machine of the state, is not the individual posited by Surrealism a mere pawn of a feckless and intractable unconscious?

It would be unfair to suggest that psychoanalysis or Surrealism necessarily promote a surrender to the unconscious: Havlíček, who was both a Surrealist and a practising psychoanalyst, argues that, on the contrary, Surrealism's aim is a form of self-recognition that can 'anchor' us within the 'flow of instinctually unconscious ... forces, whose plaything we really are'.[43] Yet in itself, the psychoanalytic and Surrealist model does complicate humanist conceptions of an active, self-determining subject. Furthermore, as recent critical accounts of Surrealism have emphasised, the 'subject' of Surrealism is barely a determinate property at all, and certainly not a coherent one, riven as this subject is by the split between conscious and unconscious, by the inherently diffuse nature of the unconscious itself, and by the role of external influences in the shaping of identity.[44] To understand the challenge that

40. Ivan Sviták, *Man and His World: A Marxian View*, translated by Jarmila Veltruský (New York: Delta, 1970), p. 80. See also Robert Kalivoda, 'Avantgarda a humanistická perspektiva', in *Literární noviny*, Vol. 14, No. 50, 1965, p. 5.

41. Kosík, in Liehm, *The Politics of Culture*, p. 399.

42. Sviták, *Man and His World*, p. 58.

43. Havlíček, *Skutečnost snu*, p. 208.

44. See Margaret Cohen, *Profane Illumination: Walter Benjamin and the Paris of Surrealist Revolution* (Berkeley: University of California Press, 1993); David Lomas, *The Haunted Self: Surrealism, Psychoanalysis, Subjectivity* (New Haven; London: Yale University Press, 2000).

Surrealism offers to humanist ideas, one needs only to think of the historical connection between Surrealism and Lacan's work, which postulates a subject caught up in the play of signifiers and always in conflict with itself, or of the avant-garde's importance for Kristeva, who dissolves the subject into a plurality of desires and positions.

Such philosophical tensions are played out within the New Wave itself. While a certain humanist essentialism may be implicit in the very philosophy of auteurism that underpins the New Wave, with filmmaking considered a means of expressing an integral or unique self, there are nonetheless some New Wave films, including Juráček's films and certainly *Daisies*, that lead us in an anti-humanist direction. Where the New Wave 'avant-garde' films seem most in accord with the Marxist humanists is in the assertion of the utopian function of the imagination. (This function will be considered in relation to *Valerie and Her Week of Wonders*, but it can also be observed in *The Miraculous Virgin, Martyrs of Love, Birds, Orphans and Fools* and *See You in Hell, My Friends!*). The idea that the imagination can construct speculative social images contradicts the orthodox, Leninist theory of 'reflection', in which consciousness and thus artistic expression is seen only passively to mirror an objective socio-historical reality.[45] For Sviták, '[p]oetry is man's rebellion against literal reality, ... the revolt of his imagination against a given order of facts'.[46] This echoes Karel Teige's assertion from the 1930s that 'miracles of the imagination are an effective imputation of desolate social reality'.[47] If Effenberger's postwar Surrealists were generally deeply sceptical about possibilities of liberatory political change, the utopian spirit that had originally characterised Surrealism was extensively resurrected within sections of the Sixties counterculture. So-called 'father of the New Left' Herbert Marcuse, who referred to Surrealism more than once and who seems to have been influenced by the movement, argued that the imagination (and its objectification by art) could offer images of a new, free, and non-repressive way of life.[48] In its 'constructive' utopian dimension as much as in the force of its 'irrational' instincts, the inner world comprises a disruptive, politically troubling phenomenon.

---

45. James H. Satterwhite, *Varieties of Marxist Humanism: Philosophical Revision in Postwar Eastern Europe* (Pittsburgh; London: University of Pittsburgh Press, 1992), p. 138.
46. Sviták, *Man and His World*, p. 115.
47. Karel Teige, quoted in Karel Srp, *Karel Teige*, translated by Karolina Vočadlo (Prague: Torst, 2001), p. 26.
48. See Herbert Marcuse, *Eros and Civilization: A Philosophical Inquiry into Freud* (Boston: Beacon Press, 1966), p. 149; Marcuse, *An Essay on Liberation* (Harmondsworth: Penguin, 1972), p. 38; Ben Agger, 'Marcuse and Habermas on New Science', *Polity*, Vol. 9, No. 2, Winter 1976, p. 168.

This last section of the introduction has suggested ways in which the New Wave's absorption of avant-garde ideas and practices has been politically critical and subversive. It has also shown how that subversive aspect might emerge from form, from changes in the language of cinema, as well as from direct, critically inflected representation or the construction of alternative, utopian realities. Throughout the ensuing, close analysis of the various films, the subversive qualities or ideas sketched in here will be explored in greater detail, though of course in such measures and configurations as the specific films demand. This exploration is intended to develop and reinforce the assertion, made throughout this introduction, that the 1960s Czechoslovak cinema's engagement with Surrealism and its sibling movements was a profound and fruitful one.

Prior to the analysis of the films, Chapter One will provide a short history of the Czech avant-garde, itself a sorely neglected subject, and sketch in the political, cultural and institutional context of the 1960s cinema.

Chapter Two, focusing on Pavel Juráček's *Josef Kilián* and *A Case for the Young Hangman*, will reveal the intertwined influences of Surrealism and the Absurd in Juráček's work. It will be suggested that these films can be read not only as bizarre satires on socialist bureaucracy but also as explorations of such wider themes as desire, the constitution of the self and language (the latter theme representing an important point of connection between the Surreal and the Absurd). In their representation of desire and identity in terms of lack and their assertion of the polyvalence of language, Juráček's films will be related to Lacanian psychoanalytic concepts. Lacan's theory of transference ('the subject supposed to know') will help connect the psychoanalytic dimension and the exploration of political authority in Juráček's work.

Chapter Three focuses on Jiří Menzel's *Closely Observed Trains*, and specifically examines the influence of the 'post-Surrealist' work of Bohumil Hrabal, who wrote the novella on which Menzel's film is based. It will be argued that Menzel largely retains the spirit of Hrabal's work, while making his film more explicit in its critique of fascist and Stalinist ethics. This chapter draws on Georges Bataille, whose ideas (themselves comprising an 'alternative' tradition of Surrealism) offer an appropriate framework with which to examine Menzel's concern with materiality, his valorisation of 'expenditures' or wasteful activities, and his exploration of the connections between sexuality and sacrifice.

Chapter Four deals with Věra Chytilová's *Daisies*, and introduces further influences such as Dada and 1960s 'happenings' (though the Surrealist influence is still evident). At the same time, the film's experimental formal practices will be read in terms of the Russian Formalist notion of 'estrangement'. In *Daisies*, estrangement operates in both aesthetic and socio-political terms, serving on the one hand to foreground the processes of aesthetic construction and on the other to satirise greed and inequality and denaturalise socially defined identities. It will be argued that Chytilová's violation of aesthetic norms not only defies traditional realism but also enables her to found a superior 'realism' that provides social insight and exposes the constructed and unnatural.

Chapter Five turns to Slovak New Wave cinema, focusing specifically on Juraj Jakubisko's *The Deserter and the Nomads* and *Birds, Orphans and Fools* (and, to a lesser extent, Elo Havetta's *Party in the Botanical Garden* (*Slávnosť v botanickej záhrade*, 1969)). It is worth examining the specificity of the Slovak New Wave aesthetic, with its combination of folk and avant-garde, and local and international, influences. This chapter will suggest how certain aspects of Jakubisko's cinema, such as his concern with dissolving binary distinctions, his interest in 'Otherness' and his themes of history, oppression and utopian possibilities, both look back to the avant-garde and anticipate the postmodern. The particularly intensive study of *Birds, Orphans and Fools* will explore the configuration of Jakubisko's hopeless view of history and revolution, the founding of alternative lifestyles and the embrace of the imagination and madness. Surrealism and the Sixties counterculture comprise two of the film's points of reference, yet it will be suggested that Jakubisko at once evokes and debunks Surrealist and countercultural valorisations of madness.

Chapter Six deals with Jireš's *Valerie and Her Week of Wonders*, another adaptation of a novel, in this case Vítězslav Nezval's eponymous work of classic Surrealism. This chapter will show how Jireš draws out the book's psychoanalytic dimension, and uses the story to illustrate Freudian notions of the family romance and the uncanny. Yet it will also be shown how Jireš's treatment of Nezval's 'dream text' fosters the play of meaning and enables the viewer to construct his or her own interpretation. The film will be analysed as a broad political allegory of repression and liberation that also asserts the liberatory power of art. Finally this chapter will explore how the film speculates upon, without wholly affirming, possibilities of utopian change. It will be argued that the film's formal practices and utopian vision owe as much to Poetism and the Sixties counterculture as to Surrealism proper.

Chapter Seven examines the short films of Švankmajer and concentrates on Švankmajer's multi-faceted engagement with the issue of language. It will be shown that Švankmajer is concerned with forging a kind of non-verbal 'language', though one that exceeds and sometimes defies a merely symbolic or unambiguously denotative function. This 'language' will be explored in relation both to Švankmajer's interest in the communicative properties of objects and to the creation of a sensuous, affective formal language; Kristeva's concept of 'semiosis' will be deployed in the discussion of this formal language. Švankmajer's preoccupations and formal practices will be linked to aspects of contemporary Czech Surrealism, as well as to other avant-garde traditions, such as Poetism and Czech Informel. It will be shown that Švankmajer's approach to language and expression is a subversive factor in his work, as is evident both in his rejection of the authoritarian codification of language and in his attempt to express the 'analogical' thought processes of the unconscious.

CHAPTER I

Inspirations, Opportunities: Cultural and Historical Contexts

Marching In Step, Swimming Against the Current: The Troubled History of the Czech Avant-Garde

The story of Surrealism has been told many times and in numerous languages. Yet that standard history comprises only one story, a story in which the Surrealist movement is rendered synonymous with a small group of avant-garde artists and intellectuals who lived in Paris between the wars. Famous émigrés from Germany or Spain generally comprise a few of the lead characters, though that is as far as the coverage of Surrealism's international dimension goes. The story of Czech Surrealism has never received a comprehensive telling in English, and in so far as the Czech movement is even mentioned it is in the guise of a subplot complementary to the larger narrative of 'true' Surrealism. For this reason the names of the Czech avant-garde's key representatives are much less well-known than they should be. Yet Czech Surrealism can claim 'authenticity' on two fronts, as not only was it closely linked with the French movement, it also grew organically out of a native avant-garde. The persistence of the movement in the face of extraordinary pressures reflects how deeply rooted Surrealism is in Czech culture, but this persistence also belies a history that is complex and convulsive, marked by numerous upheavals, shifts and schisms. Once we take into account all its legacies and deviations, twentieth-century Czech Surrealism is revealed to encompass many different aesthetic and political positions: it has embraced both realism and abstraction, Marxist–Leninist utopianism and world-weary ideological scepticism. Sometimes the movement's practitioners have questioned the extent to which they are Surrealists at all, and for more than twenty-five years of the movement's history no self-titled Surrealist group actually existed.

The prehistory of the Czech Surrealist Group comprises an entire chapter in itself, and traces of this prehistory are still visible in Surrealist works of the postwar era, as well as in a number of films influenced by the avant-garde. While Czech modernism in general can be dated back to around the turn of the nineteenth and twentieth centuries, the specific constellation of artists and intellectuals that would later comprise the Surrealist Group emerged, as did Western European Dada, out of the devastations – and transformations – of the First World War. This group, which, rather mysteriously, called itself 'Devětsil',[1] was founded in 1920, and after dabbling briefly with a self-consciously 'primitivist' style of art, it embarked upon the groundbreaking artistic programme of Poetism.[2] Like their French, German and Italian counterparts, the young men and women who comprised Devětsil had been radicalised by the war. Where the earlier Czech avant-gardes had displayed a contemplative, mystical tendency, Devětsil was as much a political movement as an aesthetic one. However, in contrast to the nihilistic, destructive mentality of Dada, Devětsil was optimistic and constructive, founded on positive principles of change rather than on mere negation. Furthermore, Devětsil was avowedly Marxist from the beginning, as is evidenced by its interest in the latest cultural developments from the fledgling Soviet Union. If the French avant-garde's transition from Dada to Surrealism constitutes a dramatic shift in aesthetic, political and philosophical terms, then Devětsil's own transition to Surrealism appears smoother. Karel Teige, the founder and chief spokesman of Devětsil, even felt that Devětsil had formulated the same essential ideas as the Surrealists, independently of and indeed before the French, with Teige's first Poetist manifesto of 1924 appearing several months before André Breton's first Surrealist manifesto.[3]

While Surrealism and Poetism are similar in many ways, there are also, as suggested in the introduction, significant distinctions. Poetism aimed above all to be the artistic voice of modernity. Underpinned by Devětsil's commitment to the emancipatory potential of technological progress, Poetist works delight in the modern metropolis and the new wonders of the industrial world. Yet Poetism is cheery and light-hearted, lacking in the violent, portentous qualities with which the Italian Futurists celebrated the same phenomena. Perhaps more than any other contemporaneous avant-garde movement, Devětsil was enamoured of popular culture, and especially of cinema, which fulfilled central criteria in being at once a 'mass' (and thus proletarian) art form and a technological innovation. Described by Teige as a

---

1. Devětsil literally means 'nine powers', but it is also the Czech name for the butterbur, a plant believed to have curative powers.
2. František Šmejkal, 'From Lyrical Metaphors to Symbols of Fate: Czech Surrealism of the 1930s', in Jaroslav Anděl (ed.), *Czech Modernism 1900–1945* (Houston: Museum of Fine Arts, Houston, 1989), p. 65.
3. Ibid., p. 66; Karel Teige, 'Deset let Surrealismu', in *Surrealismus v diskusi, Knihovna Levé fronty*, Vol. 8 (Prague: Levá fronta, 1934), p. 11.

form of 'modern epicureanism', Poetism displayed a concern with sensuous experience that extended to the materials of artistic expression themselves. In the field of verbal art, Poetism waged war against the outdated concept of 'literature' and asserted the importance of the physical properties of words. The writing of poems was often a pretext for typographical experiment, and words were selected as much for their visual form as for their meaning. Given this preoccupation with words as objects, it is hardly surprising that Devětsil enjoyed close contact with literary theorist and linguist Roman Jakobson, who had been involved with the Russian avant-garde before settling in Czechoslovakia and helping found the structuralist Prague Linguistic Circle. It was in relation to Poetism that Jakobson first defined his notion of 'poeticity' (a notion that will be explored in the chapter on Švankmajer). Poetism was marked by a greater concern with artistic form than was French Surrealism, a concern manifested in a spirit of restless aesthetic experimentation: the so-called 'picture poem' (*'obrazová báseň'*) incorporated text into visual collages, once again underlining the physical dimension of words, and in his second Poetist manifesto from 1928 Teige proclaims his ambition of creating a 'poetry of the five senses' that would encompass a poetry of smell ('olfactory poetry'), a poetry of taste and so on.

Unsurprisingly, Devětsil also harboured cinematic ambitions, and the numerous screenplays and proclamations about film written by the group suggest that a Devětsil cinema would have extended Poetist visual experiments in the fine arts: according to Teige the Devětsil screenplays' 'central interest was picture poetry, synthesis of picture and poem, set in motion by film'.[4] To a large extent Devětsil's vision of a 'pure cinema' stripped of narrative and literary elements anticipated later developments in the American underground film: a direct link is even provided by Alexandr Hackenschmied, a filmmaker affiliated with Devětsil, who would later emigrate to the United States and, under the name Alexander Hammid, collaborate with influential avant-garde filmmaker Maya Deren. While various films did emerge from the Devětsil fold during the 1930s (including several feature films directed by the great experimental writer Vladislav Vančura, notably *On the Sunny Side* (*Na sluneční straně*, 1933) and *Faithless Marijka* (*Marijka nevěrnice*, 1934), the latter film scripted by, among others, Vítězslav Nezval and Roman Jakobson), a 'Poetist cinema' as such never materialised, thwarted by the predictable absence of sympathetic investors. Nevertheless, the avant-garde arguably infiltrated popular culture to a greater extent in Czechoslovakia than in other countries, not least through the medium of theatre. The avant-garde Liberated Theatre (Osvobozené divadlo), co-founded in 1926 by Devětsil member Jindřich

---

4. Karel Teige, quoted in Michal Bregant, 'The Devětsil Film Dream', in Rotislav Švachá (ed.), *Devětsil: Czech Avant-Garde Art, Architecture and Design of the 1920s and 30s* (Oxford: Museum of Modern Art, 1990), p. 72.

Honzl, first showcased the talents of the comic duo Jiří Voskovec and Jan Werich, whose act became extremely popular and who would go on to make a series of successful film comedies (*Your Money or Your Life* (*Peníze nebo život*, Jindřich Honzl, 1932), *Heave Ho!* (*Hey Rup!*, Martin Frič, 1934), and *The World Belongs to Us* (*Svět patří nám*, Frič, 1937)). The case of Voskovec and Werich (and that of their 1960s successors, Suchý and Šlitr) represents a minor fulfilment of Devětsil's ambitions of creating a new 'proletarian' culture that synthesised avant-garde and popular elements. Such cases might alternately be seen to suggest how the opposition between 'high' and 'low' cultures is a false one to begin with.

Devětsil's formal experiments were frequently linked to the attempt to portray and stimulate the 'inner life', and it is here that the aims of Poetism most closely approximate those of Surrealism, even if Poetism's methods were often quite different. Teige argued that by emphasising the sensuous and associative qualities of words over their denotative meaning, the poet could express the 'infrared and ultraviolet reality' of the unconscious.[5] The artists Jindřich Štyrský and Toyen established 'Artificialism', a sibling movement to Poetism in painting. Typically made up of fluid, indefinable forms that seem to inhabit some subterranean level of the mind, Artificialist paintings were an attempt at 'the concrete rendering of nonsubstantive impressions, feelings, memories, and imaginings'.[6] The Czech avant-garde did not fully embrace Freudian psychoanalytic theory until its eventual Surrealist 'conversion', which may seem surprising in view of many of Devětsil's preoccupations. Paradoxically, however, Teige's thought addressed the libidinal foundations of the imagination in a way that the puritanical Breton rarely did. Teige's proposal of an *ars una*, a modern form of *gesamtkunstwerk* that would unify the different arts, was based on his belief that the roots of the 'creative instinct' are to be found in 'the basic, life-giving and creative instinct *par excellence*, namely the sexual instinct'.[7] Unlike Breton, Teige was uninhibited by conventional morality in his personal life and often bluntly biologistic in his writing.[8] In terms of sexual morality Teige was closer to a figure like the Soviet feminist Alexandra Kollontai, and the Eros he propounded not only winged but defiantly naked.

---

5. Karel Teige, quoted in Esther Levinger, 'Czech Avant-Garde Art: Poetry for the Five Senses', *The Art Bulletin*, Vol. 81, No. 3 (September, 1999), p. 514.
6. Šmejkal, 'From Lyrical Metaphors to Symbols of Fate', in Anděl, *Czech Modernism 1900–1945*, p. 70.
7. Karel Teige, 'Báseň, svět, člověk', in *Zvěrokruh*, No. 1, November 1930, p. 11.
8. See Jaroslav Seifert, 'On Teige: A Danse Macabre in Smíchov', in *The Poetry of Jaroslav Seifert*, edited by George Gibian and translated by Ewald Osers and George Gibian (North Haven, CT: Catbird, 1998), p. 230.

Poetism was a movement designed not to contribute another 'ism' to the history of aesthetics but to transform life itself, and it sought to do this in a manner at once more precise and more ambitious than that of French Surrealism. The reverse side of Teige's anti-aesthetic stance was his desire to diffuse poetry into life, and the life of the collective rather than that of the cloistered few. Teige even imagined miraculous 'magic cities of Poetism', 'which would be the site of entertaining mischief ... , the optical pleasure of colours and forms, the pleasure of hearing noise and sounds, in short the pleasure of all the senses in a carefree style'.[9] Poetist culture was thus to contribute to the cultivation of the senses and the imagination. Yet the revolution in sensibility that Teige envisaged would need to be accompanied by political revolution, as capitalism deformed human beings' sensual and emotional life, ensuring the domination of 'the feeling of ownership' at the expense of other 'physiological and psychological feelings'.[10] Poetism in fact comprised only half of Devětsil's utopian vision. Immensely adept at absorbing and synthesising different artistic trends from all over the map, Teige appropriated Soviet Constructivism, whose principles would play the role of a rational complement to the anarchic Poetism. Constructivism's watchwords are standardisation, innovation and anti-aestheticism; the Constructivist method would ensure the greatest possible rationalisation of work and production. Teige extended his concern with rationalisation into his architectural theorising of the 1920s and 1930s, although once again the desire for functionality and formal stringency is harmonised with a concern for beauty and the cultivation of human sensibilities. The Devětsil of the 1920s may largely be founded on the synthesis of oppositions, yet there are oppositions here that seem irreconcilable, not least the tension between the philosophical playfulness of Poetism and the staunchness, if not dogmatism, with which the Devětsil artists adhered to both Marxist–Leninist ideology and its representatives in the Czechoslovak Communist Party. When a group of Czech writers left the Party in protest over its 'fractious terrorism' and 'immature fanaticism', Teige, Nezval and other Devětsil figures lost no time in publicly condemning these 'seven writers who used their literary names for a political attack against the party, which for us means life'.[11] Indeed, during the 1920s and early 1930s the Czech avant-garde maintained a better and closer relationship with the Party than Breton's Surrealist group, which is at least partly a testament to the Czechoslovak Party's cultural openness, relatively speaking of course, in the days before Socialist

---

9. Karel Teige, *Svět, který se směje* (Prague: Akropolis, 2004), p. 89.
10. 'Báseň, svět, člověk', p. 14.
11. 'Spisovatelé komunisté komunistickým dělníkům', 'Zásadní stanovisko k projevu "sedmi"', in Štěpán Vlašín (ed.), *Avantgarda: Svazek 3: Generační diskuse* (Prague: Svoboda, 1970), p. 47, p. 55.

Realist orthodoxy was established. The story of the Czech avant-garde in the twentieth century is ultimately the story of its relationship with Communist authority, and the course of Czechoslovak Communism can itself be traced in the ups and downs, the crises, redefinitions and resurgences, of the avant-garde's turbulent history.

In 1934 Devětsil reinvented itself as the Czech Surrealist Group, with many of the most important figures, including Nezval, Honzl, Toyen and Štyrský, retained from the earlier group. The immediate instigating factor for the formation of a Surrealist group was the close personal bond that Nezval had developed with André Breton, although Lenka Bydžovská suggests a number of additional, deeper factors for this transformation. In the political climate of the mid-1930s, 'the hedonistic poetry of Devětsíl' was starting to seem 'anachronistic', and the avant-garde was becoming increasingly preoccupied by the depths of the human psyche at the expense of the external and rational.[12] Furthermore, Breton's own declaration of support for Marxism and the French Communist Party in his *Second Manifesto of Surrealism* from 1929 assured the Czechs, who had earlier criticized Surrealism's 'anarchist' tendencies, that the Surrealists held 'correct' political principles.[13] Teige himself was initially reluctant to join the new group, no doubt partly out of feelings of 'rivalry' with Breton's group but also because of intellectual and artistic disagreements with Surrealism: for instance, he rejected at first the Surrealist practice of 'psychic automatism' (the transcribing of thoughts 'direct' from the unconscious), believing instead that artistic expression should comprise a synthesis of conscious and unconscious elements.[14] Yet Teige later made his peace with Surrealism and would ironically become the movement's most prominent theoretical spokesman during the 1930s and 1940s, a role for which he would be persecuted when the Communists came to power.

Faced with the Communists' misunderstanding and distrust of Surrealism on the one hand and with Breton's notorious obstinacy on the other, the Czechs sought to mediate between the French Surrealists and the Communist Parties of both Czechoslovakia and the Soviet Union. Temperamentally as well as geographically, Teige and Nezval were well-disposed to reconcile Paris and Moscow. In his speech at the Soviet Writers' Congress of 1934, Nezval argued for the compatibility of Surrealism with revolutionary struggle, but to no avail: what the Czechs had envisaged as an opportunity for rapprochement was in fact the sounding of the death knell for cultural pluralism, as it was the 1934 Congress that announced the establishment of Socialist Realism as the one

---

12. Lenka Bydžovská, 'Against the Current: The Story of the Surrealist Group in Czechoslovakia', *Papers of Surrealism*, Issue 1, Winter 2003, p. 2.
13. Ibid.
14. Šmejkal, 'From Lyrical Metaphors to Symbols of Fate', in Anděl, *Czech Modernism 1900–1945*, p. 66.

'official' aesthetic of Soviet Communism. Massively disappointed, the Czechs nonetheless clung to the scraps of comfort offered by the somewhat more open-minded approach to aesthetics propounded in Nikolai Bukharin's speech. Moreover, Teige and Nezval recognised the need for political unity in the face of fascism and maintained their conciliatory stance, though they must have recognised that this stance was almost entirely one-sided. Ever the synthesist, Teige even attempted the seemingly impossible feat of reconciling Surrealism and Socialist Realism. Teige argued that realist methods could acceptably be harnessed to the socialist cause in the USSR, where reality itself had been transformed into the 'positive human and social reality' of a 'classless society'. In the capitalist world, however, reality was still inimical to the socialist writer, and thus romantic and lyrical methods were called for in the propagation of revolutionary consciousness.[15] For Teige, a solidarity of adjectives ('socialist') was more important than a solidarity of nouns ('realism').[16]

Yet the 'human and social reality' of the Soviet Union had itself become problematic by the mid-1930s. The death sentences handed out after the first Moscow show trials violated Teige's humanitarian principles, and in early 1938 the disillusionment with Soviet reality felt by Teige and other Surrealists embroiled them in a bitter quarrel with the increasingly Stalinist Nezval. A few days later Nezval tried, by means of an announcement in the press, to dissolve the Surrealist Group.[17] The other members defied Nezval's unilateral gesture, and as a response Teige wrote the pamphlet *Surrealism Against the Current* (*Surrealismus proti proudu*, 1938), in which he unequivocally attacked Stalinist political and cultural practice. This internal crisis combined with the external fact of German occupation meant that Stalinism and Nazism had both conspired around the same time to crush Czech Surrealism. Yet they did not succeed, and even though the Surrealist Group 'proper' formally disbanded in 1942, Surrealist activity flourished throughout the years of occupation. Many defiant younger artists adopted the Surrealist creed: as Bydžovská writes, '[i]n the stifling atmosphere of the Protectorate, [Surrealism] represented, for the young generation, an alluring challenge to engage in free creative thought'.[18] The years of war and occupation were no less fruitful for Slovak Surrealism, or, as it came to be known, 'Nadrealism' ('*nadrealismus*' in Slovak being a direct translation of the French term '*surréalisme*'). Having begun as the importation of a foreign model, an imitation of French and Czech sources, Nadrealism quickly become 'a thoroughly domesticated, genuinely Slovak, literary and

15. Karel Teige, quoted in Deborah Helen Garfinkle, *Bridging East and West: Czech Surrealism's Interwar Experiment* [doctoral thesis] (University of Texas, 2003), p. 66.
16. Ibid.
17. Jakub Sedláček, in Vítězslav Nezval, *Pražský chodec* (Prague: Labyrinth, 2003), p. 170.
18. Bydžovská, 'Against the Current', *Papers of Surrealism*, p. 9.

artistic phenomenon.'[19] The rural character of much Slovak Surrealist poetry, for instance, suggests the Slovak movement's independence from the Prague-centred (and -centric) Czech Surrealists.[20] Other distinguishing characteristics were a reliance on native folk tales, a greater predilection for the 'allegorical message' and a more romantic, 'literary' sensibility.[21] Surrealism in fact became even more influential and important within Slovakia than Czech Surrealism was in its own national context, and that importance only grew 'during the period of the clerico-Fascist state of the 1940s'.[22]

In many ways, the Czech Surrealism of the postwar years comprises a profound reinvention, both aesthetically and philosophically, of the earlier movement. By the time of the Communist takeover in 1948, many of the key players in the Surrealist movement of the interwar and Occupation years had either died (Štyrský), emigrated (Toyen, the poet Jindřich Heisler) or 'capitulated' to Stalinism (Nezval, Honzl). Teige maintained both his location and his avant-garde allegiances, only to be denounced by the new Communist government as a Trotskyist and relentlessly harassed by the secret police.[23] By 1951, however, a new group composed of younger Surrealists had formed around Teige. Following Teige's death that same year, writer and theorist Vratislav Effenberger assumed leadership, and the history of a new, substantially redefined Surrealism began in earnest. The attitude to Communist authority was now one of unequivocal hostility, with official ideology perceived as 'a vulgar pack of extinct and emptied-out ideas, discredited in a blindingly obvious manner by recent history and everyday events'.[24] To adapt to the present system was to forsake one's authenticity for a place in the cultural 'market' (the language of capitalism is here pointedly turned against state socialism, an indication that the new Surrealists' sympathies, for all their opposition to Stalinism and distrust of ideologies per se, remained broadly 'radical'). This antipathy was of course mutual, and the authorities denounced Surrealism as 'the Trojan horse of western imperialism'.[25] Indeed the Surrealists' determination to stay underground was something of a forced choice, as, for all but the most conservative of artists, collaboration with the system was not

19. Peter Petro, 'Dominik Tatarka: An Introduction to a Rebel', *Cross Currents 6: A Yearbook of Central European Culture* (Ann Arbor: University of Michigan, 1987), p. 281.

20. See Petro, 'Slovak Surrealism as a Parable of Modern Uprootedness', *Cross Currents: A Yearbook of Central European Culture* (Ann Arbor: University of Michigan, 1982), p. 230.

21. Petr Král, *Le surréalisme en Tchécoslovaquie: Choix de textes 1934–1968* (Paris: Gallimard, 1983), p. 60.

22. Peter Hames, 'The Film Experiment', in Hames, *Dark Alchemy*, p. 33.

23. Ibid.

24. Stanislav Dvorský, 'Z podzemí do podzemí', in Alan, *Alternativní kultura*, p. 114.

25. Král, *Le surréalisme en Tchécoslovaquie*, p. 62.

an option. The 'red future' anticipated by Devětsil had disastrously materialised, and the lyrical projection of a utopian future was exchanged for the laconic depiction of a dystopian present. The new Surrealism was mordant, satirical, full of 'black humour'; its muses are more Kafka and Louis-Ferdinand Céline than Breton and Nezval. Postwar Surrealism's key term was 'concrete irrationality', as the irrationality that had previously manifested itself in dreams and fantasies was now to be observed in the social and political systems of the real world. In the light of death camps, political prisoners and nuclear bombs, the artist could no longer retreat into a private realm of 'convulsive beauty'. The imagination was now valued most, it seems, as a means of uncovering the 'objective humour' of the social world, the irrational qualities of the real. Effenberger would later stress, however, that Surrealism's importance lay in its 'creative' character as much as in its 'critical' role.[26]

While both Breton and Teige had tried to construct their own comprehensive theoretical systems, Effenberger rejected the idea that any such system could claim universal validity. For Effenberger, 'the break-up of the integrity of the world, the break-up of universal intellectual systems – or better said: the recognition of the non-existence of this unity, integrity and universality' meant that the only credible 'unifying perspective' could be provided by the 'core' of the individual's personality.[27] The emphasis was now on 'disintegration' rather than Teigean synthesis. In 1963 Effenberger and the other Surrealists relaunched their group under the new name 'U.D.S.' (appropriately, the name stands for different things, including '*útěk do skutečnosti*' ('escape into reality') and '*Už dost surrealismu!*' ('enough now of Surrealism!')), but they stressed that the new group did not constitute any unified 'artistic movement', only a 'system' by means of which 'individual opinion-related, creative and interpretive standpoints' could interact.[28] Effenberger's thought can be considered postmodernist *avant la lettre* in its rejection of totalising theories and narratives of utopian liberation: Effenberger considered the 'utopian gestures' of both Teige and Breton to have sprung 'from despair'.[29]

The anti-doctrinal, anti-unificatory stance exemplified by Effenberger was all the more apt in that his 'official' Surrealist circle did not constitute the only attempt at negotiating the Surrealist legacy during the postwar period. The

26. See Effenberger's essay of 1966–1967, 'Variants, Constants and Dominants of Surrealism', quoted in Donna Roberts, 'Neither Wings nor Stones: the Psychological Realism of Czech Women Surrealists', in Patricia Allmer (ed.), *Angels of Anarchy: Women Artists and Surrealism* (Munich; Berlin; London; New York: Prestel, 2009), p. 75.
27. Vratislav Effenberger, quoted in Dvorský, 'Z podzemí do podzemí', in Alan, *Alternativní kultura*, p. 135–36.
28. 'U.D.S.', quoted in ibid., p. 137.
29. Vratislav Effenberger, 'The Raw Cruelty of Life', in Matejka, *Cross Currents 6*, p. 442.

'Půlnoc' ('Midnight') circle, an alternative stream that boasted the participation of such writers as Egon Bondy, Bohumil Hrabal and Ivo Vodseďálek, offered an even more unorthodox response to Surrealism, and can be considered broadly analogous to the American Beat movement. Similarly to Effenberger's own, this group, while comradely, was loose, resistant to overarching self-definition. A number of artists from these circles even published manifestos or founded 'schools' of their own: Bondy's 'total realism', Vodseďálek's 'poetry of embarrassment', Vladimir Boudník's 'Explosionism', Petr Král's 'Fire Brigade Theatre' manifesto. Poet and psychoanalyst Zbyněk Havlíček stood outside both Effenberger and Bondy's circles, a (self-)isolated figure who had nonetheless belonged to the short-lived 'Spořilov Surrealist' group during the war. On Effenberger's testimony, Havlíček was distinguished by his more 'romantic', 'lyrical' conception of Surrealism and less qualified acceptance of Freudian theory.[30] A Czech version of Informel painting emerged in the late 1950s, overlapping directly with self-declared Surrealism via the involvement of figures like Mikuláš Medek and Josef Istler.[31] Czech Informel can indeed be considered the visual analogue of the literary (or, as a stringent anti-aestheticism would dictate, anti-literary) endeavours of Effenberger, Bondy or Karel Hynek. Medek's painting, say, might be 'formalist' to an extent that these writers' works are not, comprising as it does a gestural, quasi-abstract art concerned with the 'imprint' of feelings, yet both the plastic and literary manifestations of the Surrealist-oriented avant-garde concern the materiality of the world, the obstinacy and opacity of 'brute facts', and the confrontation between subjective and objective worlds ('the mix of man and matter').[32] Plastic art operates unavoidably on the real and concrete, but even in the Surrealists' verbal output a brute externality might manifest itself directly in transposed 'blocks' of everyday reality.[33] Such tactics can of course be related to the sense, voiced retrospectively by Effenberger, that social irrationality 'burst with a humour so objective that all you had to do was place it in front of a camera or on a stage for its rationalist shell to crack open'.[34] It is unsurprising that photography, a medium capable of both documenting the real world and investigating its material textures, flourished in postwar Czech Surrealism. With a few exceptions (albeit including a world-famous one in Švankmajer), the Surrealists were never permitted to extend their concerns to cinema, although Effenberger produced numerous unfilmed scenarios to match the unstaged plays he wrote with Hynek

30. Jakub Sedláček, 'Zbyněk Havlíček – podoby surrealistické metafory', *Slovo a smysl*, Vol. 1, No. 2, 2004, p. 93.
31. Hames, 'The Film Experiment', in Hames, *Dark Alchemy*, p. 36.
32. Král, *Le surréalisme en Tchécoslovaquie*, p. 54.
33. Ibid., p. 37.
34. Effenberger, quoted in Roberts, 'Neither Wings nor Stones', in Allmer, *Angels of Anarchy*, p. 83.

(written for the flat sitting-room if not the drawer) and both he and Král indulged their interest in film with idiosyncratic, often brilliant, criticism.

The 1960s was the decade when avant-garde and Surrealist sensibilities temporarily secured a place in the mainstream, both in Czechoslovakia and internationally (although, as we shall see, this state of affairs is partly attributable to influences beyond those of the avant-garde itself). During this decade, the 'real' Czech avant-garde kept its distance from what it saw as meretricious appropriations of Surrealism, Dada or Poetism. It seems the Surrealists feared official acceptance as much as they had feared official persecution: in 1964 Surrealist writer Věra Linhartová wrote of the necessity of resisting absorption into the mainstream, and warned of the 'inner decay' that could result from 'the pressure of the public cultural market'.[35] On the other hand, the liberalisations of the 1960s did mean that Surrealist writing could be published and Surrealist art legally exhibited. The formerly beyond the pale Karel Teige received a kind of posthumous rehabilitation; a comprehensive republication of his theoretical writings was begun in 1964, although political events intervened before it could be completed. Another consequence of liberalisation was that provocative artistic practices new to the Czech context, such as performance art, took root during this time. In April 1968, the Czechs joined forces with the French Surrealists to issue a manifesto called 'The Platform of Prague', a tortuously worded but important document which upholds the contemporary relevance of Surrealism and the movement's commitment to non-totalitarian socialism.[36] Yet despite this manifestation of Surrealist solidarity, the French group disbanded shortly after the manifesto's publication (outliving its founder Breton by a mere two years). The Czech group continued under vastly more difficult circumstances: while the French had only a post-'Mai' waning of revolutionary energies to contend with, the Czechs had to face the harsh, and dispiriting, climate that the Warsaw Pact invasion unleashed. More enduringly, contacts were also established in 1968 with Slovak Surrealism, notably in the form of the young Slovak poet Albert Marenčin.[37] In 1969, with renewed repression clearly on the cards, Effenberger and his companions defiantly re-attached the name of Surrealist Group to their activities and

35. Věra Linhartová, quoted in Dvorský, 'Z podzemí do podzemí', in Alan, *Alternativní kultura*, p. 139.

36. Petr Král relates: 'the Prague group rediscovers in [the French] a hidden romanticism: almost overnight, from being sceptical and disabused dandies, we become, spontaneously, "leftists"' (Král, *Le surréalisme en Tchécoslovaquie*, p. 61).

37. According to Král, Marenčin was the first exponent of a Slovak Surrealism that could truly be considered the counterpart or twin of the contemporary Czech movement (ibid., p. 60). Marenčin also worked in the Slovak film industry, and the production group he ran with Karol Bakoš was responsible for, among other works, Uher's *The Miraculous Virgin* and Jakubisko's 1960s films. He thus constitutes one of the few direct links between Surrealism 'proper' and the movement's cinematic incarnations.

published the first issue of the journal *Analogon* (the second issue had to wait another twenty years). Czech Surrealism formally acknowledged its existence again at the very time when authority decreed that it should not exist.

Indeed, the repressions of the Normalisation period were no more effective in destroying the avant-garde than were those of the Stalinist period, and a broadly based cultural underground flourished throughout the 1970s and 1980s, ensuring exposure for its works through illegal exhibitions and Samizdat publications that were often printed in large numbers and to a professional standard. A principle of solidarity in opposition fused with diversity and an Effenbergerian 'disintegratory' spirit. The Surrealist Group itself emphasised collectivity in its creative practice during this period, devising a series of inter-subjective games and experiments (such as the famous 'tactile experiments'). The avant-garde now achieved an oppositional role in the most concrete sense, through the alignment between underground writers, artists and musicians and the dissidents who founded the Charter 77 civil rights movement. The legendary band The Plastic People of the Universe, whose incarceration provided an initial impetus for Charter 77, routinely set Egon Bondy's writings to their Zappaesque rock music: Surrealism was thus brought into direct conflict with the authorities and to the forefront of civil rights struggle. Arguably it was precisely the lack of official acceptance that enabled the Czech avant-garde to exist in such an 'uncontaminated' and closely-bound (though not repressively so) form. The fall of Communism and the arrival of free-market liberal democracy thus presented the most serious threat of all, and could have meant the dissipation or even death of Surrealism. Surprisingly, however, the group (now known as the Group of Czech and Slovak Surrealists) has continued to function at a modest level, and it remains as hostile to consumer capitalism as it once was to Stalinist dictatorship. Since Effenberger's death in 1986, the group has had no chief centralising figure or leader, which seems like a logical culmination for a narrative that has passed from a rigorous intellectual and political unity through to a tolerant relativism.

Reform, Renaissance and Revival: Czechoslovakia in the 1960s and the New Wave

The broad assimilation of the avant-garde by the Czechoslovak culture of the Sixties reflects the artistic and intellectual flourishing of a society at once liberated and galvanised by a process of political reform. Just as Surrealism and Devětsil returned to the wider cultural consciousness, so other aspects of the Sixties artistic, philosophical and political culture involved the rediscovery of traditions suppressed, if not destroyed, during the Stalinist years. So many of the cultural and political developments of this period seem at first sight radically new: the youthful New Wave in cinema, the New Economic Model that established an alternative blueprint for a state socialist economy, the political reforms, achieved or projected, geared towards infusing the Communist system with a certain level of democratic freedom and participation. Yet to a large extent the developments of the 1960s also comprise the regaining of a lost continuity. Not only was the world of arts and letters pervaded by a spirit of revival, but this decade also saw the rediscovery of the more liberal and democratic approach that had characterised Czechoslovak Communism in its early, prewar days.[38] Ironically enough, it was the loosening of political orthodoxies that enabled Marxism to live once more, to re-emerge as a dynamic, flexible human science and to find its roots again in national traditions and attitudes.

Yet Eastern Europe's period of political thaw did not begin particularly promisingly for Czechoslovakia. The stability of the Czechoslovak regime amidst the turmoil of the mid-1950s can be attributed perhaps above all to the absence of such large-scale public protests as would culminate in both Gomułka's 'Polish October' and the revolutionary government of Imre Nagy in Hungary. Meaningful reform of the system was also impeded by the involvement of Party First Secretary Antonín Novotný and other powerful figures in the excesses of the Stalinist years. Clearly these elements in the leadership reckoned that any attempt to address the crimes of the past or to establish greater political openness would have serious repercussions for their own positions. Nonetheless, minor gestures towards a thaw were made: a desultory investigation into the political trials of the period 1949–1952 began, against Novotný's wishes, and many political prisoners were quietly released. A degree of liberalisation occurred within academia and the arts, although even this modest thaw would be annulled in the late 1950s. Symptomatic of the conservative backlash was a film conference held in Banská Bystrica in 1959, at which a number of new films were attacked for their formalism, their insufficient 'optimism', and their general fixation on 'private life'.[39] Czechoslovakia thus passed into the 1960s a functioning Stalinist, or neo-Stalinist, state. In 1960 the country adopted a new 'socialist' constitution, which served both as an 'acknowledgement' that socialism had been successfully achieved, and as a means of giving Communist power a basis in law. Galia Golan describes the Constitution as 'a centralist document in which the party and the government were more intimately drawn together and the party declared "the leading force in society and in the State"'.[40]

---

38. Vladimír Kusin, *The Intellectual Origins of the Prague Spring: The Development of Reformist Ideas in Czechoslovakia 1956–1967* (Cambridge: Cambridge University Press, 1971), pp. 1–2.
39. Hames, *The Czechoslovak New Wave*, pp. 35–36.
40. Galia Golan, *The Czechoslovak Reform Movement: Communism in Crisis 1962–1968* (London: Cambridge University Press, 1971), p. 5.

The reform process thus did not begin in earnest until the early 1960s; it is often dated back to the 12th Communist Party Congress of 1962, which established a new commission for the investigation of the show trials, one that would offer a more intensive examination of the trials and would focus on the extended time period 1949–1954. While these investigations did not result in any prosecutions, a number of high-ranking Party officials lost their positions and were replaced by young, untarnished and mostly liberal successors. 1963 saw the beginning of debates about economic methods, prompted by the stagnation of the Czechoslovak economy during that year. The command economy system, in which directives were issued from the centre, was called into question both as an effective system of production and as the one pre-ordained form a socialist economy must take. The Slovak economist Eugen Loebl argued that central planning 'was not a "law" inherent to socialist society'. Against the old Stalinist view that society was 'objectively' determined by such 'laws', Loebl asserted the more humanistic view that 'socialism offered human beings the possibility to change things' as they saw fit.[41] (The rejection of determinism within the economic sphere can be seen as reinforcing contemporaneous developments within Marxist philosophy.) Another economist, Ota Šik, was charged with devising a new system of economic management.[42] Šik's 'New Economic Model', whose principles were accepted by the Party Central Committee in January 1965, involved restoring certain basic market mechanisms, granting a greater degree of autonomy to enterprises and offering rewards to the more successful enterprises. While the New Economic Model was only implemented in 1967, and partially at that, the attack on the old command structure had a significance that exceeded the economic sphere. Indeed the demand for economic reforms is often seen as the catalyst of the reform movement itself. Alfred French writes: 'What ended as a movement for wide political, social, and cultural reforms started as a set of proposals designed to promote improved efficiency, balanced economic growth, and a better use of the country's human and material resources'.[43] The call for economic decentralisation had important political implications: 'Czechoslovak communist policy had tended to absorb into the state apparatus all societal activities and organisation … The philosophy of the [New Economic Model] implied a reverse trend'.[44] Moreover, while the economic reformers had originally felt that 'economic would bring about political democratisation', 'at some stage there came an awareness that the process might have to be reversed', in other words that 'it might be necessary first to

---

41. Ibid., p. 50.
42. Ibid., p. 53.
43. A. [Alfred] French, *Czech Writers and Politics: 1945–1969* (New York: Columbia University Press, 1982), p. 212.
44. Ibid., p. 213.

reform the Party leadership in order to give the [economic] reforms a chance to work'.[45]

As the decade progressed, changes to the political system itself began to be discussed. The ossified Marxist–Leninist principles of 'democratic centralism' and the 'leading role of the Party', while never completely discarded in official circles, were subjected to much reinterpretation. Numerous advocates of reform suggested that the Party should essentially play a role of overall supervision and coordination rather than one of absolute control, and that it might still comprise the guarantor of the country's ideological direction while relinquishing such close involvement in the technicalities of political and economic life. Elements in the Party also acknowledged for the first time the existence of different social strata: orthodoxy dictated that socialism should have done away with class difference and that the Party must continue to eliminate all traces of 'antagonism', but there was a growing acceptance that social differentiation was an unavoidable facet of modern society. One of the central issues with which reformists grappled was how to enable the expression of competing group interests within the framework of Communist rule. In 1966 a committee was set up by the Institute of State and Law at the Czechoslovak Academy of Sciences to 'formulate a hypothesis for the development of the political system'.[46] Chaired by the lawyer and political theorist Zdeněk Mlynář, the committee proposed a level of democratisation that would enable the various social groups to be represented; in this regard the committee members were even prepared to consider the 'positive aspects' of the pluralistic political systems of the West.[47]

The effects of liberalisation were immediately felt in the cultural and intellectual spheres, with many writers, thinkers, artists and filmmakers promptly emboldened by the sense that change was afoot within the Party. The year 1963 was a watershed for Czechoslovak culture, offering a bravura opening round of assaults in the fight against ideological and aesthetic restriction. At the Slovak Writers' Congress of that year, a number of speakers openly criticized Stalinist politics, and the denounced Slovak poet Laco Novomeský was readmitted to the Writers' Union. A conference devoted to the work of Franz Kafka, a writer then considered by orthodox Communists to sit atop the 'cultural dung heap of reaction', was held at Liblice. According to Alexej Kusák, one of the organisers of the event, 'after the Kafka conference everything in culture was, for a time, allowed'.[48] The conference was important

---

45. Ibid., p. 216.
46. Zdeněk Mlynář, quoted in Golan, *The Czechoslovak Reform Movement*, p. 174.
47. Ibid.
48. Alexej Kusák, 'Ke vzniku konference o Franzi Kafkovi v Liblicích v květnu 1963', in *Zlatá šedesátá: Česká literatura a společnost v letech tání, kolotání a… zklamání: Materiály z konference pořádané Ústavem pro českou literaturu AV ČR 16–18. června 1999* (Prague: Ústav pro českou literaturu, 2000), p. 110.

not only for significantly broadening the scope of 'permissible' literature but also for raising the issue of the persistence of alienation within socialist society. From the world of philosophy came Karel Kosík's *The Dialectics of the Concrete* (*Dialektika konkretního*), a landmark work of Marxist humanist thought that implicitly critiques not merely the Stalinist 'distortions' of Marxism–Leninism but some basic assumptions of Leninism itself. The central concept of Marxist humanism is 'praxis': creative, and thereby self-realizing, human activity. For Kosík, the creative power that is innate to all human beings can extend to revolutionary activity, and it is here that Kosík clashes with Leninist thought, according to which only the Party can be the agent or 'subject' of history. Kosík's reformulation of Marxism involves perceiving the world as a 'concrete totality', in other words as 'a structured, developing and self-creating whole'.[49] This dynamic vision is counterposed to the vision of the world in its 'pseudo-concreteness' or 'everydayness': social reality in the latter cases is seen as finished, unchangeable, and individuals as passive objects deprived of agency. (Kosík's critique of 'everydayness' has interesting implications for the Czech New Wave's oft-noted preoccupation with everyday life: do, say, the observational films of Miloš Forman or Ivan Passer offer images of 'concrete totality' or only of 'pseudo-concreteness'?)

The year 1963 also marked the real beginning of the New Wave itself, with Forman, Jaromil Jireš and Věra Chytilová all making their groundbreaking debut features in that year (*Black Peter* (*Černý Petr*), *The Cry* (*Křik*), *Something Different* (*O něčem jiném*)). The two most famous of all the small theatres, the Semafor theatre and the Theatre on the Balustrade (Divadlo na zábradlí), had opened in the late 1950s, but during the 1960s the movement expanded, and increasingly experimental and satirical works were staged. What bound the various developments in the arts at this time was the common rejection of the role of ideological servitude that communism had imposed on culture. This could mean asserting values or ideas contrary to those of the authorities, or simply turning one's back on 'politics' (in its narrow sense) altogether. Yet artistic integrity was hardly given a smooth ride during the decade: cultural progress comprised a continuous struggle in which advances were often coupled with retreats (such as the withholding of the more problematic films, or the introduction of a stringent new press law in 1966). That culture received the degree of tolerance it did might be attributed to the fact that Novotný, though himself a hardliner, considered appeasement of the Party's liberal factions necessary as a means of maintaining power: from this point of view, the degree of cultural liberalisation that took place could be seen as one concession to the forces of reform.[50]

---

49. Satterwhite, *Varieties of Marxist Humanism*, p. 142.
50. Golan, *The Czechoslovak Reform Movement*, p. 48.

Accounts of Czechoslovakia in the 1960s often make mention of those writers who involved themselves directly in the reform movement. A relatively large amount has been written on the 1967 Czechoslovak Writers' Congress, at which a number of prominent writers (and Party members), including Milan Kundera, Ludvík Vaculík and Antonín Liehm, made speeches criticizing the Communist system, and on Vaculík's '2000 Words' manifesto, designed to encourage mass mobilisation in the interests of political improvement.[51] Yet there was a much broader spectrum of cultural activity in 1960s Czechoslovakia than is often suggested, one that stretched beyond such 'engaged', party-affiliated writers such as Vaculík and embraced such radically unorthodox figures, aesthetically and politically, as Effenberger, Bondy, the young dramatist Václav Havel and the avant-garde poet Jiří Kolář. The liberal Communist writers were not the sole representatives of an 'authentic', anti-Stalinist culture in the 1960s, nor were they necessarily the most important. According to the philosopher Ivan Sviták, himself a non-conformist Marxist and a Surrealist sympathiser, the 'true intellectual leaders' of Czechoslovak culture in the 1960s were not the 'temporarily reforming Communists' but 'members of the non-Communist intelligentsia',[52] among whom Sviták includes such figures as Effenberger, Kolář, Havel and Jan Werich. Sviták further suggests that it was these 'independent' figures that 'made the Czech culture great', by protesting 'the repressive regimentation of art' and 'promoting that organic growth of values which a totalitarian dictatorship always and everywhere hinders, no matter whether it happens to be momentarily conciliatory or aggressive'.[53]

Sviták is correct to imply that, amidst the plethora of movements and ideas that partook of the same cultural moment, many significant artists and intellectuals were unaligned with reformist politics and maintained a more independent, and aggressively oppositional, stance. Thus it would be wrong to identify too closely the aims and values of, say, Havel or the Surrealists with those of the Prague Spring. While, as we have seen, the reformists tried to reconcile their commitment to democracy and civil rights with a persistent faith in the 'leading role' of the Party, writers such as Havel, Effenberger and Hrabal espoused, whether implicitly or explicitly, a more anarchistic or, in whatever sense, 'revolutionary' stance. (Bondy was certainly a revolutionary in more than one sense, having been variously described as a Trotskyist and a Maoist.) The humanist reinterpretations of Marxism that were then appearing

51. Z.A.B. Zeman, *The Prague Spring: A Report on Czechoslovakia 1968* (Harmondsworth: Penguin, 1969); Liehm, *The Politics of Culture*; Dušan Hamšik, *Writers Against Rulers*, translated by D. Orpington (London: Hutchinson, 1971).
52. Ivan Sviták, '*The Politics of Culture* by Antonín J. Liehm and Peter Kussi' [book review], *The American Political Science Review*, Vol. 67, No. 3, September 1973, pp. 1073–74.
53. Ibid., p. 1074.

in the Writers' Union magazine, *Literární noviny*, had to compete with other, more provocative philosophical and political trends often imported from Western Europe or the USA. The writings of the radical Freudian, Frankfurt School Marxist and so-called 'father of the New Left' Herbert Marcuse, and of the French Situationists Guy Debord and Raoul Vaneigem, were immensely popular in the Prague of the late 1960s.[54] A 1965 visit by the American Beat poet Allen Ginsberg, who was crowned 'King of the May' by students of the Charles University, presaged the wide absorption of countercultural ideas and lifestyles by Prague youth: according to Alfred French, the city was known 'for a brief spell ... as the Hippie capital of Europe'.[55] Thus, in 1960s Czechoslovakia cultural life transcended the boundaries of official discussion, more closely approximating the spontaneous, 'unplanned' development of culture in democratic societies. Yet one must also acknowledge that, precisely in so far as liberals within the Party helped achieve some independence (first partial, then total) for culture, the reform movement itself was the condition for artistic and political plurality: the Party moderates sanctioned the independent radicals.

The 'disintegratory' tendency (as Effenberger would call it) of Czech and Slovak culture is evident in the diversity of the New Wave films themselves. There is no such thing as a 'Czech school' of filmmaking. The Czechoslovak New Wave has no equivalent of the Oberhausen Manifesto that launched the New German Cinema, nor did its members comprise a close group of colleagues with shared and rigorously formulated artistic tastes, as was the case with the critics-turned-filmmakers of the French *Nouvelle Vague*. The only obvious common ground between these filmmakers was their general youthfulness (although several key New Wave films were made by older figures, such as Vojtěch Jasný and František Vláčil) and their attendance at the FAMU film school. Yet the FAMU of the 1960s appears to have fostered an appetite for debate and an independent spirit more than the adherence to any aesthetic rules. Beyond their age and education, the New Wave filmmakers were united by their rejection of the prescribed aesthetics of Socialist Realism: Ivan Passer describes the New Wave as a 'conspiracy against stupidity'.[56] One might suggest that the young filmmakers were united in their opposition to uniformity itself. This individualistic mentality was obviously a reaction against the enforced homogeneity of the films of the previous decade, although it was no doubt also reinforced by the widely influential *politique des auteurs*, which promoted the idea of films as the expression of directorial subjectivity rather than as the product of collaboration or the demonstration

54. Dvorský, 'Z podzemí do podzemí', in Alan, *Alternativní kultura*, p. 141.
55. French, *Czech Writers and Politics 1945–1969*, p. 218.
56. Ivan Passer, interviewed in Robert Buchar, *Czech New Wave Filmmakers in Interviews* (Jefferson; London: McFarland and Company, 2004), p. 144.

of craft. From this perspective the filmmakers' cultivation of stylistic distinctiveness was as much a product of broad trends in film theory and practice as it was a tribute to freer political circumstances.

Institutional changes contributed further to the fostering of difference. In the early 1960s, following an internal 1962 directive, the film industry was reorganised into small, quasi-autonomous production groups, with each group headed by a major creative figure.[57] Such changes reflect the general trend towards economic decentralisation, although the specific models for the new system were the Polish 'film units', established in the mid-1950s, and the small Czech animation studios that had constituted a rare instance of autonomy within the rigidly centralised system of the Stalinist period. It is impossible to undervalue the unique situation in which Czechoslovak, Polish and Yugoslav filmmakers found themselves during this period of liberalisation: national cinemas were able to develop freely, unconstrained either by bureaucratic interference and political pressures, or by the demands of the marketplace. If, as Švankmajer has suggested, both capitalism's commercial imperatives and Stalinism's propagandistic imperatives resulted in the homogenisation of culture, it is easy to see why Czechoslovak film exhibited a greater variety at this time than at any other.

The reform process came to a head in early 1968. Liberals had by then gained increasing ground within the Central Committee and the Party's hand had also been forced by various confrontations, including the aforementioned Writers' Congress and student demonstrations in 1966 and 1967. In January 1968, Alexander Dubček, a reformist, was chosen to replace Novotný as First Secretary, and two months later, Ludvík Svoboda replaced Novotný as President. Political debate was unleashed at all levels of the Party and in public life; the 'revolution from the top' became a mass participatory process. Two independent political organisations were founded, the Club of Engaged Non-Party Members (KAN) and Club 231, comprising former victims of the Stalinist purges. In April, the Central Committee published an 'Action Programme' that outlined the new goals of the Party. According to Grzegorz Ekiert, this document 'advocated the necessity of political reforms and democratic procedures within the Communist party and other organizations', 'pointed to the need for a new electoral law ... as well as guarantees of basic political freedom for all citizens', and 'spoke of the need for other social and political organisations belonging to the National Front [a coalition of parties and mass organisations that was nominally separate from the Communist Party] to be granted autonomy and to play a larger role in the country's affairs'.[58] The Action Programme also 'supported economic reforms and the

---

57. Hames, *The Czechoslovak New Wave*, p. 27.
58. Grzegorz Ekiert, *State Against Society: Political Crises and Their Aftermath in East Central Europe* (Princeton: Princeton University Press, 1996), pp. 139–40.

democratization of economic institutions', and even 'suggested the possibility of small-scale private enterprises'.[59] Plans were announced for convening an 'extraordinary Congress' in September, at which, it was hoped, the election of a new Central Committee would rout the remaining conservatives and thereby ease the path of reform.

Sadly, Cold War politics intervened before any substantial reforms could be implemented. The formal abolition of censorship, though of course transient, was to be one of the few significant achievements of Dubček's brief reign (another successful, and lasting, reform was the federalisation of Czechoslovakia, formally declared in October 1968). Yet subsequent accounts of the Prague Spring have questioned whether the implementation of the Action Programme's proposals would have resulted in a truly democratic system: after all, the Central Committee ruled out the existence of genuine opposition parties, against which the Communists would have had to compete in elections. As Ekiert argues, the Action Programme 'was not a radical document calling for a decisive transformation of the state-socialist system': '[t]he reformers wanted to preserve the Communist party's leading role, extensive state involvement in the economy, and the dominance of collectivist property rights'.[60] Kieran Williams writes: 'the reforms of 1968, in intention and execution, amounted to only the liberalization of a Leninist regime'.[61] Be that as it may, the reforms were too radical for the Soviet Union: Brezhnev's Politburo was particularly alarmed by reports of a free media permitted to propagate anti-Soviet and 'anti-Communist' sentiments. At a July meeting between the Czechoslovak and Soviet leaderships, Dubček promised to exercise greater control over the press and to maintain Czechoslovakia's commitment to the Warsaw Pact military arrangement. The Soviets were far from reassured by subsequent developments, and another conference, this time involving all the Warsaw Pact countries, was convened in Bratislava at the beginning of August. The conference initially appeared to have resulted in a victory for the reformists: the Soviet tanks that had been stationed on Czechoslovak soil, ostensibly to practise manoeuvres, were withdrawn. Yet the tanks, along with those of the other Eastern bloc nations, were to return seventeen days later in the name of 'fraternal assistance' and the aversion of counter-revolution. The principal Czechoslovak leaders were arrested and taken to the Soviet Union, where they were forced to sign the Moscow Protocol stipulating that Czechoslovakia return to hard-line policies.

Upon his return to Prague, a shaken Dubček assured the public in a radio broadcast that something of the reform movement could still be salvaged.

---

59. Ibid., p. 140.
60. Ibid.
61. Kieran Williams, *The Prague Spring and its Aftermath: Czechoslovak Politics 1968–1970* (Cambridge: Cambridge University Press, 1997), p. 3.

Despite the almost immediate reintroduction of censorship, cultural life hardly changed in the months after the invasion. Indeed, during late 1968 and 1969 Czechoslovak culture peaked in both achievement and audacity, with the Surrealists openly pursuing their activities and with many of the most aesthetically radical and politically provocative New Wave films being made. Karel Pryl argues that the invasion stirred filmmakers to defiance, and that these later films comprised a 'conscious demonstration of a refusal to give in'.[62] By April 1969, the 'realist' Gustav Husák had manoeuvred his way to the position of First Secretary, replacing the no longer tenable Dubček. With Husák's accession, so-called Normalisation, the destruction of the reform movement and the restoration of the neo-Stalinist system, began in earnest. During the next two years thousands of high-ranking professionals lost their jobs, and hundreds of thousands were expelled from the Party. A process of screening was established as a means to test the political sympathies of Party members. As Milan Šimečka has suggested, Normalisation was a model of European civility, with not a judicial murder to Husák's name.[63] Nonetheless the regime was coldly, almost scientifically efficient in securing its objectives. In 1970, Normalisation spread to the film industry, and a number of the films that had been made during the previous two years were shelved. Many other films were also banned, and several notoriously designated 'banned forever'. The production groups were abolished, and the Barrandov film studio was placed under new management, with the hardline Ludvík Toman appointed as Barrandov's chief literary adviser. Among the New Wave filmmakers who did not emigrate to the West, the majority were dropped by the studio; some, such as Menzel and Chytilová, were later to bounce back with more conventional projects, while others, such as Juráček, effectively saw their careers and lives ruined by Normalisation. Outlining Barrandov's new artistic policy, Toman announced a 'return to the spectator', an end to excessive 'experiments' and 'modernness', and the rejection of 'scepticism, feelings of alienation, desperation, inconsiderate sexuality, egoistic bourgeois individualism'.[64] In other words, a decade of minor miracles, when avant-garde 'experiments' penetrated the mainstream and Eastern bloc socialism presented a liberal, human, if not fully democratic face, had decisively ended.

62. Karel Pryl, quoted in Hames, *The Czechoslovak New Wave*, p. 240.
63. Milan Šimečka, *The Restoration of Order: The Normalization of Czechoslovakia* (New York: Verso, 1984).
64. Ludvík Toman, quoted in Hames, *The Czechoslovak New Wave*, p. 241.

Chapter 2

Pavel Juráček's *Josef Kilián* (1963) and *A Case for the Young Hangman* (1969): From the Surreal Object to the Absurd Signifier

Before Kafka, Beyond Politics

Josef Kilián, Pavel Juráček's first significant directorial effort, appeared during the beginnings of Czechoslovakia's political and cultural thaw.[1] Despite the film's short length (it runs just under 40 minutes), it was undoubtedly one of the most remarkable and provocative Czechoslovak films to have been released for many years. Yet in a sense Juráček's Kafkaesque portrayal of impenetrable bureaucracy could not have found a more ideal context of reception than its domestic environment. *Josef Kilián* appeared in the same year as both the groundbreaking conference on Franz Kafka in Liblice, a key step towards the domestic rehabilitation of that writer's work and a significant moment in the reform

---

1. Juráček directed *Josef Kilián* in collaboration with Jan Schmidt, and the film is traditionally credited to both directors. Nonetheless, Juráček, who wrote the screenplay, is generally accepted as the film's 'authentic' creator. As Juráček had trained at FAMU as a scenarist, he was not permitted to direct his first film alone, and so he enlisted his friend Schmidt, who had studied direction and had some filmmaking experience, to collaborate. According to Juráček, Schmidt's role was not so much creative as protective: '[I]n reality I shot it myself. And Jan protected me and looked after me when I came up against the Barrandov machine.' (Pavel Juráček, *Postava k podpírání*, edited by Jiří Cieslar (Prague: Havran, 2001), p. 84). However, Schmidt himself insists that '[i]n some spots the author was singular, in others, plural.' (Jan Schmidt, quoted in Hames, *The Czechoslovak New Wave*, p. 146). Whatever the extent of Schmidt's input, the concern here is with the thematic and formal correlations between *Josef Kilián* and Juráček's other works. Thus, it is Juráček's artistic personality that will constitute the interpretive 'grid' for this discussion of *Josef Kilián*.

process as a whole, and the first production of Václav Havel's dramatic debut, the Absurdist farce *The Garden Party* (*Zahradní slavnost*). Social satire was at this time beginning to emerge on the stages of Prague's small theatres, and if such satire frequently took an absurd form, then this was surely due not only to the political necessity of offering critique through the disguises of allegory, but also to the sense that Communist reality was itself already absurd.

In his authoritative study of the 'Theatre of the Absurd', Martin Esslin suggests that while West European dramatists regarded absurdity as primarily an existential or metaphysical phenomenon, East European exponents of the genre presented it as the corollary of specific political conditions.[2] Writing of the Polish Absurd dramatist Sławomir Mrożek, Marketa Goetz-Stankiewicz observes that for an East European audience an Absurdist play could achieve 'a realism undreamt of in the West': amongst theatre audiences in Warsaw even Eugene Ionesco and Samuel Beckett were 'felt to be political writers'.[3] At the Liblice conference the writings of Kafka (arguably the most important exponent *avant la lettre* of the Absurd) were cast in similarly politicized terms. In his final overview of the conference the Czech critic Eduard Goldstücker rhetorically asks the question, 'Is Kafka contemporary?' Goldstücker responds to this question by citing the opinion of another contributor, Ernst Fischer: 'insofar as alienation has been overcome in our world, Kafka has stopped being contemporary'. Thus, Goldstücker boldly asserts, as even socialist society has not yet eradicated alienation, 'Kafka is contemporary even for us'.[4] This perspective sums up the mood of the conference, just as it sets the tone for the subsequent critical explorations of Kafka by Czech reformists. On the other hand, an important contribution by Ivan Sviták argues that Kafka's importance lies more in his concern with subjective experience than in any direct political relevance.

It is easy to see why Juráček's film has routinely been interpreted as a politicized foray into the Absurd. Its premise is as simple and striking as that of any of Kafka or Mrożek's stories. A lonely man, Herold, rents a cat from a bizarre state 'cat lending house', but when he attempts to return it he finds that the establishment has disappeared; fearful of the consequences of not returning the cat on time, Herold goes to inform the authorities, and spends virtually the remainder of the film immersed in a labyrinthine bureaucracy, as no official will assume the responsibility for dealing with Herold's problem. Concurrently with this 'quest', Herold is seeking a certain Josef Kilián, a mysterious, eternally absent figure who appears to hold a position of great

2. Martin Esslin, *The Theatre of the Absurd* (Harmondsworth: Penguin, 1991), pp. 316–17.
3. Marketa Goetz-Stankiewicz, 'Sławomir Mrożek: Two Forms of the Absurd', *Contemporary Literature*, Vol. 12, No. 2, Spring, 1971, p. 189.
4. Eduard Goldstücker, 'Shrnutí a diskuse', in *Franz Kafka: Liblická konference 1963* (Prague: Nakladatelství Československé akademie věd, 1963), p. 269.

Figure 2.1 Herold (Karel Vašíček) visits the cat lending house. *Josef Kilián* (*Postava k podpírání*, Pavel Juráček and Jan Schmidt, 1963) ©Czech National Film Archive.

official authority: a Josef K. who is no longer the victim but the agent of a social order that remains, sadly, as alienating and senseless as before. The film's Kafkaesque qualities were immediately recognised and praised (indeed those who saw the film usually considered it a truer evocation of Kafka's sensibility than Orson Welles's bravura but liberty-taking adaptation of *The Trial*, released two years earlier), as were the social and political implications of those qualities. In his 1964 review from *Literární noviny*, Antonín Liehm hints at a relevance he could not then fully spell out when he writes:

> there are young people, I do not want to estimate whether there are many or a few of them, who walk through the world, through our world, with the feeling this story expresses. This feeling is not good, it is abnormal, it is dangerous, but they didn't think it up, it objectively exists.[5]

Writing many years later, Jiří Cieslar observes how Juráček modifies or updates Kafkaesque menace, the film's air of subtle unease and 'tolerable' fear thus capturing the atmosphere of the 'soft' totalitarianism of the post-Stalinist

---

5.   Liehm, '*Postava k podpírání*', *Literární noviny*, No. 45, 1964, p. 8.

years. The film conjures up the 'uncertainty of a disguisedly totalitarian world, on the surface without visible conflicts or obvious calamities': 'no one shouts at the shy pilgrim in search of the lending house, at no point does a push await him, let alone any rougher treatment or the death which is of course prepared for Kafka's Josef K.'[6]

No doubt Cieslar's observations concerning the film's 'documentary' quality are accurate, and characterize the response that many Czechs had to the film at the time and that many survivors of the Communist era still have today. Yet is Juráček's film reducible to its topical significance? Do the currents of absurdity run no deeper than the injustices and incompetences of totalitarian experience? It is interesting to note that Juráček himself was dismayed by what he saw as the misunderstanding that greeted the film, however complimentary the reactions to it. In a diary extract from around the time of the film's release, Juráček reveals that his source of inspiration was far more intimate than was generally assumed. The roots of *Josef Kilián*, as of all his creative work, are, he asserts with some frustration, to be found in a time before Communist authoritarianism, before political consciousness, and even before his discovery of Kafka:

> I cannot explain to anyone that [*Josef Kilián*] is not Kafkaesque, that is it is mine and not a single metre of it would be changed if Kafka had never lived. This is a film which was written and shot twenty years ago with tens and hundreds of other stories, which are fixed in my memory and whose remnants come up to the surface and resemble archaeological discoveries ... I cannot say if I was happy then ... It seems to me that I was not happy. One thing however is certain: I was one hundred per cent. Never in my life will I be as complete as then. My unceasing orientation towards childhood, my dependence on it, are then a desire for lost completeness. I lived in perfect harmony with my dreams and ideas. The everyday world was for me bizarre and the bizarre seemed to me self-evident. I was able to occupy myself for days with thinking about the roundness of the globe and the horizon had for me an almost magic significance. The greatest tragedies for me were definitive answers ... recognised and attested truth reminded me of a cold, dead and immobile thing which it is necessary to abandon.[7]

During preparation for *A Case for the Young Hangman*, his second feature-length film (after *Every Young Man* (*Každý mladý muž*, 1965)), Juráček published an 'explication' of the forthcoming work: clearly he was concerned to ensure this film would be better understood than *Josef Kilián*. While he discusses here the film's literary inspiration (it is freely derived from the third part of Jonathan

---

6.   Jiří Cieslar, 'Předmluva' (Foreword), in Juráček, *Postava k podpírání*, p. 11.
7.   Juráček, *Deník 1959–1974*, pp. 333–34.

Swift's *Gulliver's Travels* (1726)) and his intentions of exploring 'human stupidity' and notions of historical progress, he also repeats, and extends, this diary account concerning his childhood and its inspirational role.

The elevation of childhood to the status of muse reveals the quintessentially Surrealist element in Juráček's work, as does the centrality of fantasies and dreams to the creative process. The Theatre of the Absurd is usually seen as dealing with external realities, at least with the void that the outer world reveals itself to be. The Absurd vision attains a social, and cosmic, perspective, notwithstanding that that vision may be mediated through the subjective factors of sustaining delusion or intense anguish.[8] Surrealism, generally speaking, is the more penetratingly introspective movement, the one preoccupied by dreams, desire and the psychic economy. This chapter does not seek to dispute that Juráček's films and the world they represent have strong affinities with the Theatre of the Absurd (and with its historical forbears), but rather to suggest that these films foreground the compatibility, perhaps even the essential identity, of the Absurd and the Surreal. Not only do the Absurd and the Surreal, in their most typical form, share some stylistic qualities and overt themes: they also share certain philosophical premises. There are thus profound as well as superficial reasons to regard Surrealism, as both Esslin and Neil Cornwell do, as a forerunner of the work of Beckett, Ionesco et al.[9] It could even be argued that the more 'realistic' and 'political' *Josef Kilián* uncovers the Surrealism at the heart of the Absurd, while the more dream-like and 'fantastical' *Young Hangman* uncovers the Absurdism at the heart of the Surreal.

Yet in what ways is the terrifying world of totalitarian Absurdity the same as Surrealism's ludic, infantile waking dreams? One might point to an identity at both a thematic and a narrative level. What should interest us in Juráček's lyrical account of his 'visionary' childhood is not so much the extent to which it enables a psycho-biographical interpretation of his films as the way that account manifests certain preoccupations and qualities already evident in the films themselves. Perhaps Juráček is less concerned here with strictly accurate reminiscence than with positing a kind of model childhood, with asserting 'childhood' as a particular state of being. Jan Švankmajer describes his childhood as his 'alter ego', thus suggesting that childhood is not delimitable to a temporal phase but rather comprises a specific form of consciousness whose thought processes are eternally present, if usually repressed. Lest his fetishization of childhood appears too sentimentalized, Juráček asserts that he was not a 'happy' child. Indeed the 'visionary' fantasies that Juráček narrates inscribe the yearning for a lost wholeness and fullness, just as they note the

---

8.   Esslin, pp. 404–5.

9.   Ibid, pp. 378–86; Neil Cornwell, *The Absurd in Literature* (Manchester: Manchester University Press, 2006), pp. 81–85.

fearful apprehension of lack. The infant Juráček fantasises about 'the roundness of the globe', yet he also imagines that the world beyond his own experience constitutes a blank, an absence, that 'the houses of distant streets are created only out of facades supported from behind by girders'.[10] At one moment he is enchanted by the 'magical significance' of the horizon, at another he senses that nothing lies beyond it, its plane thus constituting an edge or limit of the world. (This suggestive image of the horizon will be used as the opening shot of *A Case for the Young Hangman*; one might also note how the image of 'facades supported from behind by girders', recalling the two-dimensional street-fronts of cinematic yore, anticipates Juráček's future profession.) A key insight of Surrealists such as Švankmajer and Vítězslav Nezval is that childhood, for all its vitality and its inspirational qualities, is not necessarily a time of happiness, and is fraught with frustrations and the awareness of limitations. Life is already perceived to be absurd by this child, and without the aid of the totalitarian state. The world of Kafka turns out to be not so different from that of Lewis Carroll.

We can also see Juráček's anecdotes as offering a model or allegory of his films' narrative practices. His childhood self is repelled by 'definitive answers', and desires to keep all the different possibilities of 'truth' in play for as long as possible. In a sense this represents the demand for life itself to be structured like a dream, offering a multiplicity of possible meanings. Drawing on a familiar image from Czech fairy tales, Juráček writes: 'I would never have opened the thirteenth chamber'.[11] The resistance of an ultimate 'revelation' is expressed in an appropriately narrative-based image. From this perspective that unseen beyond of the horizon offers not only an existential revelation but also the opportunity for unbounded speculation. The polysemic quality of Juráček's adult works can be seen as an attempt to recuperate, if only temporarily, that thrilling sense of uncertainty with which the child experiences the world. It is perhaps this quality, more than any overtly fantastical elements, that makes his films (at least those he directed himself) such dream-like, as well as nightmarish, experiences: as both Freud and Lacan have shown in their different ways, dream representation is characterized as much by its textual practices as by its content. Polysemy, or what Theodor Adorno describes as a 'luxuriant multiplicity' of meanings, is also a characteristic of Surrealist art and, according to Adorno, the key source of its power. Yet does not such uncertainty also define the 'Absurd' experience of the subject of the Communist state? That citizen forced to deal with the machinery of such a state, or indeed with modern bureaucracy in general, is in a similar position to the child confronted with a world that is impenetrable, mysterious and obscurely threatening. It

---

10.   Juráček, 'Explicace', *Postava k podpírání*, p. 122.
11.   Ibid. The 'thirteenth chamber' generally refers, both in fairy tales and as a Czech colloquialism, to that place where the most zealously guarded secrets are kept.

could be said that, to a large extent, the 'modernist' obscurity of *Josef Kilián* derives from the fact that the bureaucratic apparatus the film portrays constitutes in itself a kind of dream text, withholding certainty from its supplicants, presenting a series of ambiguous signs and forever deferring revelation or resolution. The relay of blank-faced bureaucrats whom Herold encounters serves as an array of sphinx-like symbols, while the incongruous lecture that one senior bureaucrat gives Herold about literacy rates in Brazil can be compared with the obtuse verbiage of dream-speak. Yet little in the film's representation of bureaucracy suggests an exaggeration or a departure, and only in places, most obviously perhaps in the film's initiating premise, does Juráček seem to be striving for an overtly 'surreal' effect.

However, if the Czechoslovak experience of the 1960s enables Juráček to construct his depressive brand of phantasmagoria, his films are also preoccupied with ideas that both predate and transcend the topical-political. This chapter aims to examine how Juráček's films explore fundamental issues surrounding identity, notably the constitution of subjectivity through language and the sense of loss that process entails. While the framework of Lacanian psychoanalysis will be broadly employed to this end, this is not to suggest that Juráček was consciously influenced by such theories, but rather that the concerns explored through theoretical constructs were already implicit in Juráček's artistic influences: in fact it is this engagement with loss, lack and language that connects Juráček's work to the Absurd and the Surreal at the deepest level, and also reveals the fundamental connectedness of both 'genres'. A key term among Czechoslovakia's Marxist humanist philosophers and reformist writers in the 1960s was 'alienation', a term usually defined in accordance with the early Marx and used to denote the denial of 'praxis', of human self-realization, by modern (capitalist and Communist) societies. Yet Lacan's work and, it will be proposed, Juráček's films posit an alienation that is originary and constitutional, socially determined only to the extent that linguistic or symbolic structures are an inevitable adjunct of civilization. The various conceptions of alienation interact throughout these films, as Juráček, much in the manner of Kafka himself, exploits the metaphorical and allegorical properties of dystopian bureaucracy.

Despite Juráček's assertion that *Josef Kilián* would have been the same film even if Kafka had not existed, we need not discount the Prague writer's presence throughout these works. The rediscovery of Kafka in the early 1960s at the hands of liberal Marxist critics and philosophers, while undeniably important in paving the way for subsequent cultural liberalizations and helping set the tone for the Czechoslovak culture of that decade, was to some extent also a political appropriation. Kafka was posthumously yoked to the cause of reform socialism, and transformed into an 'engaged' writer in a way that arguably distorts or at least simplifies his work. In fact it is difficult to imagine that any particular 'version' of Kafka could ever be definitive: as Albert Camus famously remarked, 'The whole art of Kafka consists in forcing the reader to re-read.'[12] In a Stalinist culture of enforced over-legibility, that inexhaustible amenability to re-reading, the spectrum of interpretations that his work enables, may in itself constitute one of Kafka's most subversive qualities. The Liblice speakers and other Czech critics seized on particular possibilities of interpretation, yet their readings do not exhaust the meaning of Kafka's work, nor of Juráček's own deployment of the Kafkaesque. Kafka can as easily be claimed for psychoanalysis as for politics, and it is worth noting that Czech culture's original introduction to Kafka occurred via the literal mediation of Surrealism: the Czech Surrealist Group helped publish the first Czech edition of the then unknown writer's novel *The Castle* (*Das Schloß*) upon the recommendation of André Breton, subtitling the book 'a Surrealist novel' and providing a cover illustration by Toyen.[13]

As has been observed elsewhere, reformist critics such as Goldstücker tended to 'recruit' writers and artists for the struggle against Stalinist orthodoxies, and thereby asserted the ideological 'serviceability' of art as surely as did the defenders of Socialist Realism.[14] The Kafka presented by Goldstücker's account was a humanist in revolt, a revolutionary idealist who 'wanted by any means to preserve faith in mankind and its future'.[15] Kafka here becomes a proponent of social progress, whose vision is soon to be realized in present-day socialism: given that it is in contemporary Czechoslovakia that 'humanism is … winning out despite all the temporary problems, jolts and reversals', modern Czechoslovak writers are well-suited to 'adopt' and 'develop' Kafka's 'heritage'.[16] Leaving aside the value of Goldstücker's comments as literary criticism, we should observe that in the films of Juráček, one of Kafka's most significant Czechoslovak 'heirs', there is hardly such an unambiguous affirmation of progress, or of the benefits that this progress might bring to humanity. It seems that Juráček's original conception for *Young Hangman*, remnants of which remain in the finished film, was of a society developing backwards, 'advancing' into barbarism. In fact, for Juráček the only hope of a relative contentment (if not of happiness) lies not in advance but in a form of personal regression, in the return to the imaginative freedom of childhood.

---

12. Albert Camus, *The Myth of Sisyphus* (Harmondsworth: Penguin, 2005), p. 124.
13. Hames, *The Czechoslovak New Wave*, p. 139; Alexej Kusák, 'Ke vzniku konference o Franzi Kafkovi v Liblicích v květnu 1963', in *Zlatá šedesátá*, p. 103.
14. Tomáš Kubíček, 'Myšlení o literatuře v prostředí českých literárních časopisů šedesátých let', in *Zlatá šedesátá*, p. 133.
15. Eduard Goldstücker, in *Franz Kafka: Liblická konference 1963*, p. 271.
16. Ibid., p. 272.

Lost Objects, Endless Signifiers

'All drowned girls look the same.' – Lemuel Gulliver in *A Case for the Young Hangman*

A voyage of desire is charted in each of Juráček's films, even in the apparently 'sexless' and alienated *Josef Kilián*, whose protagonist appears to have no significant sexual relationships. As we shall see, this film's very absence of fulfilment and its inhumanly fetishistic character are themselves symptomatic of Juráček's Surrealist-inflected account of desire. Contemporary writing on Surrealism illuminates the parallels between the Surrealists' representations of desire and Lacanian psychoanalysis, with some critics even suggesting that 'Lacan's work bears the traces of his early surrealist associations'.[17] Of course, in the Lacanian scheme desire originates in the experience of loss that accompanies the infant's accession to the symbolic order. The price paid for one's emergence as a subject is a profound and immutable alienation, the sacrifice of a primary plenitude or wholeness.[18] The object of desire, that non-existent yet highly potent object that Lacan terms object *petit a*, is the 'missing part' of that forsaken 'being', 'the representative of our lost immortality and vitality',[19] the 'rem(a)inder' of an original (and hypothetical) unity between the infant and its mother.[20] Given that this object does not exist and can never be found, the life of desire comprises nothing but an endless substitution of real objects, of objects desired only to the extent that they seem to embody or contain object *a*: as Bruce Fink writes, 'desire is a constant search for something else, and there is no specifiable object that is capable of satisfying it'.[21] Contemporary writing on Surrealism has illuminated parallels between these Lacanian ideas and the Surrealists' own representations of desire. Many classic Surrealist texts and artworks have also revealed desire as an eternal process of substitution, in contradiction of the romantic ideals that the artists themselves explicitly espoused. André Breton may have professed his faith in the possibility of a lasting attachment to a unique love object, yet, as Johanna Malt argues in her discussion of Breton's novel *Nadja* (1928), Breton's writing presents rather an alternation between different female muses.[22]

---

17.   Johanna Malt, *Obscure Objects of Desire: Surrealism, Fetishism, and Politics* (Oxford: Oxford University Press, 2004), p. 26.
18.   Jean-Michel Rabaté, *The Cambridge Companion to Lacan* (Cambridge: Cambridge University Press, 2003), p. 120.
19.   Mark Bracher, *Lacan, Discourse and Social Change* (Ithaca: Cornell University Press, 1993), pp. 41–42.
20.   Bruce Fink, *The Lacanian Subject* (Princeton: Princeton University Press, 1995), p. 94.
21.   Ibid., p. 90.
22.   Malt, op. cit.

The fateful action of the renting of the cat in *Josef Kilián*, an action that might otherwise seem unmotivated or banal, can be interpreted in terms of a Surrealist 'narrative' of lack, desire and substitution. Herold's coming upon the cat shop by chance is comparable in this sense to the Surrealists' discovery of found objects (*trouvailles*). The found object is explicitly described within Bretonian Surrealism as 'a manifestation of objective chance, i.e., a marvelous resolution of "internal finality" and "external causality", desire and object'.[23] Yet in so far as the found object is really a manifestation of that 'lost object' that is object *a*, such a 'resolution' can never take place: '[t]he found object is always a substitute, always a displacement, that drives on its own search'.[24] Hal Foster argues that the Surrealists did, at some level, apprehend these acquisitions as part of a process of substitution impelled by lack: for instance, the supposedly fulfilling slipper spoon of Breton's *L'Amour fou* (1937) is transformed into a 'figure of lack', 'an image of desire based on an originary separation … and driven by an infinite substitution'.[25] Juráček displays a similar awareness of desire's basis in lack: the cat shop, which promised plenitude and completeness, becomes itself an absence, a 'lost object' that must be (yet can never be) refound. This disappearance also points to the object *a*'s chimerical status. Pets are actually cited by Lacan as a possible embodiment of the object *a*, and the cat's status as such in this film is particularly apt given that, within Czech culture, the possession of pets carries associations of sexual frustration.[26] Pets also have connotations of homeliness and childhood, although this is a homeliness that is alienated, literally 'unhomely' (if not authentically 'uncanny' in the Freudian sense), as the cat is, and remains, the property of the state. The motif thus serves as a satirical reflection on an authoritarian system that even encroaches upon one's home life.

Yet glimpses into Herold's lonely, drab existence point subtly to longings and forms of estrangement far removed from the realm of authoritarian bureaucracy. As Peter Hames observes, the two short scenes set in Herold's small, sparsely furnished apartment suggest an 'alienation' that is 'outside any particular time'.[27] To expand somewhat on Hames's clearly accurate comments, this alienation is as much the originary alienation propounded by psychoanalysis as the isolation of urban life. In the first of these scenes we see Herold opening a parcel from his mother and reading her letter; the mother's voice is heard reciting the letter's contents. This seemingly extraneous allusion to filial separation, and the fact of the mother's voice emanating into this atomized world from some offscreen, forsaken other place, help us to read Herold's

23. Foster, *Compulsive Beauty*, p. 40.
24. Ibid., p. 43.
25. Ibid., p. 42.
26. Bracher, *Lacan, Discourse and Social Change*, p. 44.
27. Hames, *The Czechoslovak New Wave*, p. 143.

actions in relation to the original, constitutively necessary severance of the maternal bond. Of course the voice is itself one of the most ubiquitous embodiments of the object *a*, one of the privileged registers in which the mother's desire can once again be perceived.[28] (Perhaps it is not coincidental or irrelevant that the vivacious tones of a female singer are also heard in this scene, playing over Herold's radio.) The cat's function of substituting for a human presence is suggested by its sitting in a large armchair. However, the second scene set in the apartment implies the drifting of Herold's desire away from his pet: he pushes the cat off his bed as he arranges a late-night sexual encounter over the telephone (this brief exchange representing another allusion to the abstracted part-object of the female voice).

What is implicit, if not virtually subliminal, in *Josef Kilián* becomes explicit in *Young Hangman*, and much of this cinematic journey through the crazed scientific 'utopia' of Balnibarbi is taken up with the delusions of desire. That is to say that *Young Hangman*, with its more pronounced psychoanalytic theme, is the more classically Surrealist of the two films (Jonathan Swift, whose famous work of fantasy provided the genesis of this film, was himself designated a 'Surrealist in malice' in Breton's *Manifesto of Surrealism* (1924)).[29] *Young Hangman*'s protagonist, Lemuel Gulliver (Juráček preserves the name if little of the identity of Swift's hero), is tortured by the memory of his drowned adolescent sweetheart Marketa, a narrative motif that in itself evokes the original trauma of primary separation. In Balnibarbi Gulliver encounters a

Figure 2.2 Princess Niké, AKA Tereza (Klára Jerneková) in *A Case for the Young Hangman* (*Případ pro začínajícího kata*, Pavel Juráček, 1969) ©Ateliéry Bonton Zlín, reproduced by courtesy of Bonton Film.

---

28.   Fink, *The Lacanian Subject*, p. 92.
29.   André Breton, *Manifestoes of Surrealism*, p. 26.

young girl, Gabriela, who looks exactly like the lost girl. The likeness of
Marketa later reappears as a girl called Tereza, and yet another incarnation is
discovered on the flying island of Laputa, in the appropriately exalted and
unattainable form of Princess Niké. Clearly these girls are perceived to share
that same quality, that feature comprising the object *a*, to which Gulliver was
attracted in the 'original' Marketa. (Of course, the unspoken original of all
these avatars of ideal femininity is the mother, and it is perhaps telling that a
motherly figure at whose home Gulliver stays at one point is called Marketa.)
Juráček uses a similar device, albeit less successfully, in his intermediary film
Every Young Man, where all the young girls encountered by the two soldier
protagonists of the film's first part are played by the same actress: the suggestion
is that all the girls *are* the same, to the extent that the object *a* sought by the
male protagonists appears, if only momentarily, in each of them.

Petra Hanáková describes Juráček as 'probably the most misogynistic
writer and director of the Czech New Wave'.[30] Certainly Juráček's cinema
offers little space for 'real' women, as it seems he is unable to envisage his
female characters outside of wishful projections or to judge them in any other
terms than whether or not they appear to possess the precious object *a*. Female
identity falls prey again and again to the fragmenting and fetishizing processes
of male desire. In *Young Hangman*, the unwanted brunette girl Dominika is

Figure 2.3 Dominika (Milena Zahrynowská) with Gulliver (Lubomír Kostelka)
in *A Case for the Young Hangman* (*Případ pro začínajícího kata*, Pavel Juráček,
1969) ©Ateliéry Bonton Zlín, reproduced by courtesy of Bonton Film.

30. Petra Hanáková, 'Voices From Another World: Feminine Space and Masculine
Intrusion in *Sedmikrásky* and *Vražda Ing. Čerta*', in Anikó Imre (ed.), *East European Cinemas* (London: Routledge, 2005), p. 67.

presented as a negative inversion of the blonde Marketa/Gabriela/Tereza/Niké figure: if the latter figure constitutes an idealization, Dominika represents the love object in which the *lost* object is no longer perceptible, a sexuality drained of desire. Of course it is only in the guise of Dominika that Gulliver attains any woman in the film. Within the world of *Josef Kilián*, 'whole' female characters are mostly replaced by found objects or part-objects (cats, voices, the sashaying buttocks of a girl dancing in a bar). To the extent that women are 'visible' in Juráček's films, they are perpetually subject to misrecognition and distortion, either conflated within a generalized image of 'Woman' ('Woman, object of male fantasy') or split into opposing aspects of the same self: Marketa, Gabriela, Tereza and Niké (along with the girls in *Every Young Man*) are different women, even though they appear as the same woman, while, conversely, the blonde and brunette figures in *Young Hangman* appear as distinct characters, even though they are only different perceptions of the same woman.[31] The exaltations of male desire hardly make for a meaningful tribute, for, as we have seen, the object *a* is only something believed to inhere in the actual person. Desire never embraces the totality of another person's self, only the object *a* and the qualities associated therewith.

To be fair, this inability to 'see' women in an undistorted form may be as much a comment on the nature of desire as a consequence of Juráček's own attitudes towards women, and both *Every Young Man* and *Young Hangman* are of course explicitly focalized through the eyes, and fantasies, of their male protagonists. Then again, even when Juráček's scripts deal with women as leading characters, they are seldom fully-fledged characters, and tend to appear only in a parodic or purely negative light.[32] At the very least, however, Juráček reveals some awareness of the distortions wrought by desire, the gap between reality and the fantasized promise of fulfilment. Ironically, this awareness is voiced through Princess Niké herself, who suggests that Gulliver only imagined Marketa's drowning, and that it suits him to believe in her death as this enables him to preserve his illusory image of her. This suggestion is more explicit in Juráček's screenplay, where Niké remarks: 'probably you couldn't bear the thought, that one day she will cut off her plaits [more part-objects!]…That one day you will … blacken her name in some horribly rude sentence'.[33] Had Gulliver continued to know Marketa, he would have found that she is not 'exactly what you wanted her to be'. Courtesy of the fictitious drowning, Marketa *is* now 'exactly what you wanted her to be…Dead!' It is

---

31. Bacher, *Lacan, Discourse and Social Change*, p. 44.
32. Observe, for instance, the ridiculously clichéd heroine set free from an old 'socialist construction' film in the short *Black and White Sylva* (*Černobílá Sylva*, Juráček and Schmidt, 1961) and the near-feral female survivors of nuclear war in *The End of August in the Hotel Ozone* (*Konec srpna v Hotelu Ozon*, Schmidt, 1967).
33. Juráček, *Postava k podpírání*, p. 183.

only in death that Gulliver can uphold the identity of real girl and object of desire. Furthermore, as has been suggested, the tragic back-story serves to evoke that original, maternal attachment to which adult desire is nothing but a perpetual referring back.

For all those substitutes that promise 'to plug the gap at the ... centre of our being',[34] Juráček's work finally offers only an image of desolate emptiness. While the peculiar atmosphere of these films, at once oneiric and drab, can at one level be related to the textures of state socialist experience, it can also be explained as a fusion of dream-consciousness and an all too acute awareness of lack. Emptiness and privation exceed the experience of the people's democracies. If this atmosphere is to be read only in terms of direct political critique, why then does the same sense of emptiness and alienation haunt the least 'political' and most apparently light-hearted of the films Juráček directed, *Every Young Man*? That film, at least in its slight but beguiling first part, reveals yet another environment oppressive in its very sense of absence. The deserted streets and parks and the empty restaurants with their taciturn waiters render the unnamed city scarcely distinguishable from the contemporary Prague of *Josef Kilián* or the make-believe Balnibarbi of *Young Hangman*. As with these alienating environments, we are never at home within the Lacanian symbolic order: we are always, like Gulliver, '*cizinec*', a foreigner or stranger, estranged even from ourselves. To enter the symbolic means to speak the language of the 'Other', an 'alien' language that precedes and exceeds us. Our own words betray us, and our subjectivity is never unified or stable but 'always dispersed, ... strung out along the chains of the discourses which constitute it'.[35]

The world of *Josef Kilián* comprises, literally, a world of language, a world of slippery and indeterminate texts that grotesquely affirms Lacanian theories of signification. Written words recur throughout the film, yet they seldom elucidate anything: walking down a corridor in the Clam-Gallas Palace (home of the Prague city archives),[36] Herold passes a collection of outdated Communist placards and banners, many of whose slogans are only half-legible in the darkness and clutter; when renting the cat, he is referred to a ludicrously thorough set of rules and instructions that the viewer has little time to read; and, most bizarrely of all, in an official waiting room he picks up a newspaper written in Arabic.[37] Yet the difficulty of clear communication is also asserted in the dialogue. In an early exterior sequence Juráček's camera observes various passers-by engaged in conversation; all of these conversations are concerned

---

34. Eagleton, *Literary Theory*, p. 168.
35. Ibid., p. 169.
36. Hames, *The Czechoslovak New Wave*, p. 143.
37. The problems of communication are of course compounded for non-Czech speaking viewers watching subtitled versions of the film, where subtitles can only present a fraction of that text which is legible.

with understanding, and all but the final exchange involve an admission, or an accusation, of the failure to understand (Juráček uses a freeze-frame here each time any form of the verb 'understand' is used).[38] By continually depicting the failure of communication Juráček emphasises the ambiguous nature of language; moreover, by locating that failure within everyday life he emphasises that this ambiguity is an inherent quality of language, not merely an effect of officialese or the doublethink and mystifications of Communist discourse.

The idea that signification is nothing more than the revelation of self-evident meaning, with each signifier chained 'naturally' to its signified, is presented throughout the film as a fallacy. In a celebrated moment one of the supplicants in the waiting room opens the shutters of a large window, only to be presented with a brick wall: this image, while suggestive of the mystifying opacity of the bureaucratic world and the inaccessibility of power in a totalitarian society, can also be seen as refuting the commonsense conception of the signifier as a transparent window on the world. The incorporation of written text into the film, as well as the use of foreign languages (Arabic, Russian in one of the fragments of everyday conversation), makes us aware of words as material objects, and thus draws our attention to the 'act of enunciation' itself, to signification as process. From this perspective even the apparently arbitrary lecture on the high percentage of illiteracy in Brazil by one bureaucrat takes on a certain relevance: in constructing Brazil as a savage Third World 'Other' of enlightened socialist societies, these remarks can be seen as a bizarre exercise in self-serving propaganda, but at another level this construction conjures up fantasies of a 'pure' life without language, where reality would not be mediated, 'distorted', by signifiers.[39] If *Josef Kilián* is, of all Juráček's films, the one most preoccupied with signification in terms of verbal language, we could also describe the reality of all three films as essentially a 'linguistic' reality, constructed as it is out of mysterious or unreadable signs. That description is particularly apposite to *A Case for the Young Hangman*, Juráček's most emphatic attempt at replicating dream reality. The world of Balnibarbi comprises a cryptogram without a key, a world filled with images, personas and activities that maintain the appearance of symbolism in spite of Juráček's refusal to divulge what they actually symbolize.

The preoccupation with language, and the assertion of its problematic status, comprises one point of contact between the Surreal and the Absurd. It is in its linguistic dimension, in its verbal playfulness and opacity, that the Theatre of the Absurd perhaps reveals its greatest indebtedness to the earlier Surrealist movement. To speak in general terms, the Absurd seems concerned with investigating the 'Other' of the social domain, which appears to us as an omniscient entity, a 'big Other', that registers the truth of our statements and

---

38. Hames, *The Czechoslovak New Wave*, p. 143.
39. Fink, *The Lacanian Subject*, p. 50.

authorizes our desires and beliefs. The diverse forms of the Absurd are bound together by the revelation that such an ultimate authority is non-existent, illusory. The classic Absurd theme, whatever the explicit subject, is the death of God, the absence of objective rules or standards, the free-standing nature of all beliefs and commitments. Slavoj Žižek concurs with that vision when he declares that the Other (no less than the obsessive Surrealist protagonist) is itself lacking and '"hasn't got it", hasn't got the final answer'.[40] The big Other may manifest itself in the Absurd as divine power, as society or as legal or bureaucratic structures (as in Kafka), yet preponderant throughout all these variations is the attack on the big Other as the final judge of linguistic or symbolic meaning. The representation of language as inherently ambiguous or polysemic is something that unites Absurdists East and West, politically and metaphysically oriented. As will be argued throughout this study, the fluidity of meaning is central to Surrealism, and arguably even more so to Poetism and Artificialism, Czech forms of proto-Surrealism. In these cases, of course, the cultivation of polysemy is often linked to the attempt to portray the working of dreams and the primary process. Yet the exchanges of many Absurdist plays would suggest that dreams have no monopoly on confusion, and would thus seem to reinforce the Lacanian view that '*all* our discourse is in a sense a slip of the tongue',[41] that even our everyday utterances have unintended associations and implications. To paraphrase Marx, what was lyrical and poetic in Surrealism repeats itself as grim farce in the Theatre of the Absurd. What was hidden away in unconscious processes breaks out in social interaction. The Absurd asserts 'the basic impossibility of communication',[42] as witness the comedy of cross-purpose mined by Absurdist playwrights: the failure of mutual understanding in Ionesco, the pointed reliance on *double entendre* and obfuscation in Pinter and Albee.

In *The Rebel* (*L'Homme révolté*, 1951), Albert Camus claims that the absurdity of existence consists in 'that hopeless encounter between human questioning and the silence of the universe'.[43] Yet in many classic works of the Absurd, that silence manifests itself as the babble of confusing or impenetrable signifiers. Sometimes language is taken as the direct subject of the Absurd, as in Havel's 1965 play *The Memorandum* (*Vyrozumění*), concerning the introduction into official life of a synthetic language designed to eliminate all the ambiguities of normal speech though one which proves impossible to learn. Implicit in this conceit is the impossible fantasy of stable, univalent signification. Moreover, language is often the implicit subject of the Absurd even when a work's explicit focus is the political sphere: what distinguishes

40. Slavoj Žižek, *The Sublime Object of Ideology* (London: Verso, 1989), p. 122.
41. Eagleton, *Literary Theory*, p. 169 (italics added).
42. Esslin, op. cit., p. 146.
43. Albert Camus, quoted in Neil Cornwell, *The Absurd in Literature*, p. 117.

such a 'political' play as the aforementioned *The Garden Party*, another Havel piece, is the way Havel dissolves ideology into language, revealing the 'progressive' transformations in official socialist thought as little more than the exchange or redeployment of signifiers. Is this an attack on the hollow, nominal nature of reform socialism or an assertion that ideology is inherently linguistic? *Josef Kilián* asserts the textual basis of ideology quite literally: in that early scene in the basement of the Clam-Gallas Palace, Juráček presents the ethos of high Stalinism (abandoned now, or merely lying dormant 'underground'?) as a collection of texts, a set of slogans and images. This point has subtly subversive implications: the authorities could scarcely have been comforted by the suggestion that no ideological system has any support or referent outside of language. Of course, this does not mean that Juráček is blind to the often terroristic material practices through which political regimes impose their ideologies. An air of real menace haunts the hollow symbolism of *Josef Kilián* and even the dreamlike *Young Hangman* has its share of political arrests and a busload of execution victims: empty signifiers are reinforced by the 'fullness' of state violence.

In the next section we will examine more closely the voyage taken by Juráček's protagonists through the world of political or bureaucratic authority. While this world is, quintessentially and almost exclusively, the territory of the Absurd, that voyage does share certain properties and revelations with the quests of the Surreal.

Big Brother or Big Other? The Absence of Power

Who is Josef Kilián? Does he even 'exist'? At least one of these two questions is bound to confront the first-time viewer of Juráček's first film. Yet such questions are perhaps less important than the very fact of Kilián's absence, the paradox of the character who dominates the fictional world even while remaining invisible within it. The idea of the cipher who occupies a central role, the 'absent' personage who is overbearingly present, is a trope much beloved of the Absurd genre. In this respect a fictional scrap by the Russian proto-Absurdist writer Daniil Kharms, 'Blue Notebook No. 10', is paradigmatic: Kharms appears to begin narrating a tale about 'a red-haired man', only to strip away all physical attributes from this 'character' (even his hair!), so that finally nothing remains except language itself, the act of verbal identification. The figure of the literal non-entity is especially prominent in the work of Samuel Beckett, and the eponymous, never-seen saviour of his play *Waiting for Godot* (first English publication 1954) remains arguably the most famous absence in literature and no doubt comprised as much an inspiration for Juráček's conception of Kilián as anything from Kafka. Yet the work of Kafka himself (as of Nikolai Gogol, Flann O'Brien, and many other exponents or antecedents of the Absurd) also abounds in absent, empty and 'bodiless' characters. For Carlos Fuentes, the 'carapace' of the man-turned-beetle Gregor Samsa in Kafka's 1912 story *The Metamorphosis* (*Die Verwandlung*) negates corporeal presence and enjoyment: 'the body is absent, its presence and its pleasure postponed'.[44]

As we have seen, the Lacanian subject is also an empty, disembodied creature; language 'submerges' the subject, and 'hollows being into desire',[45] the eternal compulsion to restore one's lost fullness. Thus, whatever other connotations it may have, the Absurdist trope of a kind of living non-existence or emptiness can be linked with the vintage Surrealist motif of the fleeting, chimerical object of desire. If we read Kilián's non-presence as indicating an absence or lack within the subject, then we might suggest that what Herold and the other supplicants of officialdom finally confront, in the form of a bare office room from which Kilián has apparently fled, is their own emptiness. After all, an identification is established between Herold and the object of his search. Kafka's own 'Josef K.' was of course himself the persecuted victim of bureaucracy, and even in the construction of this fictional alter ego we find an identity between persecutor and persecuted: as a high-ranking official of the Workers' Accident Insurance Bureau in the Prague of the Habsburgs, what was Franz Josef Kafka, the original 'Josef K.', if not a representative of bureaucratic power? The notes that accompany Juráček's 1962 synopsis for the film reveal that Herold's original name was 'Jan Kilián'.[46] (Josef Škvorecký, in his account of the film, even misremembers Herold as Kilián.) The very fact that Kilián occupies a position of authority, that he is situated at the centre of this society, underlines Herold's lack or absence as systemic and universal, as the lack that pervades the symbolic order and the subjectivities founded therein.

Here the psychoanalytic resonance of Juráček's film meshes brilliantly with its satirical qualities. Totalitarian bureaucracy itself can be seen as enacting a form of 'disembodiment' upon the individual. In his essay on Kafka, Milan Kundera relates the true story of a Prague engineer wrongly accused of slander and defection to the West; the engineer goes to the Ministry of the Interior to rectify the mistake, but is informed that official mistakes are never retracted. According to Kundera, this story is authentically Kafkaesque because it strikes at the essence of modern bureaucracy, an essence that Kafka was the first to represent artistically. The bureaucrat's world, consisting of 'unknown persons' and files, is '*the world of the abstract*'.[47] Because Kafka understood this, his novels evoke the 'poetry' of bureaucracy. In modern bureaucracies, 'the file takes on the role of a Platonic

44. Carlos Fuentes, *Myself With Others*, p. 96.
45. Fink, *The Lacanian Subject*, p. 52; Jacques Lacan, quoted in Eagleton, *Literary Theory*, p. 168.
46. Juráček, *Postava k podpírání*, p. 85.
47. Milan Kundera, *The Art of the Novel*, translated by Linda Asher (New York: Harper & Row, 1986), p. 113.

idea', it becomes 'true reality', and a person's flesh-and-blood existence becomes a mere 'shadow cast on the screen of illusion'[48] (even if, as in the engineer's case, existence becomes the shadow of a mistake). Needless to say, in societies where essentially all of social and economic life has been subsumed into state bureaucracy, the replacement of the corporeal by the 'abstract' self is even more pervasive. (The 'disembodying' character of state socialism perhaps helped instigate, as a kind of compensatory backlash, the return to material, private pleasures in the Czechoslovakia of the 1970s.) As an oppressive yet de-corporealized authority, Kilián constitutes the perfect representative, an aptly 'personless' personification, of the abstract realm of bureaucratized socialism. Indeed Kilián (and by extension Herold) is directly comparable to the subject of bureaucracy whose 'real life' is reducible to the text of his official file: for what reality does Kilián ultimately have but that of the signifier? In spite of Herold's exhaustive quest, all that finally materializes of Kilián is, in a literal and non-Lacanian sense, a chain of signifiers: the name 'J. Kilián' written in many different styles on an endless series of doors. These doors serve not to indicate a presence, an individual waiting behind them, but only to conjure phantoms of language; as screens or surfaces, the doors entomb a death-like absence. 'Josef Kilián' thus constitutes the signifier(s) which 'represent' the subject and thereby swallow up his or her existence.

Absence continues to make itself felt even after the 'revelation' of Kilián's non-existence. Another of the film's suppliants of bureaucracy, a man carrying a boiler, continues in the quest for official 'presence' and, in a particularly bizarre moment, he attempts to mount a flight of stairs while in reality only going downwards (the domain of officialdom as space-distorting funhouse of the Absurd). Meanwhile Herold leaves the building; a shot of him walking the streets is accompanied, non-diegetically, by the sound of the boiler falling noisily to the ground. Peter Hames informs us that the spot from which Herold is shown walking away 'once boasted the largest statue of Stalin in Eastern Europe'.[49] That statue was destroyed in 1962, only two years before the film's release, so this shot would certainly have registered with most Czechoslovak viewers at the time as the paradoxical visualization of an absence. Juráček here confronts us with another non-existent 'Josef/Josif' (Stalin), another absence that has usurped the place of ultimate political authority. That Stalin is the authority that the film symbolically 'erases' in this way has especial significance: Stalin was after all the concrete, material representative of Communist ideology, a role in which no other leader, at least in the Eastern Bloc countries, really replaced him. Žižek even relates the mythology surrounding Communist leaders to the idea of 'the king's two bodies', to the belief that the leader's 'ordinary transient' body 'envelops' and 'supports' another body, a 'sublime' body.[50] The Communist leader thus directly incarnates 'the objective Reason of

---

48. Ibid., p. 102.
49. Hames, *The Czechoslovak New Wave*, p. 145.
50. Slavoj Žižek, *For They Know Not What They Do*, p. 260.

History'; this, according to Žižek, is the meaning of Stalin's famous vows to Lenin: 'We, the Communists, are people of a special mould. We are made of special stuff.'[51] Žižek identifies that invisible, immaterial 'stuff' with object *a*, 'the sublime object, the Thing within a body'.[52] What *Josef Kilián* registers is not so much Stalin's physical death as the death of this mythology: it is the mythical, idealized Stalin of political propaganda that is seen 'buried' in the Clem-Gallas Palace and that is absent in the form of the obliterated statue. The literal absence inscribes that loss of faith in the sublime Communist body that has taken place in the disillusioned world of post-Stalinism. As with the phantom cat shop, the disappearance of a deity-like image of Stalin represents the illusory, impossible nature of object *a*. This moment thus complements and underscores the failure or futility of the Surrealist quest.

The original Czech title of *Josef Kilián*, *Postava k podpírání*, is best translated as 'a figure to support'. On one level this title can be seen as alluding to the need for support in an arduous and impossible 'Sisyphean' endeavour, such as Herold's struggle with bureaucracy comprises. Sisyphean imagery recurs throughout the film, first in the opening image, depicting 'a statue of an Atlas-type figure carrying a heavy burden',[53] and then in the absurd yet poignant image of the man carrying his portable shower inexorably downwards. (In turn, these allusions establish a link with one of the key philosophical texts of the Absurd, Albert Camus's *The Myth of Sisyphus* (*Le Mythe de Sisyphe*, 1942).) Yet we might also interpret that 'figure' of the title as Kilián, the representative of power whose authority is not self-evident but is present only in the 'supportive', cult-sustaining belief of Herold and the others. Why this need to 'believe in' authority, and what is the nature of that authority? Here we again encounter power in the guise of the big Other, an illusory agency that may well manifest itself as an individual 'subject supposed to know'. In psychoanalysis that subject is, of course, the analyst, whom the analysand believes to be capable of definitively diagnosing his or her symptoms, of 'reading' his or her cryptic speech. As we have seen, this 'transferential' relationship of subjects to authority is founded on an illusion: no institution or community can possess the authority believed to inhere in the big Other, no individual can truly be the subject supposed to know. This is not least the case with regard to that place where the 'true' meaning of our words and symptoms is registered, for signification always resists any final interpretation.[54] It is the illusion of the analyst as a 'God-like ... all-knowing Other' that the unorthodox techniques of Lacanian clinical practice attempt to dismantle.

51.   Ibid., p. 257.
52.   Ibid.
53.   Hames, *The Czechoslovak New Wave*, p. 141.
54.   Fink, *The Lacanian Subject*, p. 67.

The narratives of both *Josef Kilián* and *A Case for the Young Hangman* culminate in the exposure of an illusory or defunct authority. Kilián's illusory status represents the illusion that is 'all-knowing' authority itself; alternately his literal non-appearance suggests that Kilián is at once nobody and everybody, that the authority his name signifies is attributed rather than inherent. In this sense the names written on the multitude of doors suggest not only his absence but also his promiscuous presence. Herold faces each new functionary with the renewed good faith that the prestige of officialdom will reflect an authentic knowledge. Kilián's non-appearance (or the inability of anybody to incarnate him) amounts to the realization that the socio-political system itself is headless, disordered and incoherent, that nobody in charge

Figure 2.4 *Josef Kilián* (*Postava k podpírání*, Pavel Juráček and Jan Schmidt, 1963)
©Czech National Film Archive.

really knows about the cat shop, or how or why it disappeared. The aberrant cat, which we discussed before as a manifestation of the object of desire, is thus also an obvious token of lack, of the incoherence and inadequacy of 'the system'. Beyond the need of resolving his immediate dilemma, Herold seeks an authority who will offer enlightenment, and even make sense of the slippery and Absurd reality (existential as well as political) in which he lives: after all, the fantasy of Kilián is one that Herold is shown to believe in even before he rents his cat. One silent official who sits high above Herold in a darkened room has the same dauntingly unresponsive demeanour as that of the model Lacanian analyst, just as Herold's confused, fragmented, timidly defensive speech evokes the discourse of the analysand ('Myself, in your place, I would find it so ... I don't know how it could have happened'; 'I'm a normal man'). The fallacy of a 'subject supposed to know' is implied even in the allusions to the specific political context: the one who might seem to be the ultimate incarnation of such a subject, the figure of Stalin, is conspicuous by his absence, notwithstanding his single appearance as a dead relic in the Clam-Gallas Palace.

Authority is shown to derive more from social or professional status than from personal qualities: when the man with the boiler steps into the office and answers the ringing telephone, does not his literal occupation of Kilián's place in fact transform him into Kilián? The telephone's presence hints at how authority exists only in and through the interpersonal: the right of decree and judgment depend upon another's faith in one's wisdom or expertise. Power thereby becomes materially effective even as it remains impotent. The character of King Mateuš, in *Young Hangman*, provides a similar commentary on illusory authority to the motif of Kilián. Mateuš is believed to reside on the flying island of Laputa and to rule over the land of Balnibarbi below (the conceit of Laputa, derived from Swift, serves here both as a metaphor for imperialism, and as an image of a regime that has 'theologized' itself and cut itself off from the people it governs). Unlike Kilián, Mateuš does seem to have a substantial reality – portraits and newsreel films exist of him – but he is no longer operative as leader. Not only does he have no say in the governance of Balnibarbi, having left years ago, he is also believed to work as a porter in a Monte Carlo hotel. While arguably less successful in its exploration of authority than *Josef Kilián*, *Young Hangman* has the advantage of revealing that faith in an 'all-knowing Other' to be symptomatic of more than a few individuals: all the subjects of Balnibarbi believe in Mateuš's omnipotence.

What makes both films so striking and unusual is that they not only present authority in its coercive guise but also reveal it as something bound up with fantasy and psychic need. In *Josef Kilián* especially, the more 'realistic' of the two films, this illustration of authority as fantasy construction can inevitably be seen to comment on the mentalities induced by Communist totalitarianism.

The horrors of Stalinism have often been explained in terms of a kind of collective moral transference whereby people abdicated responsibility for their participation or complicity in state crime. The fantasy of Kilián as omniscient subject is a means for Herold and the others to disavow that they too are agents of the social order, and that they bear some responsibility for its present state, if only through their acquiescence. According to Jan Žalman, the film finally suggests that 'a man on whose behalf "society does all the thinking" does not only find himself in an absurd situation, he is involuntarily instrumental in bringing society to the same condition'.[55] At the political, economic and philosophical level the Party posited itself as *the* subject supposed to know; it presented itself as the sole agency capable of discerning the course of history and of offering the true interpretation of Marxism. This construction is directly comparable to the fantasmatic construction of the analyst, dependent as it is on the idea that there exists a univalent truth waiting to be uncovered by the expert. (Poststructuralist criticism would, of course, assert that there is no true Marx, only a plethora of interpretations.) In this context Juráček's films are subversive for portraying power precisely in its weakness, a weakness that does not, however, compromise its terrifying strength. On the other hand, as Lacanian theory would suggest, the fallacy of ultimate authority is something not delimitable to authoritarian societies or their political leaders: doubtless Herold and the others would still be looking for Kilián, for some manifestation of Kilián, even in the event of political reform.

From this account it might seem that Juráček's films are despairing works, with their protagonists bound up in eternal and illusory quests, whether for the fulfilment of desire or for an all-knowing authority figure. However, we must note the distinction in the roles played by the protagonists of *Josef Kilián* and *A Case for the Young Hangman*, one that makes the latter film the more positive work. At the end of *Josef Kilián* Herold is shown still to believe in the idealized figure of Kilián. In the film's final scene set in a beer garden, he asks a middle-aged patron whether he is Kilián. Jan Žalman's argument that this man really is Kilián misses the point, as we finally see that this man is also in unauthorized possession of a cat: he is yet another helpless, frightened supplicant of the Law. (The omnipresence of cats or other such 'guilty' objects also implies the universality of desire and its substitutes.) Herold remains at once trapped in an irreparable guilt and caught up in his own tormenting delusions of wise authority. By contrast, at the climax of *Young Hangman* Gulliver reveals to the people of Balnibarbi that King Mateuš is no longer in power on Laputa, and thereby destroys the illusion of a supreme, all-knowing power. This revelation is perhaps as close as any of Juráček's characters ever come to a 'revolutionary' gesture: Jiří Cieslar writes that 'while [Gulliver] is not transformed by this shocking truthfulness into any hero, he is now no

---

55. Jan Žalman, *Films and Filmmakers in Czechoslovakia* (Prague: Orbis, 1968), p. 74.

longer the passive *Jedermann*, the inconspicuous "little Czech" who just lets himself get dragged around'.[56]

Moreover, a certain degree of contentment is suggested by the serene ending of *Young Hangman*, in which Gulliver leaves Balnibarbi on a horse-drawn wagon driven by a genial madman. The pocket watch that Gulliver retrieved from the dead hare Oscar at the beginning of the film now appears to be going backwards, yet, the madman remarks, 'is it not enough that you can hear it ticking?' Indeed regression, the journey backwards into childhood, may be necessary to preserve the vitality of experience. The restoration of an early 'completeness' is suggested, though this is to be understood not as the (impossible) fulfilment of desire but as a rejuvenation of the imaginative life

Figure 2.5 Gulliver and the genial madman in *A Case for the Young Hangman* (*Případ pro začínajícího kata*, Pavel Juráček, 1969) ©Ateliéry Bonton Zlín, reproduced by courtesy of Bonton Film.

---

56. Cieslar, 'Předmluva', in Juráček, *Postava k podpírání*, p. 22.

that made the young Juráček feel 'one hundred per cent' and that comprises a crucial part of our existence. On the one hand, this return to childhood means embracing a vision of life as open-ended, multivalent, forever fluid in its significance: the vision articulated by Juráček in his diaries, when he describes his childhood wonder at the horizon. Gulliver's 'insurrection' is a hermeneutic, indeed a textual, one: the rejection of the authority figure as subject supposed to know is tantamount to accepting the fluidity of signs. On the other hand this ending could be seen to reveal how Gulliver has come to terms with the visions, dreams and childhood memories that constituted the world of Balnibarbi (Cieslar observes that this world contains echoes of Juráček's own Příbram childhood);[57] fantasy and childhood experience are reintegrated into a now subtly 'shifted' adult reality, indeed a 'surreality' that synthesizes the previously illustrated states of, respectively, reality and dream. We might even suggest that, just as Swift's hero drastically changes his view of humanity after his bizarre experience of the Yahoos, so Gulliver's re-engagement with fantasy prompts him to see the real world in a new light, the light of the Absurd.

The 'revolutionary' quality of the films themselves consists as much in their acceptance of the form and substance of dreams as in their directly critical aspects. What *Josef Kilián* helped inaugurate into Czechoslovak cinema, along with such contemporaneous works as Štefan Uher's *Sunshine in a Net* (*Slnko v sieti*, 1962) and Vojtěch Jasný's *When the Cat Comes* (*Až přijde kocour*, 1963), was not simply a new political outspokenness but also a new set of aesthetic and philosophical concerns. As we examine the work of other New Wave filmmakers we will observe a recurring preoccupation with fantasy, sexuality and the psyche, and with representing these themes in an aesthetic language that is complex and ambiguous: in other words we will trace the connections forged with the rich heritage of the avant-garde. Juráček's aesthetic subverts Stalinist norms while providing the only apt response to neo-Stalinist societies. Authority insists on an extreme transparency of communication even though its own institutions are opaque; Communist totalitarianism refuses to acknowledge the irrational or fantastic, even though it has authored a reality that is manifestly absurd. In the words of Carlos Fuentes, '[l]aughter is crushed when the joke is codified by the perfection of the law'.[58] One of the great ironies of *Young Hangman* is just that discrepancy between a professed extreme rationalism and the irrational reality of Balnibarbi: the Balnibarbian poet is sentenced to death for writing a poem about a hare that wears clothes (this poem, he reveals, is considered 'foreign to our spirit'), even though besuited hares were really kept by the government on Laputa. Juráček's films constitute an artistic revenge on totalitarianism, complementing the more obviously political gestures that would ensure his

---

57. Ibid.
58. Fuentes, *Myself With Others*, p. 176.

eventual dismissal from the film industry and his exile from Czechoslovakia. In holding up the mirror of the Absurd to his own society, he presented it in the terms it most despised.

CHAPTER 3

Jiří Menzel's *Closely Observed Trains* (1966): Hrabal and the Heterogeneous

From *Midnight* to Daylight:
Bohumil Hrabal and the New Wave

The work of Bohumil Hrabal, author of the 1965 novella *Closely Observed Trains* on which Jiří Menzel's 1966 film is based, provides one of the few immediate links between the postwar Czech avant-garde and the cultural renaissance of the 1960s. Born in 1914, Hrabal was loosely affiliated with the underground group of writers and visual artists that 'published', Samizdat style, the cultural anthology *Midnight* (*Půlnoc*) in its various instalments during the first half of the 1950s. The Půlnoc group included two more deeply influential figures in Czech culture, Hrabal's friends the poet Egon Bondy (Zbyněk Fišer) and the 'Explosionalist' artist Vladimir Boudník. Although Půlnoc established itself as a 'renegade' deviation from the 'orthodox' Surrealist circle of Vratislav Effenberger and Karel Teige and explicitly renounced Surrealist poetics in its manifestos, the group's output can nonetheless, as Martin Machovec suggests, be ranked with 'the creation of those who were engaging, as if anew, with the urgent heritage of Surrealism'.[1] Machovec observes in *Midnight* the persistence of such Surrealist traits as 'the poetics of the "found object"', 'the conception of dream equalling life (and of course life equalling dream!)', 'the inability to hierarchize values', and even a 'faith in socialist revolution (of course of an anti-Stalinist, Trotskyist type)'.[2] At the same time, the work of such figures as Bondy, Boudník and Ivo Vodseďálek reflects an organic, critical response to the corpus of interwar Surrealism, as in their own way do the activities of the other

---

1. Martin Machovec, 'Od avantgardy přes podzemí do undergroundu', in Alan, *Alternativní Kultura*, p. 158.
2. Ibid., p. 159.

underground groupings, not least Effenberger's own. That response consists, for *Midnight*, in the attempt to reformulate Bretonian precepts in the light of both the horrors of Czech Stalinism and the drab, plebeian environments of these artists' work-a-day lives, whence both the pronounced emphasis on sarcasm and 'black humour' and the pursuit of some form of realism, however idiosyncratic. (It will later be suggested that these reformulations have much in common with the alternative, anti-Bretonian 'tradition' of Surrealism represented by Georges Bataille.) Bondy proclaims an aesthetic of 'total realism', although his is a realism that embraces the reality of subjective experience: committed to expressing the 'definite poetic subject in the definite moment', Bondy conceives his work as a polemic against Socialist Realism's fallacious objectivity, its naïve faith in the 'point of view of the outside observer'.[3]

Marked, at least initially, by Bondy's influence, Hrabal's fiction also pursues a phenomenological, subjectively mediated realism. His narrative voice mixes the colloquial with the lyrical, and the fragments of ordinary life that compose his stories are made phantasmagorical in the dense aggregation of incidents. Hrabal's incorporation of personal experiences and actual snippets of ('rough', colloquial) speech into his writings comprises a specific literary analogue to Boudník's foundation of an abstract-expressionist art on the use of discarded, everyday or industrial materials (scraps of metal, nails, old walls). Marie Klimešová underlines the importance of Hrabal's early experiences working at an iron works in Kladno, where, in a manner not dissimilar to the original Surrealists, Hrabal first observed the fantastic qualities manifest in the everyday: in the lives of his fellow workers 'he saw a raw pathos, which replaced the lost *myths, allegories* and *symbols*'.[4] Hrabal himself later wrote, 'I am here and here only, in the nerves of reality, which is for me just as miraculous as Breton's beauty, which is just as full of revolt and the desire to live in a glass house.'[5] The embodiment of the Surrealist imagination in a faithfully observed reality, as well as the conviction that the utopian (Breton's glass houses) is always a potentiality of the quotidian and 'low', remain evident in both the novella and film versions of *Closely Observed Trains*. While the story's setting, a station in occupied Bohemia through which Nazi munitions pass, would suggest a most non-quotidian reality, at its core is the coming of age of its protagonist, young signalman Miloš Hrma, and the (mainly erotic) misadventures of Miloš and his colleagues. Playing off the story's grave background against its 'frivolous' foreground, both works illustrate the pleasures of ordinary life in contrast to the horrors of 'significance'.

3.   Gertraude Zandová [Zand], *Totální realismus a trapná poezie: Česká neoficiální literatura 1948–1953*, translated by Zuzana Adamová (Brno: Host, 2002), p. 113.
4.   Marie Klimešová, 'České výtvarné umění druhé poloviny 20. století', in Alan, *Alternativní Kultura*, p. 382.
5.   Hrabal, quoted in Klimešová, ibid.

Figure 3.1 Miloš (Václav Neckář) and Máša (Jitka Bendová) in *Closely Observed Trains* (*Ostře sledované vlaky*, Jiří Menzel, 1966) ©Ateliéry Bonton Zlín.

Though technically Hrabal's work was first published 'overground' during the limited, and aborted, cultural thaw of the 1950s, it was the 1963 publication of the short story collection *Pearls of the Deep* (*Perličky na dně*) that caused a sensation, indicating a new direction for Czech literature and culture. Alfred French claims that although, by the 1960s, 'soc-real literature had long gone out of fashion', 'it was only with the advent of Hrabal that the dynamite below its pedestal seemed finally and irrevocably to have been ignited'.[6] Škvorecký describes Hrabal's emergence in similar terms, as a 'revolution'.[7] Hrabal helped reorient Czech literature from the 'collective good' to the individual good, from the future to the present, and from the portentous to the inconsequential.[8] The inconsequentiality of Hrabal's protagonists themselves is foregrounded by his defiance, if not simple lack of interest, in traditional narrative structure, with his stories often lurching arbitrarily from one incident to another or rambling to a close without climax. Though mainly devoid of direct political commentary, Hrabal's characters

---

6. French, *Czech Writers and Politics 1945–1969*, p. 208.
7. Josef Škvorecký [under the pseudonym Daniel S. Miritz], Introduction to Bohumil Hrabal, *The Death of Mr. Baltisberger*, translated by Kača Polačková (London: Abacus, 1990), p. xi.
8. French, *Czech Writers and Politics 1945–1969*, p. 209.

and his own literary persona represent an individualism and self-adopted marginality as challenging to a totalitarian order as they were inspirational to Sixties youth culture: Hrabal's affirmation of non-conformity and 'dropping out' *avant la lettre* made of him a kind of middle-aged, blue-collar, Czech Kerouac, an inspiration to the emerging domestic counterculture.

Hrabal was no less inspirational, of course, for the filmmakers of the New Wave. Within two years of the publication of *Pearls of the Deep*, a portmanteau film of the same name appeared, in which five Hrabal stories were brought to the screen by a range of the New Wave's most significant talents. While only patchily successful, the film is notable as both a mark of Hrabal's popularity (Hrabal himself makes a number of cameo appearances, and Boudník shows up to demonstrate his artistic techniques) and as the closest thing to a collective statement of purpose from the new generation of filmmakers. Appropriately, given the diverse, desultory grouping that the New Wave actually comprised, the film runs the gamut of styles from casual realism to near-Expressionism, though this also reflects the range of stylistic possibilities enabled by Hrabal's texts: it could be argued that Hrabal's influence is as much apparent in the formal experiments of a Němec or a Jireš as in the naturalistic comedy of a Forman. If Jiří Menzel has become Hrabal's cinematic representative courtesy of his several feature adaptations of Hrabal's work (*Closely Observed Trains*, his first feature, then *Larks on a String* (1969), *Cutting it Short* (*Postřižiny*, 1980) and *I Served the King of England* (*Obsluhoval jsem anglického krále*, 2006)), then this is a title doubly deserved, for Menzel has proved to understand Hrabal's debunking of the false opposition between fantasy and realism.

Menzel brought Surrealist and avant-garde credentials of his own to the filming of *Closely Observed Trains*: he had directed the pop-Dadaist double-act Suchý and Šlitr at the Semafor theatre, and his 1965 short *Crime in the Girls' School* (*Zločin v dívčí škole*) boasts some Surrealist trappings, albeit superficial, stylistic ones. Yet Menzel has consistently asserted that his aim as a director is to do no more than 'serve' his source material. The transformation of literary texts into films is conceived not as a process of imaginative extrapolation, but rather as an act of transposition that combines maximum fidelity with a more general directorial self-effacement. Menzel repudiates most of the techniques and mannerisms that would commonly be thought characteristic of Surrealist or avant-garde cinema, such as overtly fantastic imagery, trick effects and non-linear narrative: another filmmaker, let loose upon *Closely Observed Trains*, might have sought to approximate cinematically the novella's rambling, associative structure, yet Menzel eschews the bravura time-scrambling editing techniques of a Jireš or an Alain Resnais. In interviews, Menzel argues that it is necessary to hide art and contrivance:

For me artistic work is predominantly service ... A person must be humble, if he wants another to listen to him ... I don't like it when the director is seen too much. I want the viewer to forget while watching the film that it is directed ... It makes the viewer sick when the directorial – or actorly, pictorial, musical – exhibition takes precedence over the story and the idea ... I myself, at the theatre or cinema, want to submerge myself in what I see and hear. Spontaneously.[9]

In contrast to many of the great works of 1960s European cinema, *Closely Observed Trains* stands as a model of transparency. Thus, while Menzel's film is in most respects an act of exemplary 'service' to Hrabal, its straightforward manner of exposition lays Menzel open to the charge of imposing censorious order on the novella's temporal and narrative dislocations, of domesticating and thereby neutering Hrabal's anarchic original. Certainly, the film's accessibility must have helped gain Menzel his 1967 Oscar for Best Foreign Language Film.

Thus, Menzel's films might seem vastly removed from the notion of Surrealist cinema, and Menzel has even denigrated cinema's capacity truly to master the interior world generally seen as Surrealism's true province: 'Film is too imperfect to be capable of recording everything that takes place in our fantasy when we read Hrabal's texts.'[10] Yet the Surrealists themselves, as both spectators and practitioners, were frequently entranced by the cinema precisely in its concreteness and objectivity, in its avoidance of 'avant-garde' effects: it suffices to recall Vratislav Effenberger's praise for the Czech documentarist Karel Vachek, Petr Král's love of technically primitive silent film comedies, and such examples of cinematic Surrealism as the documentaries of Georges Franju and Humphrey Jennings. The claim has been advanced by Susan Sontag that the photographic medium is inherently Surrealist, and the 'manipulation or theatricalization of the real' is therefore unnecessary or redundant.[11] From this perspective a Surrealist conception of cinema is, strangely, not so divergent from a Bazinian insistence on preserving the ontological authenticity of the image. Photography may serve to uncover the immanent poetry of the real, though it is equally a means of exploring the world's material qualities (the latter function is heavily exploited in, for instance, the work of the Czech postwar Surrealist Emila Medková). *Closely Observed Trains'* visual affinities with Surrealism are thus to be found in the film's taste for surface and texture, for the sensual appeal and multivalent significance of objects. It must be conceded that Menzel's work has never regained that sense of the enchantment of phenomenal reality exhibited here.

---

9. Menzel, quoted in Kateřina Poštová, *Jiří Menzel* (Prague: Český filmový ústav, 1992), p. 38.
10. Menzel, quoted in Hames, 'The Film Experiment', in Hames, *Dark Alchemy*, p. 29.
11. Susan Sontag, *On Photography* (New York: Farrar, Straus and Giroux, 1973), p. 52.

The visual concern for surfaces and bodies is replicated at the level of narrative and character, and developed into a sustained exploration of the claims of materiality and the subversive qualities of the erotic: unproductive sexual activity represents the ultimate challenge to political systems (Nazi fascism is only the most directly implied) that reduce the body to its use value. Menzel's film is all the more polemical and pointed for staging this exploration upon the hallowed ground of national resistance, the favoured location of Czech Socialist Realist narratives. To be sure, much of what makes the film politically provocative is already present in Hrabal's original text; it could be said, however, that the film presents the ideological or ethical oppositions in the story with a greater lucidity (this is partly a result of the expanded role of the Nazi administrator Zednicek), even if Menzel also smoothes away some of the rawer and less palatable conceits and images of the novella. *Closely Observed Trains'* close examination of bodies – vital and dysfunctional, horizontal in copulation, inactivity and death – can be linked with the ideas of Surrealism's great 'enemy from within', Georges Bataille. Menzel's cinema, with its charm, gentle humour and vignettes of everyday life, is easily characterized as 'humanist', and it might for that reason seem perverse to connect one of his films with a figure as dark, as forbidding, as apparently insistent on the inhuman as Bataille. The partial or limited nature of that connection, no less than the differences in tone and sensibility between Menzel and Hrabal, must be stressed. Yet it will be shown here that *Closely Observed Trains'* explorations of materiality, the conflict between eroticism and instrumentality and the links between sex and death (as well as sex and sacrifice) can profitably be examined through a Bataillean lens of heterology, the study of 'base' matter and 'waste' economy.

Grunting Pigs and Grand Ideas: Hrabalian Baseness

One of the qualities that Josef Škvorecký most admires about Menzel's film is its dedication to capturing 'the essence of the visible reality'.[12] In his fascination with the concreteness of reality, Menzel succeeds in communicating the 'taste' or feel of the story's phenomenal world: 'This *is* how life *does* look on a tiny station somewhere in central Bohemia. One can almost smell the smoke of locomotives.'[13] The viewer need not espouse Bazin's faith in the veracity of moving images in order to note and admire the enchanted attention that Jaromír Šofr's camera pays to the material surface of the world. The snug fictional terrain of the station comprises a libidinal, sensually inviting world

---

12. Josef Škvorecký, *Jiří Menzel and the History of the Closely Watched Trains* (New York: Columbia University Press, 1982), p. 73.
13. Ibid., p. 72.

that draws the viewer into it in an act of cinematic seduction. There is, as Peter Hames observes, a consistent 'eroticization' of *things* throughout the film, a process that takes place not only through overtly phallic symbolism but also through the film's privileging of particular objects and its fastidious rendering of textures: torn leather and torn skin are equal objects of the filmmaker's delectation.[14] Even the more conventionally erotic moments are filmed with an uncommon sensitivity towards the tactile, whether in regard to animate or inanimate surfaces. In the justly famous scene where the station's lascivious dispatcher, Hubička, rubber-stamps the backside of the young telegrapher Zdenka, lamplight caresses the bodies of the performers, highlighting the soft, goose-bumped textures of Zdenka's skin; the room's clock, scale and ever-active tape machine become sentient little contraptions, mysterious and beautiful in chiaroscuro. Miloš's suicide attempt is arguably as significant a physical and tactile event as it is a narrative one, offering a painful yet compelling mix of wood grain, soft flesh, steam and blood, as well as the steady sounds of the running tap and the workman's hammer.

We have already suggested the connection that might be made between the rapturous materiality of Menzel's film and Surrealism. In particular, much of the art of Czechoslovakia's postwar Surrealist movement seems preoccupied with the world as the sum of its material qualities: indeed this tendency will emerge prominently in the discussion (in Chapter 7) of the bona fide Czech Surrealism of Jan Švankmajer. (While such qualities are, obviously, a given of the film medium, they are qualities that Menzel, like Švankmajer, consciously heightens or foregrounds.) The 'materialist' strand of the Czech avant-garde profits better from being interpreted in Bataillean terms than in the more standard Bretonian ones. Bretonian thought is resolutely idealist, Surrealism being defined in Breton's *Second Manifesto of Surrealism* as the quest for a 'certain point of the *mind*' at which contradictions are synthesized.[15] A renegade from Breton's original group, Bataille counterposes to this Hegelian bent his own, 'anti-philosophical' system of base materialism. Bataille's project concerns the reassertion of the bodily, of the coarsely material, at the expense of ideas and ideals: in the words of David Lomas, he 'espouses a materialism whose whole direction is downwards, *de*sublimatory'.[16] This act of descent is at once topographical and metaphorical: Bataille's literal preoccupation with the lower parts of the body reflects his resistance to the 'elevated' bodies of classical representation and to the sublimation of sexual instincts into nobler, 'higher' activities. The scatological, grotesque and generally 'low' images of Bataille's writing are conceived as an attempt at '*sub*verting' the idealism of philosophical

---

14. Hames, *The Czechoslovak New Wave*, p. 179.
15. Breton, *Manifestoes of Surrealism*, p. 117 (italics added).
16. Lomas, *The Haunted Self*, p. 130.

and ideological systems;[17] spit and squashed insects represent for Bataille the real 'formlessness' of a world that has not been garbed in the 'frock-coat' of thought, with its categories and laws.[18] In his essay 'The "Lugubrious Game"' ('Le "Jeu lugubre"', 1929), Bataille celebrates the 'human brute' who rebels against the shackles of 'the idea' – 'the idea in the form of, among other things, a piece of paper adorned with the arms of the State'.[19]

Hrabal's novella offers this eminently Bataillean statement, a complaint made by the stationmaster about the feckless Hubička: 'For me there is a God! But for that grunting pig nothing exists but pork, dumplings and cabbage...'[20] This remark counterposes the high (God in heaven, the spiritually elevated) and the low (the horizontality of the animal with its gaze fixed upon the ground, the satisfaction of one's 'base' instincts), the ideal (moral and spiritual principles) and the material (eating and, by implication, sex); in addition, one is reminded of Bataille's own assertion that 'it is impossible to get worked up other than as a pig who rummages in manure and mud uprooting everything with his snout'.[21] The metaphorically low is transposed onto the topographically high, as when the characters' sexual fantasies are seen 'projected' onto the sky. Such transpositions can be seen at one level as valorizing or recuperating low phenomena, at another as collapsing the very hierarchies that divide high from low. We might even consider Hrabal's characteristic disruption of the order and linearity of classical narrative form in terms of Bataillean provocation: 'the dislocation of forms leads to that of thought',[22] Bataille suggests in a passage on the grotesque bodies of Picasso's paintings. It is worth emphasizing that, as far as Hrabal is concerned, the model for this artistic and philosophical reformulation of Bretonian Surrealism did not come from Bataille himself (there is no evidence Hrabal was aware of the Frenchman's work) but from the working class culture in which Hrabal immersed himself. Hrabal's materialism and earthy directness comprise a heightening of '*čecháčkovství*', the culture of the 'little Czech' (according to Ladislav Holý 'the typical representative of the Czech nation', 'the embodiment of ordinariness and healthy common sense').[23] A strange affinity is thus revealed between a native plebeian folksiness and the self-consciously transgressive intellectualism

---

17. Allan Stoekl, Introduction, in Georges Bataille, *Visions of Excess: Selected Writings 1927–1939*, translated by Allan Stoekl, Carl R. Lovitt and Donald M. Leslie, Jr. (Minneapolis: University of Minnesota Press, 1985), p. xv.

18. Bataille, *Visions of Excess*, p. 31.

19. Ibid., p. 27.

20. Bohumil Hrabal, *Closely Observed Trains*, translated by Edith Pargeter (London: Abacus, 2001), p. 24.

21. Bataille, *Visions of Excess*, p. 24.

22. Ibid.

23. Ladislav Holý, *The Little Czech and the Great Czech Nation* (Cambridge: Cambridge University Press, 1996), p. 72.

of Bataille. Hrabal's 'modernist' narrative constructions derive from the form of the idle anecdote, with its digressiveness and temporal muddling. Menzel's own cultural roots lie in much the same place as Hrabal's, as is evident from such non-Hrabal projects as *My Sweet Little Village* (*Vesničko má středisková*, 1985), an exemplary study of small-town *čecháčkovství*.

As we have seen, in *Closely Observed Trains* Menzel does discipline the 'formlessness' of Hrabal's narrative style, albeit without imposing too tight a narrative corset on the story's action. Nonetheless Menzel's film can be read in terms of Bataillean baseness: in fact the film version makes for a more explicit study of the struggle between idealist systems and sensuous pleasures, being aided in this by the emphatic material presence of objects and the illustration of that conflict in terms of character. The quisling administrator Zednicek (played by Vlastimil Brodský) is established as the film's philosophical foil not only because he espouses the principles of Nazism, but also because, more broadly, he stands for a pallid, 'disembodied' idealism. A character who plays a more significant role in the film than in the novella, Zednicek is described in Menzel and Hrabal's published screenplay as 'an inconspicuous human being, inspired throughout with the great ideas of Nazism, Mission and Providence sparkling from his eyes'.[24] Zednicek makes his first appearance bearing documents with which the station staff will ratify their commitment to the German cause; the 'great ideas' for which Zednicek stands are precisely such ideas as come 'adorned with the arms of the State'. When Zednicek attempts to justify the Nazis' historical project, the lofty, intangible abstraction of the terms of his defence, the redemption of 'civilization', is counterposed to the sensualism and concrete immediacy of the station-workers' pleasures and preoccupations.

That confrontation of high and low is staged more ribaldly as the sabotage of law and order by the nether regions of the body: the presentation of Zdenka's 'defiled' bare bottom by her angry mother in the courthouse, the station-master's appearance at the disciplinary hearing presided over by Zednicek in overalls copiously stained with pigeon droppings (a base affront both to Zednicek's idealism and to the ordered, purified bodies of Nazi ideology). One could see such assertions of the base body in less than absolute terms, and suggest that Menzel and Hrabal do not so much reject the ideal as seek to supplement it with a sense and sympathy for the concrete and corporeal: after all neither Menzel nor Hrabal are themselves immune to the ideal or lyrical. A more precise formulation of both authors' stance is perhaps to be found in Menzel's 1969 Hrabal adaptation *Larks on a String*, where a much kindlier incarnation of Zednicek, Vlastimil Brodský's librarian turned labour-camp inmate, falls into a latrine following an impromptu citation from Kant. 'This is man's glory,' he concedes: 'his head is full of ideals and his feet are stuck in shit.'

---

24. Menzel and Hrabal, *Closely Observed Trains*, p. 46.

Figure 3.2 The station master (Vladimír Valenta) in *Closely Observed Trains* (*Ostře sledované vlaky*, Jiří Menzel, 1966) ©Ateliéry Bonton Zlín.

The station's world is an infantile, libidinal one, animated not by intellectual principles but by sensual obsessions: even the forever moralizing, supposedly high-minded stationmaster is a secret voluptuary preoccupied with sex and the compensatory pleasures of his suits and fabrics. Throughout the film characters relate to one another in a tactile manner that is sometimes lewd, sometimes merely familiar (Máša's lecherous uncle runs his hand along a line of girls, the stationmaster slaps Zdenka's cheeks). The crude yet seductive figure of Hubička unself-consciously serves as the film's key proponent of 'materialism', and to this extent presents a provocative inversion or parody of Socialist Realist convention. Hubička in many ways resembles the traditional Socialist Realist figure of the older 'mentor' whose narrative function is to initiate the young protagonist into the Party's wisdom. Through the inculcation of Marxist–Leninist doctrine, the mentor, himself typically a senior Party member, completes the protagonist's transition from 'spontaneity' to 'consciousness', which might be described as a transition from feeling to thought, from the affective to the intellectual. Hubička's 'initiation' of Miloš is anything but an intellectual one, as the older man comprises mainly a sexual role model for the gauche Miloš. Furthermore, even though Hubička will eventually initiate Miloš into the Czech resistance and entrust him with a grave political mission, he is pointedly never shown to be a Party member, nor to espouse any political principles, Marxist or otherwise. Interested less in 'grand ideas' than in the sensuous and concrete, Hubička stands in counterpoint to Zednicek, who in his self-assumed 'instructive' role comes closer to the Socialist Realist trope. If Zednicek is 'inconspicuous', then Hubička represents triumphant physical presence, largely courtesy of actor Josef Somr's performance. The American critic John Simon writes: 'There is something so spontaneous, unconcerned, and complete about such a performance that it affects our entire sensorium – finger tips, nostrils, and palate no less than eyes and ears.'[25]

As representative of the low, Hubička is also responsible for the 'corporealization' of language, that crucial bearer of abstractions and ideals (the German language, of which Zednicek declares Hubička's stamping of Zdenka an 'abuse', of course constitutes the language of idealism par excellence). This process, whereby language is introduced into the bodily or material domain (or where, conversely, the body insinuates its way into the linguistic sphere), can be observed in other Hrabal and Menzel works: it is evident as the compacting of books in the hydraulic press in the 1977 novella *Too Loud a Solitude* (*Příliš hlučná samota*) (the words of religious and philosophical texts are 'made bloody flesh',[26] revealed in their fragile, abject materiality) and in the grating, compulsive, obscenely present speech of Uncle Pepín in the novel and film versions of *Cutting It Short* (1974/1980). The stamping of Zdenka represents the merging of the linguistic with the bodily both because of the actual words on the rubber-stamps, which are inscribed on Zdenka's flesh, and because the stamps have themselves been invested with a signifying function courtesy of Zednicek's account of military strategy, which transforms the stamps into representatives of the German armies. Of course the stamps also ensure the binding nature of all the station's documents. Hubička prepares us for his erotic use of the stamps during the ratification of the stationmaster's forced agreement, blowing on them with insolent languor before passing them to Zednicek. (He will repeat this gesture with Zdenka.) This provocative gesture at once mocks the portentousness of the official procedure and soils that procedure by conferring on the stamps an obscene material quality, a 'bodily' contamination.

Ironically, however, the erotic use of these stamps also reveals the unwitting or disavowed truth of Zednicek's symbolic demonstration, courtesy of a literalized metaphor. As Škvorecký reminds us, the phrase 'to head for the ass' (*'jít do prdele'*) is a Czech colloquialism meaning to face disaster. That Hubička applies the stamps where he does thus underlines the fact that the Nazi troops are themselves 'heading for the ass', that the Germans are 'fucking up the

25. John Simon, 'A Track All Its Own', in Menzel and Hrabal, *Closely Observed Trains*, p. 12.
26. Hrabal, *Too Loud a Solitude*, translated by Michael Henry Heim (London: Abacus, 1993), p. 32.

war'.[27] It seems that the corporeal or erotic domain, even conceived as the foil for the linguistic and symbolic, cannot help but speak provocative truths. As we shall see in the next section, the world of the erotic also potently expresses or epitomizes the Bataillean notion of 'heterogeneous' economy, and more generally the principles of self-sufficient enjoyment and individual worth valorized in this film.

The Sacred and The Profane: Utility and Expenditure

Bataille sometimes refers to his ubiquitous base matter as that which is 'heterogeneous' to meaning. But the 'heterogeneous' also has a more directly political meaning, signifying all that with which fascism, capitalism and communism would not sully itself, those activities excluded from the 'homogeneous' order of modern economies. 'Social homogeneity', propounded in classical theories of economy, consists in the reduction of human individuals to a mere exchange value, to instruments of production and social advancement deprived of any self-sufficient meaning: 'According to the judgement of homogeneous society, each man is worth what he produces; in other words he stops being an existence for itself: he is no more than a function.'[28] Bataille presents this principle of homogeneity as characteristic of both capitalism and Stalinist Communism, with the distinction that in Stalinism the transformation of individuals into objects is both more profound and more conspicuous, lacking the 'deceptive appearances' of a meaningful, autonomous subjectivity fostered by capitalist mystification.[29]

The 'heterogeneous', by contrast, is defined in terms of those experiences and activities that resist assimilation into a socio-economic order dependent upon functionality and usefulness. Heterogeneous acts are those that are not subordinated to any purpose, but represent ends in themselves; the quintessence of heterogeneity is the 'unproductive expenditure', the enactment of deliberate and profligate waste. In *On Nietzsche* (*Sur Nietzsche*, 1945), Bataille discusses the difficulties that the dominant political and ideological systems have in conceiving states of pleasure or 'ardour' as their own justification: 'Lacking any relation to material benefits such as power or growth of the state (or of God or a Church or a party)', such states 'cannot even be comprehended' and manifest themselves merely as 'empty consummations'.[30] Bataille identifies the realm of

---

27. Škvorecký, *History of the Closely Watched Trains*, p. 73.
28. Bataille, *Visions of Excess*, p. 138.
29. Bataille, *The Accursed Share, Volumes 2 and 3: The History of Eroticism and Sovereignty*, translated by Robert Hurley (New York: Zone, 1993), p. 368.
30. Bataille, *On Nietzsche*, translated by Bruce Boone (New York: Paragon House, 1994), p. 20.

the heterogeneous, though not exclusively, with the realm of the erotic. Distinguished by Bataille from sexuality in its procreative and thus 'purposeful' guise, eroticism is characterised by its utterly gratuitous waste of energy and by its rupture of the limits of the self, its dissolution of the boundary between subject and object. Moreover, in Bataille's view sexual urges have an inherent tendency towards excess, towards ever-greater waste, and the sense of waste is itself seen as integral to the pleasurable erotic experience.[31]

The essential originality, and danger, of Bohumil Hrabal's work consists in the choice of 'empty consummations' and purposeless ardours (and not only erotic ones) as the dominant territory of his fiction. Alfred French considers Hrabal one of the most subversive Czech authors of the 1960s in the sense that his work (unlike that of many well-intentioned reformist writers) abandons the homogenous realm of 'socialist construction'. His characters are not self-denying ciphers concerned with work and productivity but feckless sensualists and daydreamers leading committed lives of eventful idleness, active in their non-activity. Hrabal drew for his aesthetic on such aimless, meandering anecdotes as are recounted in pubs, on that freewheeling, detail-dense yet strictly pointless form of storytelling that Hrabal defines as 'palavering' (*pábitelství*). Courtesy of a cut-and-paste approach that elides incidents together, a Hrabal story typically resembles a feast of scraps, an assemblage of weightless follies in which effects seldom follow causes. If we choose to define Hrabal's aesthetic as a kind of plebeian modernism, then this is partly because modernism has been seen (by Fredric Jameson at least) as a rejection of the instrumentality inherent in commercial art forms, the 'means/ends differentiation' evident, for instance, in the practice of reading a story for the sake of an ultimate revelation.[32] Menzel faithfully transfers Hrabal's vision to the screen, portraying the station workers' carefree lifestyles with a similar indulgence. In the film as in the novel, Miloš unabashedly indicates his lackadaisical agenda early on, an agenda that has also characterized his work-shy forbears: 'everyone knows I want to be [a signalman] because I don't want to do anything but stand on a platform with a signal disc and avoid hard work'. It is often tempting to politicize the activities of Hrabal's characters, especially when, as with Miloš and Hubička in *Trains*, they are also involved in political resistance movements. Yet this interpretive move risks reducing pleasurably gratuitous activities to instrumental ones in the service of higher ends. Indeed, such a line of argument would be comparable to Zednicek's threats to prosecute Miloš's self-mutilation and Hubička's stamping of Zdenka as acts of sabotage. Of course, Zednicek's charges ludicrously misrepresent the real meaning of those actions, as Zednicek himself is well aware: the Czechs'

---

31. Bataille, *Eroticism*, translated by Mary Dalwood (London: Marion Boyars, 2006), p. 170.
32. Fredric Jameson, *Signatures of the Visible* (London: Routledge, 1992), p. 12.

Figure 3.3 *Closely Observed Trains (Ostře sledované vlaky,* Jiří Menzel, 1966) ©Ateliéry Bonton Zlín.

behaviour is 'political' or subversive only to the extent that it rejects the instrumentalist values of Nazism (and, by implication, Stalinism).

If Hrabal's characters lead relatively carefree lives, then they must often snatch their pleasures from the representatives of repressive order: in *Larks on a String* (or rather the 1965-published stories 'Strange People' ('Divní lidé') and 'Angel' ('Anděl'), the primary inspiration for Menzel's film), the customary frolics even take place within the confines of a Communist labour camp. Such fictional worlds suggest a Surrealist utopia (though, of course, of a distinctly unideal, anti-heroic and quotidian kind) hemmed in by twentieth-century dystopia. The deployment of historical context in this way enables Menzel and Hrabal to counterpose the protagonists' libidinal 'expenditures' with a totalitarian economy of bodies that represents the principle of homogeneity at its most extreme and brutal. Arguably that counterpoint is even more fully developed in Menzel's adaptations than in Hrabal's works. While the political relevance of *Closely Observed Trains* may not seem apparent due to the film's Occupation setting, it must be remembered that the 'ethical' dimensions of Stalinism and fascism are largely the same as regards the human individual. As Eagleton suggests, both systems are founded on the mass homogenization of bodies, whereby individuals are rendered as identical objects to be used or discarded as extraneous (of course, this levelling of individuals also takes place in a less extreme way through the exchanges of the capitalist marketplace).[33] When Miloš visits Zednicek's office to report his absence, Zednicek witheringly contrasts Miloš and Hubička's sexual preoccupations with the selfless fighting spirit of the German soldiers:

> The most noble people of Europe go to the front to fight for peace. Risking their lives, their blood. And how do you thank the Reich? You stamp imprints on the telegraphist's rear end, and slash your wrists because of a girl.

The transformation of the body into a military instrument constitutes a brutal application of the principle of homogeneity, a merciless extraction of the individual's 'use-value'. By contrast, the Czech characters' activities signify pleasurable, purposeless expenditure (the stamping is non-procreative sex-play that expends official ink rather than semen, and even carries intimations of sodomy, that original Sadeian affront to reproductive sexuality) and a wilful, strictly non-redemptive self-destruction. Paradoxical here is the contrast between the constructive, and thus life-affirming, quality of the soldiers' deaths and the nihilistically wasteful, and thus deathly, sexual activities: Nazi troops march to their battlefields in the service of 'peace', while Miloš's sexual problems prompt him to attempt suicide. The eroticized depiction of the suicide attempt itself, Menzel's location of the scene in a cut-rate brothel and the image of Miloš's wounds bleeding luxuriantly and uselessly away, irresistibly evokes Bataille, in particular his well-known comments concerning 'the truth of eroticism': 'Our only real pleasure is to squander our resources to no purpose, just as if a wound were bleeding away inside us.'[34]

---

33. Eagleton, 'Bakhtin, Schopenhauer, Kundera', in Ken Hirschkop and David Shepherd (eds), *Bakhtin and Cultural Theory* (Manchester: Manchester University Press), pp. 234–37.
34. Bataille, *Eroticism*, p. 170.

While the station characters' commitment to the momentary and self-sufficient is, of its nature, expressed spontaneously, the conflict of values attains a more polemical character in the scene where Zednicek first visits the station, a scene invented by Hrabal and Menzel in their screenplay for the film. Using his threadbare map and the station's rubber stamps, Zednicek explains, in highly positive terms, the German army's current strategy for the conquest of Europe. However, Hubička can only respond to this report of the latest military 'masterstroke' by asking, 'But why?' Believing the question to evidence merely a dull-witted failure to understand the Germans' tactical logic, Zednicek explains how the withdrawals will effectively set a trap for the 'enemy'. Yet this apparently definitive explanation is greeted once again by a quietly posed 'Why?' Zednicek is visibly irked by the repetition, perhaps because it seems gratuitous, perhaps because it subtly suggests an incomprehension concerning less the tactical means being employed, than the value or necessity of the military venture itself. The quisling replies, in a polite yet proselytizing tone, 'In order that we can all live well, yes?' This matter neatly resolved, Zednicek urges the stationmaster to sign the declaration that will officially bind the station to the Nazi cause. The stationmaster wishes to change out of the unfinished suit he is wearing, yet Zednicek insists, 'When the ultimate victory is being fought for, clothes don't matter. We will leave finery until the attainment of peace.' This remark provides yet another occasion for the soft-voiced but grating refrain, delivered now by Miloš: 'Why?' This is the most flagrantly nonsensical instance of questioning, and also the most profound, attacking not only the worth of the cause itself, but the entire 'rational' allocation of value, the scale that opposes victory and frippery. Škvorecký describes all this questioning as a 'quintessential' example of the Švejkian gesture so ingrained in Czech culture and behaviour: the deliberate resort to stupidity as a form of covert mockery. In this case, Škvorecký argues, the aim is to '[ridicule] the concept of the sub-human nature of non-Germanic peoples stipulated by Nazi racism'.[35] While the scene undoubtedly is Švejkian (in fact it is directly modelled on a scene from Hašek's novel), the purpose of these questions is more complex than Škvorecký suggests. To begin with, does not the very 'stupidity', the oafish short-sightedness, of Miloš's question betray a precise ethical position? Why, indeed, are the pleasures of clothes, of fabrics or flesh, secondary to the exigencies of history?

Such a question, so phrased, may seem frivolous, yet it is in this scene that Menzel strikes at the heart of Stalinist ideology and political practice. That Zednicek's literal faith is Nazism offers the thinnest of alibis for Menzel's critique, directly vocalized though this is in Miloš's meek monosyllable. The request that a utilitarian, 'homogenous' society at least acknowledge the

---

35. Škvorecký, *History of the Closely Watched Trains*, p. 55.

repressed, hedonistic 'Other' of the heterogeneous is provocative when posed by a Bataille. Such a request, however, must appear especially subversive or unwelcome in the context of Stalinism (or even its Thawed-out contemporary equivalent), a ruthlessly instrumentalizing political system that yoked virtually all of social and human existence to the demands of socialist construction and historical 'progress' and denied the value not only of individual moments but also of individual lives. Menzel's satirical representation of Zednicek reveals how such disregard for the finite and personal is an inherent danger of any conception of history as narrative, whether this manifests itself as Stalinism's pseudo-scientific 'historical necessity' or as Nazism's mystical 'providence'. Paradoxically, the transpersonal force of history can only realize itself through conscious material force: continuous violence and coercion are required to keep 'destiny' on its correct path. Thus Zednicek can cite the Fuhrer's belief that 'providence will not abandon us', while simultaneously urging the signing of a document that spells out the severe consequences for those who impede the 'course of history': 'neglecting one's duties' at the station will mean ten years in prison, and 'in the worst circumstances, life – or death'.

The amusing alternation of 'life or death' in their apparent equivalence illuminates the central contradiction in Zednicek's brand of homicidal millenarianism: the commitment to universal happiness, to life at its grandest and most joyful, sanctions and even necessitates the worst sufferings, the devaluation of human lives in their particular, concrete significance. The value of the moment is surrendered to an endlessly deferred eternity. In his 1957 essay 'Responsibility and History' the Polish philosopher Leszek Kołakowski reveals the radical nihilism that constitutes the underside of Stalinist utopianism:

> If historical necessity is seen as an unlimited process without a defined final stage, or if an ultimate goal is attributed to it that has not yet been attained but constitutes merely a promise for the future, and if at the same time moral judgements are subordinated to the realization of historical necessity – then there is nothing at all in daily life that can be an end in itself.[36]

Another way of looking at Hubička and Miloš's repeated questioning is as a means to parody the nihilistic logic of historical necessity. The repetition of the question 'Why' constitutes the *reduction ad absurdum* of a process of reasoning in which nothing is permitted to stand for itself, in which every end is only the means of yet another end. Zednicek responds confidently to Miloš, 'Why? In order for us to save civilisation.' But this is only for Hubička to follow with another insolent 'Why?' What is the cause that impels the Grand Cause itself? Abstraction now pushed to breaking point, Zednicek can offer

---

36. Leszek Kołakowski, *Towards a Marxist Humanism* (New York: Grove Press, 1968), pp. 143–44.

nothing, and resorts to the authoritarian principle of unquestioning obedience: 'Because that is the Fuhrer's wish, and that is enough!' It is in this aspect that the scene is authentically Švejkian, as Švejk's exaggerated stupidities and follies are always designed to reveal the stupidities and follies of the political and military establishment. The tradition of Hašekian absurdity on which the film draws can be seen as a kind of populist Dada, spinning comic riffs out of the irrationalities of power.

Tellingly, within the Communist world *Closely Observed Trains* fell foul of the very instrumentalist ethos that the film illustrates. Although the film was not actually banned in Czechoslovakia until the onset of Normalization, Peter Hames observes that the 'association of sex with the theme of national liberation was one of the most politically 'subversive' qualities of the film, undercutting the traditional (and inhuman) convention of the noble Resistance fighter'.[37] Škvorecký informs us that '[i]n the Soviet Union the film was found to be an insult to the anti-Nazi resistance movement' as it broached the 'heretical idea' that, 'even in times of revolutions, young men, besides being preoccupied with the sacred matters of the nation, also give some thought to the well-guarded sanctuaries of their girls'.[38] Perhaps not unjustly, Škvorecký attributes this disapproval of the film to Soviet puritanism: 'This is … understandable as it is well known that in the Soviet Union children are brought by a stork.'[39] Yet, at a more fundamental level, it could be argued that the film caused offence by mingling homogenous and heterogeneous orders, by soiling the sanctified realm of Resistance with the obscene spectacle of waste. Of course, the film's 'insult', such as it was, was not to the sporadically efficient, disorganized coalition that comprised the real Czech opposition to Nazi rule, but to the Sovietized iconography of Resistance that constituted the great ideological fiction of Communist Czechoslovakia. As is evident in the cult created around the autobiographical writings of Julius Fučík, a Communist Resistance member imprisoned and executed by Protectorate authorities, the mythical image of the Resistance fighter is one of rigorous self-discipline, fervent idealism and steadfastness throughout almost superhuman suffering. Such national martyrs as Fučík may possess an individual specificity, but that does not make the mythic image that Fučík embodied any less inhuman. The great irony in *Closely Observed Trains*, of course, is that the affirmation of the disciplined body 'utilized' for war is voiced not by the Resistance-associated Czech characters, but by their Nazi enemy. Menzel's aim here is not to pursue historical revision for its own sake, but to attack Stalinist ideology upon the terrain of one its most beloved and ubiquitous cultural manifestations.

Yet if we contented ourselves with conceiving this attack as a mere

---

37. Hames, *The Czechoslovak New Wave*, p. 155.
38. Škvorecký, *All the Bright Young Men and Women*, p. 170.
39. Ibid.

'desacralization' of the Resistance hero, we would be ignoring the centrality of the sacred to Menzel's vision. In fact the film is concerned not with denying the sacred but with reclaiming it for Surrealism and heterogeneity. The heterogeneous and the sacred are virtually interchangeable terms in Bataille's writing, as sacral status is conferred on such activities as represent ends in themselves, as enact significant loss and waste. Indeed religious rituals comprise quintessential unproductive expenditures, and thus the 'sacred' and the 'profane', as convention would have it, are not diametrically opposed phenomena but rather diverse manifestations of a single essence, heterogeneity. Throughout *Closely Observed Trains*, Menzel redefines the sacred in these transgressive terms with a surprising explicitness: the surname of Zdenka, participant in the film's central erotic misdemeanour, is *Svatá*, meaning 'saintly', 'holy'; a Renaissance image of the Virgin Mary hangs incongruously on the wall of the brothel bedroom in which Miloš tries to kill himself, while his rescue at the hands of a builder is quite self-consciously staged as a pietà, the prone, tousle-haired Miloš naked but for his bandaged wrists and a towel shrouding his genitals. The chimes of the stationmaster's clock, themselves a ceremonial salute to ephemerality, lend each erotic episode a solemn, ritualistic character; Hubička even waits for the chimes, marking the commencement of midnight, before kissing Zdenka. This aspect of the film deepens Menzel's polemic with Socialist Realist traditions, and comprises one of the ways in which Menzel subverts or challenges Socialist Realism's own division of phenomena into sacred and profane.

Of course, the sacred or transcendental realm of Socialist Realism is not the spiritual world but History, in its capitalized, millenarian guise. Katerina Clark discusses Socialist Realist aesthetics in relation to the concept of a mythic 'Great Time', a notion developed by the anthropologist Mircea Eliade in his studies of traditional societies. Great Time denotes a period 'when life [will] be qualitatively different from present-day reality', a period of great events, of grand heroic action or convulsive historical change.[40] The Great Time of Soviet and East European Communist discourse can comprise a revolutionary past, mythified and monumentalized, or a promised 'Great and Glorious Future', but never the quotidian present. There is little place here for time as it is ordinarily experienced, for time as a flow of bathetic, trivial events: as Clark notes, 'ordinary time' constitutes 'profane time'.[41] Yet literary and cinematic works must, on occasion, portray present-day reality; moreover, the experiences of ordinary individuals represent the lifeblood of fiction, especially of such a self-consciously 'demotic' and propagandistic sort. Socialist Realism forestalls any potential lapse into the 'profane' by means of symbolism: the

---

40. Katerina Clark, *The Soviet Novel: History as Ritual* (Chicago; London: University of Chicago Press, 1981), p. 40.
41. Ibid., p. 175, p. 40.

Figure 3.4 The lesson on military strategy. *Closely Observed Trains* (*Ostře sledované vlaky*, Jiří Menzel, 1966) ©Ateliéry Bonton Zlín.

stuff of everyday experience finds its purpose and meaning in its capacity to represent the events of Great Time. According to Clark, '[a] hierarchy is thus established in which present moments are not valuable in themselves but represent modest, particular instances of Great Moments'.[42] Clearly this ethos could not be more divergent from that of Hrabal, for whom value and beauty inhere precisely in the everyday. Socialist Realism can be seen as an aesthetic analogue to Stalinist instrumentality, in that a story's overt diegetic content can never be interesting or important enough on its own terms: 'material from present-day reality', reduced to its symbolic value, 'need not be particularized'.[43] In a manner akin to mystical experiences, Great Time reveals itself as incarnated in everyday life, which is thereby 'redeemed' from its condition of 'profane' contingency and insignificance.

Menzel's film offers a particularly stinging riposte to this aesthetic formula, not only valorizing 'ordinary time' in all its pettiness and ignobility, but doing so in the midst of Great Time itself: Clark notes that the Second World War was 'added to the list' of the Soviets' 'canonized' Great Moments,[44] while for Communist Czechoslovakia the period of Occupation and subsequent Liberation constitutes something of a founding myth. It might seem paradoxical to claim that Menzel and Hrabal situate the 'profane time' of the present within the Great Time of the past, yet Clark's distinction between past and present time should be considered more an ontological than a chronological one. In fact, the film's one obvious illustration of Great Time takes place when Zednicek 'enacts' the German army's military strategies using his map and the station's stamps. This 'epic' representation of the war is symbolic rather than direct, deploys National Socialist rather than Communist teleology, and serves as a parody of the fateful struggles and immense panoramas of Great Time on

42. Ibid., p. 175.
43. Ibid., p. 41.
44. Ibid., p. 40.

which Socialist Realism ultimately sets its sights. Zednicek's tattered map comprises a tawdry imitation of the vast political canvas implied in even the most modest Socialist Realist narratives. Moreover, as we have seen, the lofty allegorical cipher is soon contaminated by its erotic implementation.

The transpersonal dimension of Zednicek's symbolic military manoeuvres has its obverse in the grotesque expansion of body parts and sexual images. In a recurrent motif from Hrabal's novella, a character appears to see a recent sexual experience 'replayed' against the expanse of the sky like a cosmic movie image: the private fantasy writ large against the surface of the world. Such lewd, delusionally narcissistic imagery has a long history in Surrealist art and evokes perhaps most specifically Karel Teige's collages of the 1930s and 1940s, which obsessively integrate monstrously overscaled female body parts into natural landscapes, thus rendering pornographic cut-outs as fleshy monuments in a libidinal, utopian neverland. Referring to Surrealism, the Czech critic and psychoanalyst Bohuslav Brouk writes that the artist (in contrast to the pornographer) 'extend[s] the reign of his sexuality over the entire world': 'He pisses a sea, shits a Himalayas, gives birth to cities, masturbates factory chimneys'.[45] Perhaps the ultimate theoretical source of such images is Dalí's 'critical paranoia', the commitment to reinterpreting or 'discrediting' objective reality in the light of neuroses and phantasies, one's personal irrational 'system'. On one level, Hrabal's deployment of the Surrealist motif can be seen as ribald mockery of the delusional qualities of fascism and Stalinism themselves: as Freud himself noted, all attempts to construct totalizing theoretical systems can be construed as paranoiac (while Zednicek's faith in the Nazi military victory is more overtly deluded). What is most crucial, however, is the status of these delusions, and Hrabal's images express the earnest desire to subordinate the collective myths of political totalitarianism to the subjective imaginings of Surrealism.

While Menzel does not attempt directly to accommodate Hrabal's fantastic conceit within his scrupulously realistic realization, he nonetheless subtly approximates it in a variety of ways. Hubička's post-coital mornings are spent staring dreamily into the sky, and on one such occasion, after the stamping incident, Menzel's inspired editing supplants a winter sun with the circular imprint of the stamp on Zdenka's behind (a conceit that cannot but evoke the author of an essay entitled 'The Solar Anus' ('L'Anus solaire', 1927)). In an even more striking example during Zednicek's military presentation, Menzel cuts from a close shot of Zdenka scratching her chest to an overhead shot of the map, Zednicek's hands now depicting the German entrapment of enemy armies. Momentarily, the hands cup themselves into the shape of breasts, and an unwitting gesture of erotic appreciation dwarfs whole continents. However,

---

45. Bohuslav Brouk, 'Afterword', in Vítězslav Nezval and Jindřich Štyrský, *Edition 69*, translated by Jed Slast (Prague: Twisted Spoon, 2004), p. 116.

the film is arguably most powerful in this regard when it relies on the distorting properties inherent to cinema itself (one source of its 'delirious' quality and its fascination for the original Surrealists), with the detailed close-ups of the stamping scene transforming the surfaces of the body into lunar landscapes of skin. Menzel's film thus more closely approximates an authentic 'concrete irrationality' than Hrabal's novella, exploiting the identification between subjective and objective worlds that cinema can foster. The film's brand of Surrealism can be defined in terms of a warping of scale, an absence of proportion, the usurpation of the public and global by the private and local. Menzel and Hrabal underline the humanist implications of their warped scale by defining it against the discourse of Socialist Realism, whose 'correct' sense of proportion involves denying the value of specific individuals.

The Secret Life of Stalinism

If there is any convergence between the discourses of Soviet Communism and Bataillean Surrealism, it consists in their portrayal of erotic activity as excessive squandering. While Communist attitudes towards the erotic can be linked on the one hand to an overall Stalinist 'ethics' of instrumentality, of the subordination of means to ends, they can on the other be traced to a sense of sex as a specific and great threat to social or political endeavours. No less a personage than V.I. Lenin, in his correspondences with Clara Zetkin, discusses the danger posed to revolution by the magnitude of erotic 'expenditures': castigating Zetkin for the preoccupation with 'sex problems' within her youth organizations, Lenin warns that '"[t]his nonsense is especially dangerous and damaging to the youth movement. It can easily lead to sexual excesses, to overstimulation of sex life and to *wasted health and strength of young people*."'[46] Lenin later remarks, '"I will not vouch ... for the men who run after every petticoat and let themselves in with every young female. No, no, that does not go well with revolution."'[47] Of course, what is valorized in Bataille is feared and loathed in Lenin and the Soviets, and with apparently good, 'scientific' grounds. 'Classical' Soviet psychology, as represented by the vulgar Freudianism of Aron Zalkind, postulates a single pool of 'energy' upon which the entire spectrum of human activities depends. With sexual activity a serious drain on resources, Zalkind argues that sexual instincts are best channelled, or in Freudian terminology sublimated, into 'healthier' pursuits such as sport and, of course, politics.[48] In an ironic inversion of such prescriptions, the morose-

---

46. Clara Zetkin, 'My Recollections of Lenin', in V.I. Lenin, *On the Emancipation of Women* (Moscow: Progress Publishers, 1972), p. 104 (my italics).
47. Ibid., p. 106.
48. H. Kent Geiger, *The Family in Soviet Russia* (Cambridge, MA: Harvard University Press, 1968), pp. 85–88.

looking doctor of *Closely Observed Trains*, played by Menzel himself, recommends that Miloš think about sport as a means of improving his sexual performance. Of course, the climax of Menzel's film thoroughly subverts the traditional representation of Resistance hero as self-denying ascetic, and to that extent the film could even be seen as a reproof to the Soviets' insistence on the incompatibility of sexual fulfilment and revolution, love and war. Miloš's successful sexual performance seems to create the condition for his revolutionary 'performance', endowing him with newfound strength and confidence. His act of sabotage is presented not as the sublimation of his sexual desires, but as a complement to the sex act, a convulsion in the political sphere to echo the shudders of orgasm.

Bataille's work, like Zalkind's, addresses 'energy', though Bataille conceives that energy in social and material, as well as psychic, terms, and concentrates more frequently on the excess of energy than on its scarcity. Whereas Bolshevism and Stalinism condemn unsublimated sexual license as a counter-revolutionary threat, Bataille insists on the necessity of recognizing and disposing 'correctly' of the surplus energy. In the absence of relatively harmless expenditures (such as feasts or vigorous erotic activities), the irrepressible need or tendency to squander might express itself through the darker expenditures of, say, murder or war. Yet for all such 'ethical' considerations (mainly expressed in such late works as *The Accursed Share* (*La Part maudite*, published in French in 1949)), the unsettling implication of Bataille's writings is that the most satisfying expenditures are the cruellest and most destructive ones. Bataille's work revels in a fearsome iconography of human sacrifice, blood rituals, deviance and criminality, while his discussion of expenditure extends to modern warfare and the arms proliferation of the Cold War. While fascist movements often barely disguised their irrational elements and their glorying in violence for its own sake (hence Bataille's early fascination with Mussolini), even the most brutal Communist regimes have generally presented themselves as the culmination of enlightened, rational civilization. For this reason Menzel's film is perhaps even more recognizably a critique of Stalinism than of Nazism: the idealistic, intellectual Zednicek surely resembles more an inconspicuous Communist Party secretary than he does an adherent of Hitler. Yet Bataille's discussion of expenditure suggests how far such a putatively rational, goal-oriented political order might partake of its abjected, heterogeneous Other. Is not the attraction towards violence as self-sufficient gesture furtively apparent in Stalinism's obsessively deployed imagery of martyrdom, its ceaseless rhetoric of war and conflict? The great Czech critic Václav Černý toys with this heretical insight in his pungent critique of the Fučík cult. For the Communist youth 'seduced' by the legend of Fučík, the political significance of Fučík's self-sacrifice was secondary to the act itself, to the martyrological ecstasy of impending annihilation: 'Not by the nature, content, or significance of his resistance activity did Fučík seduce, but rather by the way in which ... he rushes with zealous joy to face death.'[49]

From a Reichian perspective the joys of violence, war and martyrdom would be judged compensations for denied libidinal pleasure. Conversely, for Bataille sex seems to become all the more pleasurable the nearer it approaches the experience and condition of death. Bataille makes much of the fact that one French nickname for orgasm is 'the little death'. As we have seen, the specific pleasure of 'eroticism' consists in its nihilistic, self-destructive aspect. Sex and death are similarly intertwined throughout *Closely Observed Trains*. All the film's sexual incidents are presided over by the stationmaster's grand ornamental clock, whose chimes measure the onset of death. The recurrent motif (in both novella and film) that links virility with farm animals also yokes sex to the slaughterhouse.[50] The marks left on Zdenka's body after her encounter with Hubička and the rubber stamps form a counterpart to Miloš's suicide scars, themselves the consequence of sexual failure. Daniel López argues that the two sets of markings 'are a kind of mutilation and indicate that sex initiation can be either torture, or pleasure' – or both at once?[51] Etymologically and philosophically, it is but one short step from the sacred to the sacrificial, and at such moments eroticism approaches the condition of sacrifice in the Bataillean sense of pure loss and self-destruction, while of course opposing itself to Socialist Realism's representation of sacrifice as instrumental political act. Yet, in view of Bataille's insight into the heterogeneous aspects of 'rational' political systems, the film is perhaps as much an exploration of the Stalinist unconscious, Socialist Realism's scandalous 'unsaid' dimension, as an embodiment of the Surrealist 'Other'. Indeed Menzel shows how far the heterogeneous phenomenon of sacrifice extends into the martial and political spheres: the scars resulting from Miloš's 'irresponsible' suicide attempt are mirrored in the scars of the Nazi soldier, who quickly discerns a kinship of transgressive humanity over and above national or political differences; in Zednicek's admonitions to Miloš we can perceive a fetishistic, and typically fascist, preoccupation with blood; and both the final explosion and an earlier Allied bombing are greeted with bursts of raucous, wasteful laughter (Bataille describes laughter as another manifestation of the heterogeneous).

Indeed the film's ultimate representation of sacrifice, in which Miloš dies sabotaging a German munitions train, also serves this dual purpose of both transgressing Stalinism's explicit norms and foregrounding the heterogeneous aspect of Communist martyrology. The subversive enactment of Socialist

---

49. Václav Černý, quoted in Peter Steiner, *The Deserts of Bohemia: Czech Fiction and its Social Context* (Ithaca; London: Cornell University Press, 2000), p. 98.
50. Peter Hames, '*Ostře sledované vlaky/Closely Observed Trains*', in Peter Hames (ed.), *The Cinema of Central Europe* (London: Wallflower Press, 2004), p. 125.
51. Škvorecký, *History of the Closely Observed Trains*, p. 76.

Realist convention is easily dismissed as a capitulation to narrative orthodoxy. This charge has been levelled at Hrabal's work itself. The novella of *Closely Observed Trains* was an intensive reworking of a more obviously 'transgressive' piece which Hrabal wrote in the late 1940s called *The Legend of Cain* (*Legenda o Kainovi*). No doubt largely because of its apparently 'positive' representation of its protagonist's death, *Closely Observed Trains* has been considered a domesticated version of the earlier work (which remained unpublished until 1968), written with an eye towards official acceptance. Hrabal has recounted a taxi-driver's remark to him apropos the difference between the two stories: "'So they've outsmarted you, haven't they? You wanted to be a *poète maudit*, and they've turned you into a socialist realist. That's what I call an achievement!'"[52] Even Škvorecký wonders whether Hrabal decided on such an ending 'to make his oversexed story more acceptable'.[53] Superficially this viewpoint is easy to understand. Where *The Legend of Cain* was preoccupied with death and suicide in their overtly heterogeneous, wasteful dimension, Miloš's death is linked to resistance and national liberation, and would thus suggest an instance of heroic Great Time. It is a death *for* something, even if that 'something' is more the preservation of concrete freedoms than the 'big ideas' of a terrorizing utopianism. In the film Menzel juxtaposes Zednicek's assertion that the Czechs are a 'nation of grinning beasts' with the explosion of the munitions train, as though offering a refutation of the quisling's opinion and forcing upon us a revised impression of these 'over-sexed' characters.

Yet what makes this ending so subversive is the way it evokes the Socialist Realist model only to contaminate it with tokens of the heterogeneous. Miloš's cap, with the force of the explosion, blows back to Máša, a detail that links Miloš's death to the other occasions when his cap is removed: his successful sexual encounter and his eroticized, sexually motivated suicide attempt. Herbert Eagle considers the wearing of this cap a sign of 'repression';[54] one could also see the cap as standing for homogenous principles and the end-oriented world of work. (Incidentally, Petr Král reveals the rich symbolic resonance of hats as they appear in silent film comedies.)[55] Most importantly, Miloš's martyrdom is accompanied, again as in the sexual episodes, by the clock's chimes, which make their last bittersweet homage to finitude and irretrievable loss. Just as the erotic had its mortal component, so death is eroticized, and in this Menzel points up the shared nature of sex and sacrifice, which may be considered as respectively the comic and tragic guises of the heterogeneous.

---

52. Hrabal, quoted in Škvorecký, ibid., p. 38.
53. Ibid., p. 33.
54. Herbert Eagle, quoted in Hames, *The Cinema of Central Europe*, p. 121.
55. Král, *Groteska čili Morálka šlehačkového dortu* (Prague: Narodní filmový archiv, 1998), p. 140.

However, for all the film's subversive qualities, there is a serious instance of compromise in its final scenes, one in which Menzel shies away from the novella's exploration of the heterogeneous at its most troubling. In the novella Miloš's loss of his virginity at the hands of the Resistance fighter Viktoria Freie (who delivers the bomb that Miloš will use to blow up the munitions train) coincides with the firebombing of Dresden: the night sky is now decorated not with erotic hallucinations but with the red light of the bombs. This shocking example of mordant Hrabalian humour serves to align the atrocity with the sexual encounter. (Indeed the Allied devastation of Dresden lends itself to being interpreted as a supreme instance of expenditure in Bataille's terms.) Here Hrabal most pointedly indicates that the heterogeneous is often far from benign, that the Bataillean enactment of loss frequently brings much in the way of real loss. With the exclusion of this incident, Menzel's version of the sequence is perhaps more simplistic in its implied identification of personal and political 'liberation', as well as in its refusal to implicate an Allied democracy in heterogeneous violence. To be fair that identification is already suggested by Viktoria's name, which Menzel derives from the novel: while this codename obviously serves as a talismanic invocation of the 'victory of freedom', Škvorecký informs us that, when 'pronounced in the Czech way', the name also has connotations of 'drinking and fornication'.[56]

There are other ways in which the film compromises or attenuates its transgressive quality. Perhaps most notable among these is its approach to sexual politics. Predictably, the film's evocation of a 'formless' materiality is realized in relation to the female rather than the male body, and thus for all its artistic sophistication the role that the film offers its female characters is little better than that of sex object. Hubička may be the film's chief exponent of sensualism, yet even he is allowed the benefits of a subjectivity, albeit a lascivious one. In theoretical parlance, he is allotted the 'gaze': in one early scene he looks longingly at a local countess as she mounts her horse, and Menzel cuts between the countess's fleshy buttocks and the observing Hubička. If the world of the station seems to evoke a libidinal, and pre-Oedipal, state, then the film's finale can be seen rather to affirm a 'phallic' potency. Miloš's achievement of a functioning genital sexuality is synchronous with, and in fact enables, his attainment of a newfound bravery and moral strength; in this sense the association of resistance and military struggle with masculinity is symbolically reinforced. Although Viktoria Freie is a resistance member too, she is portrayed only as the means through which Miloš achieves his heroic status, just as she is the means by which, in sexual terms, he 'becomes a man'. It must be noted, however, that a progressive attitude towards gender is far from a universal characteristic among Surrealists (Andrea

---

56. Škvorecký, *History of the Closely Observed Trains*, p. 33.

Dworkin, for one, condemned Bataille's own sexually explicit novel *The Story of the Eye* (*L'Histoire de l'oeil*, 1928) on such grounds).[57]

A more surprising charge that might be made, in view of the long association between author and filmmaker, is that Menzel does not fully capture the spirit of Hrabal's novella. Karel Vachek criticizes Menzel for only offering '"castrated" Hrabal'.[58] As previously suggested, to some extent the film constitutes a 'repression' of the darkest elements of the book, just as Hrabal's novella was in some ways a repression of *The Legend of Cain*. Peter Hames compares Menzel's film favourably to the work of the great French filmmaker and Surrealist fellow traveller Georges Franju, though the comparison tempts one to speculate about what Franju would have done with the same source material. Franju is arguably cinema's pre-eminent example of a Bataillean filmmaker, and as the creator of that remarkable poetic exploration of the abattoir, *The Blood of Beasts* (*Le Sang du bêtes*, 1949), he would no doubt have done much with the novella's recurring motif of animal cruelty and its preponderant carcasses.[59] Because it avoids the 'base' and 'formless' in its most horrifying manifestations, *Closely Observed Trains* cannot perhaps be called a truly Bataillean film (an 'honour' that would go to Franju's *The Blood of Beasts* and *Eyes Without a Face* (*Les Yeux sans visage*, 1959), as well as to Yasuzo Masumara's alarming study of tactility and self-destruction, *Blind Beast* (*Môjuu*, 1969)), even if it lends itself to explication in terms of Bataillean concepts. Such 'shortcomings' could be seen as indicating the limits of culture and politics (including sexual politics) in 1960s Czechoslovakia, yet we must also reckon with Menzel's own directorial personality. To wish for a different film is essentially to wish for a different filmmaker. Menzel's films are old-fashioned and cheerfully sexist in their attitude to women, and they never stray into the terrain of visceral horror so favoured by contemporary cinema (Menzel is known to disdain such films as David Lynch's *Blue Velvet* (1986)). Yet the overt amiability of Menzel's cinema might also be seen as a subversive quality in itself: after all, when has the domain of 'wasteful' eroticism appeared so seductively sweet?

---

57. Susan Rubin Suleiman, *Subversive Intent: Gender, Politics and the Avant-Garde* (Cambridge, MA: Harvard University Press, 1992), pp. 79–80.
58. Karel Vachek, interviewed in Buchar, *Czech New Wave Filmmakers in Interviews*, p. 157.
59. See Adam Lowenstein, 'Films Without a Face: Shock Horror in the Cinema of Georges Franju', *Cinema Journal*, Vol. 37, No. 4. (Summer, 1998), pp. 37–58.

CHAPTER 4

Spoiled Aesthetics: Realism and Anti-Humanism in Věra Chytilová's *Daisies* (1966)

Morality Play or Stylistic Play?

In 1975, frustrated by her situation as a politically dubious filmmaker whose projects were continually and systematically scuppered by the authorities, the ever-outspoken Věra Chytilová wrote a letter to President Gustav Husák appealing for the right to practise her chosen profession. In the course of this long letter, Chytilová reiterates her allegiance to socialism, dismisses official criticisms made of her work, and summarizes her career as a director to date. Whether attempting to allay any fears of the ideological dangers that her return to the film set would present, or simply to demonstrate the unconditional artistic validity of her work, she explains briefly the philosophical import of each of her films. Her 1966 film *Daisies* (*Sedmikrásky*) is described as a 'morality play', in which the 'roots of evil' are shown as 'concealed in the malicious pranks of everyday life'.[1] The raucous, deceitful behaviour of the film's 'heroines' is typical of 'young people' when they are 'left to [their] own devices', when their unfulfilled creative needs turn into destructive impulses. As an audacious act of professional expedience, Chytilová's writing of this letter is to be applauded (even if we will never know what role the letter played in securing Chytilová's return to work the following year, with *The Apple Game* (*Hra o jablko*)), yet does this case of auto-interpretation as self-defence yield any valuable or accurate critical insights into such films as *Daisies*?

Strangely enough, Chytilová's comments on this film evoke nothing so much as the forthright moralizing, the didactic transparency, of Socialist Realism. The description of *Daisies* as a kind of contemporary fable on malign youth would suggest, to those unfamiliar with the film, an inoffensive and

---

1. Věra Chytilová, 'Letter to President Gustav Husák'. Full text of the letter available on the Facets 2001 DVD release of *Daisies*.

blandly 'responsible' work, conventional in medium as in message: after all, the condemnation of hooliganism, nihilism and political disengagement, in such a manner as rejects either ambiguity or a chance for transgressive enjoyment, hardly constitutes a radical departure from official cultural and political discourse. Whatever Dr. Husák's thoughts ultimately were on the matter, many of those who have seen *Daisies* would certainly challenge Chytilová's claims to such artistic simplicity and to such a narrowly conceived responsibility. Even those who have not seen the film might be tempted to ask how the safe, even platitudinous, work she describes could have caused, in roughly equal measure, so much elation and hostility, delight and disgust.

Must we take Chytilová's comments on board? Certainly, in the context of a letter effectively seeking the renewal of official favour, this particular account of her work can be seen as mechanically disingenuous, as though Chytilová were playing the obligatory role of the *engagé* (a term she applies several times in the letter) but obedient artist, yet she has reiterated this 'moral' interpretation of the film elsewhere, in one interview even describing it as a 'parable'.[2] Personally speaking, Chytilová's 'ethical' interpretation seems one of the least convincing or sustainable among the range of extant readings of *Daisies*. This discrepancy between the work and its creator proves strangely apposite however for a film whose groundbreaking poetics so gleefully undermine the identity of author and authority. Indeed *Daisies'* multivalent, multifaceted nature is precisely the reason why the film cannot be considered in terms of the parable, a form characterized by stark, exhortatory clarity. To adopt poststructuralist terms, *Daisies* reveals a certain 'excess' of meaning, an intractability to unitary interpretation, and even, in places, that libidinal expressiveness *beyond* meaning that comprises Kristeva's *signifiánce*: the surfeit of meaning culminates in its transcendence, a process abetted by remarkable visual effects and photographic experiments unseen anywhere before or since in the Czech 'mainstream' cinema, and paralleled by occasional flights into a near-abstract plasticity that has its equal only in animated, underground and avant-garde cinema.

Critics, Czech and otherwise, have demonstrated a wide variety of responses to the film's formal and hermeneutic complexity, from simplification

---

2. Chytilová, quoted in Škvorecký, *All the Bright Young Men and Women*, p. 108. See also Chytilová's comments in Yorick Blumenfeld, *Seesaw: Cultural Life in Eastern Europe* (New York: Harcourt, Brace and World, 1968), pp. 52–53. It should be noted, however, that Chytilová's own attitude towards *Daisies* and towards filmmaking in general is not entirely consistent. Peter Hames observes: '[Chytilová] claims that if the meaning is sometimes "invisible" and certain scenes not understood, this reflects badly on the film. On the other hand, she demands freedom for herself as a creator, and freedom for the audience as spectators, intending that the interplay between the two should be active' (Hames, *The Czechoslovak New Wave*, p. 196).

on the one hand to outright incomprehension and rejection on the other. Displaying good faith in authorial intentionality, some critics, such as Zdena Škapová, have doggedly attempted to apply Chytilová's interpretation to their reading of the film. Škapová describes the film as 'a critical examination of women', specifically young, irresponsible and selfish women, and, like Chytilová, sees it as akin to a 'mediaeval morality play'.[3] While Škapová rightly recognizes that the film's visual style makes for 'a work of unchained imagination', its aesthetic realization is essentially considered a means for Chytilová to 'disguise' this serious social commentary 'as a charming and playful spectacle'; the film's ambiguities signify a refusal to 'patronise the audience with a directly moralistic work'.[4] Milan Kundera regards the film as 'a parable about vandalism',[5] albeit one with a greater polemical sting than Chytilová herself suggests. More interestingly perhaps, Brigita Ptáčková discerns in the film 'a strife between ethics and aesthetics', a tension between the attempt to communicate an 'ethical' message and the cultivation of formal play for its own sake. It is worth asking to what extent that 'ethical' project is made evident in the film, and to what extent Ptáčková, on the basis of Chytilová's own comments, simply assumes it to be there. In one of the most damning critiques of *Daisies*, Surrealist leader Vratislav Effenberger fails to see any real purpose, critical, moral or otherwise, in the film, which he berates for offering flamboyant surface without depth. In an attack which anticipates critiques of postmodernism, Effenberger accuses Chytilová of an opportunistic eclecticism, describing the film as nothing more than a shallow assemblage of 'fashionable' artistic styles divorced from their true subversive function:

We find here everything that the international art market is capable of accepting (of course in a degenerated form) from the development of modern art and through which today's artistic racket blooms: pop-art, op-art, happenings, scriptural decorations, absurdity in the style of the 1920s and other forms of decorative cynicism, from which has fled the force of sarcasm. Everything that was once the work of imaginative protest returns now ... as decorative formalism ...[6]

---

3. Zdena Škapová, '*Sedmikrásky/Daisies*', in Hames, *The Cinema of Central Europe*, p. 132, 131.
4. Ibid., p. 130, 134.
5. Milan Kundera, 'Appendix: Speeches made at the Fourth Congress of the Czechoslovak Writers' Union June 27–29, 1967', in Hamšik, *Writers Against Rulers*, p. 173.
6. Vratislav Effenberger, 'Obraz člověka v českém filmu', *Film a doba*, pp. 349–50.

Figure 4.1 Marie I (Jitka Cerhová) and Marie II (Ivana Karbanová) in *Daisies* (*Sedmikrásky*, Věra Chytilová, 1966) ©Ateliéry Bonton Zlín, reproduced courtesy of Second Run DVD.

Effenberger's charge of 'eclecticism', his characterization of the film as an assortment of borrowed styles, actually hit the nail of the film's aesthetic peculiarity on the head: Chytilová flaunts the 'assembled' character of her work, appearing to treat artistic styles as though they were pre-existent or 'ready-made' discourses to be appropriated and combined at will. Another aspect of *Daisies* that has created many critical problems, beyond the style of the film, is the authentic nature of the protagonists themselves, the 'real' identity of these girls who even lack consistent names (only in the screenplay are they identified as Marie I and Marie II; they are designated thus in most commentaries on the film, as, for the sake of convenience, they will be here). Are these girls feminist practitioners of gonzo satire or 'bad girls' in need of punishment? Are they agents or objects of the film's critique? I would gravitate more towards the former interpretation (like both Herbert Eagle and Petra Hanáková in their excellent readings of the film), while also conceding the girls' resistance to even that totalization. The film's ambiguity in regard to its protagonists is not only the result of directorial subtlety, but also of the grotesque mutability, indeed manipulability, of these puppet-like figures, dragged as they are through a breakneck variety of guises, attitudes and cinematic idioms. Just as, for a commentator such as Effenberger, there is nothing beneath the film's cut-and-paste amalgam of aesthetic tropes, so its protagonists might confront us with a nagging, almost uncanny feeling of surface without depth, of body without soul, of a plethora of dazzling appearances in search of a substantial essence.

Chytilová's refutation both of the author as origin point and of the original, unitary self, implied in the aesthetic choices just mentioned, is among the film's most enduringly subversive qualities. From this perspective Effenberger is at once correct and off the mark when he lambasts *Daisies* as a patchwork of borrowed aesthetic styles. Chytilová's film brazenly yokes together different artistic movements, and different modes of filmmaking, in a rude, even jarring, manner, but in so doing foregrounds the idea of artistic creation as the deployment and arrangement of collective codes, in contrast to more traditional notions of art as transcendent self-expression, the outgrowing of a unique, coherent, originating subjectivity. That principle of assemblage is also a means to expose the constructed nature of the film's diegetic reality. As one technique jostles with another, as one shot is arranged ill-fittingly alongside another, the seams and fissures of the fictional world are opened up and the continuous fabric of cinematic 'space-time'[7] is transformed into a jagged mosaic of discrete fragments. Identity itself succumbs to this fragmentation. Neither of the protagonists presents any semblance of a coherent character, hence the futility of attempting to provide a definitive interpretation of their actions. The sum of their different functions, the girls appear in a variety of ontological registers, sometimes as live-action cartoons, sometimes as mere Bressonian models, and sometimes even as 'realistic' characters. To what extent is our subjectivity also an assemblage of discourses, a collage of disparate elements?

Effenberger dismisses the film as a work of mere ersatz avant-gardism, lacking the truly subversive qualities of the artistic movements that it ostentatiously refers to. Alternatively, we might suggest that that emphasis on the fragmentary, the constructed and the inauthentic in itself connects Chytilová's work with the most radical and troubling dimensions of the avant-garde. The original project of Dada, undertaken in the interest of political revolution, was also to expose the constructed nature of discourse, to 'de-naturalize' ideological representations. Margaret Cohen, in her study of Bretonian Surrealism, reveals the Surrealist subject as one whose 'fissuring' far exceeds the Freudian split between conscious and unconscious, a subject constituted by multiple external determinations.[8] We could adapt Chytilová's own claims for her film by observing that the cultivation of such an overdetermined, anti-illusionist aesthetic comprises a politically 'engaged', even a moral, project all by itself. For it is at this formal level that Chytilová

7.　Herbert Eagle, 'Dada and Structuralism in Chytilová's *Daisies*', in Ladislav Matejka (ed.), *Cross Currents 10: A Yearbook of Central European Culture* (New Haven; London: University of Yale Press, 1991), p. 223.

8.　Margaret Cohen, *Profane Illumination*, see chapters 3 and 4 (pp. 57–119).

both attacks humanist conceptions of authorship and subjectivity, and punctures the claims of any discursive act to the unmediated representation of the world. Critic and filmmaker Luc Moullet once asserted that 'morality is a question of tracking shots';[9] for Chytilová, a radical ethics is no less bound up with decisions regarding aesthetic practice.

Living Satire and Really Existing Socialism

One of the great virtues of the Czechoslovak New Wave is commonly considered to be its 'realism'. For many commentators on the movement and for many of the key filmmakers themselves, the New Wave's central achievement, and its most subversive aspect, was its ushering in of a new truthfulness after the distortions and mendacity of the Socialist Realist films made in the previous decade. The buzzwords of 'truth', 'truthfulness', 'authenticity' and so on recur throughout cinema-related articles and interviews from the period.[10] This concern with expressing the 'truth' is often identified with New Wave filmmakers' pursuit of stylistic realism, with their forging of a greater naturalism through technical innovations (the absence of a musical score, the use of improvisation and non-professional actors), and, unsurprisingly, with their interest in the new *cinéma vérité* methods then being pioneered in European and American cinema. Yet Chytilová also makes claims for the truth-value and realism of her films. While these claims were most frequently made in her early interviews and thus in relation to her more obviously 'realist' and *cinéma vérité* influenced works (*A Bag of Fleas* (*Pytel blech*, 1962), *Ceiling* (*Strop*, 1962), *Something Different*), she seems to adopt a similar view towards *Daisies*, which she describes as a 'philosophical documentary in the form of a farce'.[11] As previously shown, Chytilová's own descriptions of her work are not always entirely reliable, yet is it so absurd to suggest that a film like *Daisies* attains its own kind of realism?

9. Luc Moullet, 'Sam Fuller: In Marlowe's Footsteps', in Jim Hillier (ed.), *Cahiers du Cinéma, Volume 1: The 1950s: Neo-Realism, Hollywood, New Wave* (London: Routledge, 1985), p. 150.

10. See, for instance, the following *Film a doba* pieces: Jaromil Jireš, 'Vlna pravdy ve filmu' ['The Wave of Truth in Film'] (*Film a doba*, No. 8, 1965) and an article of the same name by Ivan Sviták (reprinted in Sviták's unpublished 1996 collection *Vlna pravdy ve filmu*, available at FAMU's library), which cites Chytilová's statement that 'The truthfulness or untruthfulness of a film does not consist in the conception of the method of the realization, but in the conception of the idea of the realization' (*Vlna pravdy ve filmu*, p. 22); Jozef Vagaday, 'O autentickom filme a o veciach okolo hovorí Štefan Uher: Rozhovor s Štefanem Uherem' [Štefan Uher Talks about Authentic Film and Other Things: A Conversation with Štefan Uher] (*Film a doba*, No. 6, 1963).

11. Chytilová, quoted in Hames, *The Czechoslovak New Wave*, p. 187.

Of course, we must here consider, indeed reconsider, what we understand by 'realism'. It is worth noting that Chytilová herself never espoused an orthodox conception of realism, even at her *vérité*-influenced stage (in a 1964 interview she praises Resnais's *Last Year at Marienbad* (*L'Année dernière à Marienbad*, 1961) for capturing the 'reality' of the 'subconscious'). Russian-born Formalist (and then Prague-based Structuralist) Roman Jakobson has argued that virtually all the major artistic movements, from 'classicists', 'sentimentalists' and 'romanticists' to 'modernists', 'futurists' and 'expressionists', have 'steadfastly proclaimed faithfulness to reality, maximum verisimilitude – in other words, realism – as the guiding motto of their artistic program'.[12] While realism is all too often identified with an established set of conventions, with the so-called Realist movement of the nineteenth century, according to Jakobson the concern to supplement or intensify our apprehension of reality has been the impetus underlying the overall development of art history.[13] For the Russian Formalist tradition itself, the truth-value of a work of art consists, strangely enough, in its capacity to 'deform', in the extent to which it 'defamiliarizes' the world as it is commonly experienced. While artistic development may generally be impelled by a certain need to violate established perception, there are of course particular movements that embrace the project of defamiliarization more fully, systematically and penetratingly than others: 1970s counter-cinema springs to mind as a contemporary example.

The Russian Formalists were generally politically disinterested in their writings, but the aesthetic practices they identify have often arisen out of a radical political programme, as is the case with counter-cinema, Dada and Brechtian 'epic' theatre. Brecht, in fact, appropriated the Formalist concept of defamiliarization with an eye to its political usefulness, evolving it into the theory, and practice, of his famous 'alienation' or 'estrangement' (*verfremdung*) effect. Not only does Chytilová's film utilize the specific strategies of defamiliarization identified by Formalist critics, including metaphor, exaggeration and the 'laying bare' of technique (in which techniques stand revealed as techniques): as will be argued throughout this chapter, it too can be seen to employ these strategies for political ends. If the Formalists themselves pointed towards any potentially subversive aspect of defamiliarization in their work, then it was towards the way exaggeration and estranged representation can expose the real nature of society and its institutions. The Formalist critic Victor Shklovsky writes that art exists 'to make one feel things, to make the stone *stony*';[14] defamiliarization, in

---

12. Roman Jakobson, 'On Realism in Art', in Ladislav Matejka and Krystyna Pomorska (eds), *Readings in Russian Poetics: Formalist and Structuralist Views* (Chicago: Dalkey Archive Press, 2002), p. 39.

13. Ibid.

14. Victor Shklovsky, 'Art as Technique', in *Russian Formalist Criticism: Four Essays*, translated and edited by Lee T. Lemon and Marion J. Reis (Lincoln: University of Nebraska Press, 1965), p. 12.

Chytilová's hands, can serve to make exploitation feel exploitative, to make greed *greedy*. In *Daisies*, exaggeration often has the same polemical function as in a Swift or a George Grosz. As we shall see, however, even this function does not exhaust the political usefulness of the aesthetics of defamiliarization.

In the remarkably condensed images of *Daisies'* title sequence, Chytilová intimates a connection between the film's radical aesthetic practices and such a political agenda. First we see a rotating flywheel, shot in a blueish monochrome and in close-up, and accompanied by a drum-laden martial theme. Images of the flywheel are intercut at regular intervals with aerial shots depicting wartime bombing runs (the Second World War? Vietnam?), degraded newsreel or documentary footage strikingly colourized with a garish red-orange hue. Already, we are confronted here with different levels of defamiliarization or estrangement. Most obviously, the meaning of these images is itself 'estranged'. Collapsing a number of competing associations and affects, this sequence represents intellectual montage at its most sophisticated, of the kind that Eisenstein theorized though arguably seldom realized in his own films. The images must be worked on for their contents to emerge; meaning is not self-evident here, nor 'obvious', but instead demands the critical participation of the spectator. Despite their formal and ontological disparity, one can read the two sets of images as connected, blending together as cause and effect: by a *coup* of creative geography, the mechanical actions of the flywheel become the force that drives the bombing campaigns. Perhaps it is not too fanciful to see these images as comprising a sexual trope, a device of what Shklovsky calls 'erotic defamiliarization', with the flywheel driving an unseen piston which prompts these orgasmic 'explosions'. This conceit of sex-as-machinery, of such great significance for Dada, here presages the film's anti-humanist interrogation of gender roles that posits sexual identity as itself an 'artificial' construct. Yet most importantly perhaps, this opening also makes for a mini-treatise on the coexistence, indeed the cause and effect relation, between numbed passivity and raw violence. For Shklovsky, art, with its power to defamiliarize, was the key weapon against the 'automatization' of perception. As a consequence of over-familiarity, reality grows subject to ever more mechanical apprehension: 'And so life is reckoned as nothing. Habitualization devours work, clothes, furniture, one's wife, and *the fear of war.*'[15] Here, then, the mechanical nature of perception is transformed into a literal image. If the flywheel causes the bombings, then, by analogy, it is the mechanizing of our response to reality, the automatization of human consciousness, that enables wars and atrocities to continue unchecked. At the same time, the actual violence of the bombing run is estranged or distanced

---

15. Ibid. (italics added).

through the indistinct visuals of the newsreel footage and the tinting of the footage into unreal colours; these real conflagrations are presented virtually as beautiful abstractions. It is the images of the banal flywheel, with its grindingly monotonous movement, that are the more oppressive, and it is these images, perversely enough, that are accompanied by the ominous martial score. The silent flowerings of warfare thus appear almost as points of respite or release. From this perspective the violence represents an assault on an insidiously 'mechanical' consciousness, a break in routinized, reified existence. The aesthetic distortion of these images suggests that Chytilová is interested in violence not as a physical act but as a textual event, as the 'deforming' practices of avant-garde art.

The following scene, and the film's first scene 'proper', offers a similar alternation of the passively mechanical and the violently revolutionary. Here the protagonists appear for the first time, yet the introduction of human elements signals neither the beginning of narrative, nor, at first sight, a clear break with the mechanized world of the previous sequence. Marie I and Marie II appear sitting side by side against the wooden wall of the bathing pool, a location that will recur throughout the film. At first sight, the girls' lifeless posture, blank expressions and attractively contrasting bikinis render them as mere dolls, abandoned to the toybox and awaiting the life-bestowing magic of play. Then they start to move, in a sequence of abrupt, stylized call-and-response gestures; the creaking sounds that are dubbed to accompany these movements evoke long-unused marionettes or rusty automatons. The scene's blue-tinged black and white photography emphasizes the connection between these non-entities and the flywheel. The two girls initially suggest a vicious, Godardian caricature of numbed social acquiescence; with their seemingly involuntary, manipulated movement, vacant expressions and stylish accessories (the coordinated bikinis, the chessboard bath towel the girls are sitting on), they appear to be mindlessly obedient pleasure-seekers, blank consumers of life. Yet this is not to suggest that Chytilová's transformation of her protagonists into puppets or automatons has only this relatively superficial satirical function: as we shall see, the film's imagery of automatized or artificialized humans also illustrates the notion of 'assembled' identity. In addition, the overt rendering of the film's performers as puppets in this introductory scene signals that these protagonists are not to be treated as flesh-and-blood characters but as ciphers, pawns in the filmmaker's formal and intellectual manoeuvres: Marie I and II are 'born', or activated, simultaneously with the beginning of the film, roused to animation by the purpose of the puppeteer-director.

In the ensuing dialogue, the girls establish the subversive game that will comprise the film's only real thread of 'story'. It seems this game will consist in the attempt to match the world's moral ugliness blow for blow: 'If everything is spoiled...So...We will be...Spoiled...As well', the girls gleefully declare in a crescendo of alternating speech fragments. As the scale and depth of their enormities escalate, the protagonists will strive, as part of their game, to respond only with a blithe indifference. 'Does it matter?', one Marie asks the other after each fresh misdemeanour, to be met by the only response that 'habitualized' or mechanized consciousness can offer: 'It doesn't matter'. This line also suggests some reflexive refrain of political cynicism, targeting those citizens who have grown inured to corruption and abuse because these things are part of the system. We even find in this opening dialogue some evidence for Chytilová's claim that the film is an exploration of youthful nihilism: such lines as 'We can't do anything', 'Nobody understands us' and 'Everything is spoiled for us in this world' at first sight reiterate such justifications as might be used for a destructive spree.

As previously suggested, it would be mistaken to attribute any consistent 'motivation' to the characters themselves, to 'fix' them as revolutionaries, nihilists or anything else. The affectless, rhythmic quality of the girls' speech here, spread evenly between the two as a flowing recitative duet, already puts paid to any illusion of inner depth. It *is* reasonable to see the girls' dialogue, at least at this point, as articulating Chytilová's own concerns, and their consequent actions as a mirror, a *mise-en-abyme* representation, of the film's own projects. The girls have even been discussed as direct stand-ins for the film's female co-authors, Chytilová and writer and designer Ester Krumbachová. Petra Hanáková informs us that Krumbachová's 'pranks at school' with 'her best friend Marie' are 'sometimes taken as a possible source of inspiration for [*Daisies*]', and that 'the two Maries have been seen by some as reflections of the blonde Ester and the brunette Věra Chytilová'.[16] This literal identification is perhaps less trivial than it might seem, for it could be seen as foregrounding the symbolic significance of the film's female authorship, and alerting us that the film will inscribe a 'feminine' discourse of semiotic disruption and libidinal play. Herbert Eagle also finds in the film's opening a clear allusion to Dada and its own commitment to 'spoiled action' as a response to 'rapid industrialization and the First World War' (represented here by the flywheel and the bombing run respectively).[17] As with Dada and the other avant-gardes, the girls' response to the evils of their world seems to be essentially *aesthetic*: one kind of spoiling, the deformation of society, necessitates another, the deformation of art. In their professed ambition to counter evil with yet more evil, the protagonists demonstrate their faith in the subversive power of representation. Their concern is with the staging, the visualizing, of evil in a manner that will unmask it to its own perpetrators and collaborators (whether

---

16. Petra Hanáková, 'Voices from Another World', in Imre, *East European Cinemas*, p. 76.
17. Eagle, 'Dada and Structuralism in Chytilová's *Daisies*', in Matejka, *Cross Currents 10*, p. 226.

the captive audiences in the restaurants and cabarets or the film's own viewers). Clearly, then, the aesthetic project is not merely aesthetic, but might have a shattering real-world effectivity: Marie II blows her toy trumpet and, as a scrap of stock footage intimates, real walls fall down.

What form does this aesthetic protest take? The 'spoiled action' comprises a series of outrageous public pranks that play on the (apparent) contrast between formal, 'civilized' settings and the girls' delinquent, 'savage' behaviour. Most famous, or notorious, among these pranks are a series of 'dates' at which the girls dine lavishly and gluttonously at the expense of wealthy older men, before brusquely sending them packing. While the pranks in themselves appear spontaneous and anarchic, the overall sequence depends on the repetition of motifs (notably food) and structures, and follows a logic of escalating outrageousness. It is this sense of premeditation and control that indicates the 'artistic' and symbolic nature of these actions. Eagle, correctly, discusses these pranks as instances of Happenings. Usually seen to have its roots in Dada and the theatrical assaults of the Cabaret Voltaire, the Happening is a form of conceptual public performance that abandons the usual hierarchical divisions of theatre (theatrical space and auditorium, performers and spectators). Happenings flourished in Europe and the US during the 1960s, when they were embraced by conceptual artists such as Joseph Beuys, Jean-Jacques Lebel and George Maciunas (founder of Fluxus) and by countercultural-political groups such as the Yippies. They also attained high visibility in the Czechoslovak art world at this time, most notably through the performances of Milan Knížák.

While it may be objected that the actions in Chytilová's film are merely simulated, thus 'safe', Happenings, one could also suggest that Chytilová's extensive use of improvization in the film, with the action guided only by a skeletal script, at least pushes the film further towards the Happening's peculiar dialectic of structure and spontaneity, art and 'real life'. If the Maries' pranks appear mean-spirited, abusive towards the 'innocent' bystanders-dupes, it must be remembered that Happenings were virtually by definition confrontational and provocative events, often somewhat cruel in their interplay with those technically 'outside' the performance. The purpose of the Happening was sometimes a kind of living satire that directly incorporated the satirical targets themselves into the spectacle: a celebrated example is when Abbie Hoffman and the Yippies floated dollar bills onto the floor of the US Stock Exchange, provoking an orgy of craven, grasping acquisitiveness amongst businessmen only too willing to visualize, to 'visibilize', their own greed. Chytilová could herself be considered complicit in the protagonists' 'bad' behaviour through her defiance of cinematic 'etiquette', the profligate, 'senseless' over-indulgence of technique approximating the girls' wastage of food. In her use (or misuse) of food and dining as recurrent motifs, Chytilová also draws on a tendency of cinematic and literary Surrealism that images the existing corpus of social conventions through mealtime ritual. In late Buñuel, for example, as here, revolution and subversion are more than once envisaged as the contravention of table manners.

These provocative performances disguised as gold-digging dates comprise variations on a theme, attacking specifically the tacit 'understanding' whereby young attractive women exchange their favours for material comforts, and more broadly the patriarchal attitudes that support, sanction and even necessitate such relationships. As gonzo performance artists seeking an ever more 'defamiliarized' representation, Marie I and II push their routine ever further into the realm of the grotesque. The contours of the basic sexual situation, a transaction between established age and nubile, helpless youth, are thus rendered as ever more pronounced and cartoon-like: with each 'date' the material comforts are yet further extended, the girls grow greedier and more callous and the 'older' men become ever more superannuated and unattractive. Indeed the last such meeting is authentically grotesque, the girls' final 'sugar daddy' resembling rather a frail, kindly grandfather indulging two young granddaughters with baby-talk. Yet the baroque freakishness of these scenes only reveals an inherent ugliness: are not such mismatched, self-serving and exploitative relationships, to which we are inured by routine and even sympathetic representation, already grotesque? In so far as the method succeeds, the shock of Chytilová's work is as much the shock of suddenly clarified perception as of aesthetic assault: 'Exaggeration in art is unavoidable …; in order to show an object, it is necessary to deform the shape it used to have.'[18] Chytilová and her protagonists also reveal and mock patriarchally defined roles through this heightened representation. The traditionally masculine role of economic provider is interpreted with an insolent expansiveness, with both girls cribbing vast meals and finally piles of newspapers and magazines off each man. As a response to the near-infantilized status of women (one of the dates refers to the girls as '*dívenky*', 'little girls' or 'girlies'), the Maries become literally infantile, playing with their food and eating messily, wearing twee matching outfits and using childish word-play. Conversely, the paternal role allotted to men (implicit in such terms as 'sugar daddy') is grotesquely emphasized by the men's age, and, in a touch of punning overstatement, the final date even resembles T.G. Masaryk, founder of Czechoslovakia's First Republic and thus symbolic 'father of the nation'.

These restaurant scenes both contextualize and prepare us for the grand finale of the banquet sequence, the film's most explicitly 'subversive' scene. Here Chytilová transfers her critical sights from the bourgeois dining table, its own presence here a sufficient indictment of a society putatively committed

---

18. Jakobson, 'On Realism in Art', in Matejka and Pomorska, *Readings in Russian Poetics*, p. 44.

Figure 4.2 The final dinner date. *Daisies* (*Sedmikrásky*, Věra Chytilová, 1966) ©Ateliéry Bonton Zlín, reproduced courtesy of Second Run DVD.

to eradicating all inequalities, to the banqueting tables of official functions. Given the national context, it is difficult not to see this ornately furnished hall as the setting for an abundantly and expensively catered Party function. Most critics have interpreted the scene in this way, though Eagle points out that the table would equally well seat a Party presidium or a board of directors, and thus usefully implies that the film has broader relevance than that of mere 'anti-Communist' critique. On the other hand, of course, the very interchangeability of capitalist officialdom and Communist officialdom hardly reflects well on a nominally egalitarian state. It is shown here that the gross materialism and the cultivation of elite exclusivity through taste observed in the film's expensive restaurants are no mere overhang from a bourgeois past but constitute an institutionalized standard of this 'new class'. There are no other characters present in this sequence, which enables the Maries, as in the wildest fantasies of Kafka's heroes, to penetrate to the political centre of this society, but authoritarian sensibilities make themselves firmly felt, enshrined in pompously baroque décor. The patriarchal critique developed through the restaurant motif is here translated into political terms: masculine paternalism finds its parallel in state paternalism, sexual exploitation in the exploitation of labour, double standards governing sexual probity in double standards concerning politically 'correct' lifestyles. Far from the enlightenment customarily received in Socialist Realism, the girls' initiation into the Party's inner sanctum yields only the mirror image of their own gluttony, a primal avarice here sublimated into ceremony. As with the Yippies' pranks, the ensuing orgy of feasting represents the staging of greed as a means of making it legible. The girls' disregarding of courses and their smushing and mashing together of the elaborately arranged dishes helps to detach dining from its symbolic and ceremonial status: greed is greed, cloaked in ritual or not. In the confrontational spirit of Happenings, the film's gross spectacles set a trap for the viewer, with those who declare themselves appalled by the protagonists' behaviour only revealing themselves as complicit in the social political systems that Chytilová condemns: why should we lament the vandalization of the luxurious surroundings that are themselves the fruit of exploitation?

Thus the punishment ultimately meted out to the girls and their subsequent 'reform' can only be seen as deeply ironic. After all, their 'crimes', for which they are dunked in water by an unseen force of 'justice', are hardly grave, at least by this society's standards. The flagrant wastage of food in slapstick debauchery does not affect what would have been a waste even under respectable circumstances. Moreover, for the powers that be, such feasts are not a momentary transgression but a matter of course(s). The girls' culinary 'expenditures without return' certainly do not compare with the murderous, state-orchestrated waste of arms proliferation and warfare (footage of a bombing run recurs at the very end of the film). A further layer of irony was added by the angry official response that Chytilová's film received, not least by the now notorious speech made in the Czechoslovak National Assembly accusing the film itself of wasting food. Perhaps the girls' real crime is the representation of their society's sins in a clear form. As the girls thrash about in the water, taunted by the long poles that drift in and out of their reach, a caption appears across the screen: 'They could only end up like this'. Indeed, maybe things could only have turned out thus, but less because the punishment is just than because the ruling powers will always guard vigorously against such subversion, demonizing its practitioners as troublemakers and degenerates (indeed the girls' treatment evokes the persecution of that archetype of threatening female Otherness, the witch).

The girls then attempt to 'make good' on their vandalism, as though they have drowned and been promptly condemned to some monochrome purgatory in which to atone for their sins. One of the film's most stylistically over-worked scenes with its sped-up movement and incomprehensible audio collage of whispered lines (a kind of aural counterpart to the mashed-up food), this moment of amendment has been recognized by most critics as parodic (according to Stanislava Přádná, the film's ending only reiterates the inability of these 'degraded heroines' to 'reform').[19] Nothing is ultimately set right: the food remains as revoltingly inedible as before, despite the fastidious re-ordering of the table. Can a subversive representation be 'undone', or is the damage wrought by artistic 'deformation' irreparable? At the same time, if the feckless gormandizing represented a parodic vision of official corruption and greed, then these restorative actions can be seen as parodying an illusory official reform, a rectification that takes place in formal terms, while neo-Stalinism's ugly essence, the nasty taste of bureaucratized power, is left untouched.

The film's apocalyptic conclusion, with the falling of the banquet hall's vast chandelier appearing to herald nothing less than the end of the world, suggests a cautionary sting in the tale that would justify Chytilová's claims for the moralistic nature of her enterprise. Yet, as Peter Hames points out, this catastrophe occurs only after the girls have finished making amends, and thus not as a consequence of their 'bad' behaviour. Satisfied, and self-satisfied, over their apparent good work, Marie I and II lie together on the table and declaim their happiness. In a sense closure has been achieved, for Chytilová's multiform representation of the protagonists has been brought full circle: as is suggested by the recitative quality of the dialogue, the girls' frontal placement before the camera and the blue-tinted monochrome photography, the girls appear once again as the consumerist mannequins that they embodied in their first scene, superficially content in their own numbness. Dialogue and delivery suggest once again a 'mechanized' consciousness: the line 'We are truly happy' can alternate with the habitual 'It doesn't matter', as this is a negative, affectless happiness, founded on the indifference that ensues from impeded sensation. Just as Shklovsky's automatized perception resurfaces, so does war, yet the devastation glimpsed in the opening bombing runs now returns as apocalyptic conflagration: the political-military organization marches on towards self-annihilation, in spite of desultory and superficial gestures towards its 'improvement'. While the protagonists' subversive actions may hold out the promise of explosive change, what might actually obliterate the world, Chytilová seems to suggest, is that same affectless complacency, that failure or insufficiency of perception, that her own artistic endeavours seek to rectify.

Spoiled Performances: Denaturalization and Deformation

So far this chapter has discussed the girls' and the filmmakers' subversive 'performances' in terms of their directly satirical function. It can be argued that satire, indeed any form of polemical representation, always depends on some level of defamiliarization, in so far as exaggeration and over-emphasis are

---

19. Přádná, Škapová and Cieslar, *Démanty všednosti*, p. 206.

necessary in order to reveal social reality. Surrealism, especially Czech Surrealism, has often deployed its heightening of representation for such a satirical purpose. However Chytilová's defamiliarizing practices are also de-naturalizing ones, forcing our awareness of codes as codes and exaggerating the contours of social and gender identities until these identities become parodies of themselves. To defamiliarize or 'make strange' a phenomenon is to make it seem unnatural, to make it jar against the textures of our 'ordinary', everyday experience. Here we find yet another subversive function of defamiliarization, one scarcely reckoned with by the Russian Formalists themselves though subsequently elaborated, in his theoretical writings at least, by Brecht. Chytilová's deployment of these practices is informed by her sense of identity as performance: for what is a parody if not an appropriation, an inauthentic imitation? Through its establishment of performance as an ontological principle, Chytilová's film, in a manner that was years ahead of its time, creates a bridge between the avant-garde and Marxist aesthetic practices of the interwar years and the conceptualization of the 'performative' by contemporary gender theory. By means of this intensive defamiliarization at both a representational and a formal level (the process of 'laying bare'), reality is revealed as itself a construction, a work of art and artifice, as something historically determined and therefore changeable.

The dinner table is the perfect setting for these de-naturalizing spectacles, in so far as the observance of mealtime rituals represents an adherence to a culturally specific definition of 'good' or civilized behaviour. As a ceremony of instinctual satisfaction, dining provides an apt motif through which to express the relative nature of social conventions: in a celebrated scene from Buñuel's *The Phantom of Liberty* (*Le Fantôme de la liberté*, 1974) the social ritual of eating and the private activity of defecation exchange status, and the very mention of food or hunger is forbidden in polite company. The correctly observed meal also offers a confrontation between raw, pre-cultural instinct and the materiality of the body on the one hand, and the artifice of socialization, the historical forms through which behaviour is shaped, on the other. It is surely for these reasons that not only Surrealist filmmakers such as Buñuel and Švankmajer but also Brechtian, politicized filmmakers such as Rainer Werner Fassbinder have so frequently used the dinner table as their chosen terrain for social examination. Chytilová and her heroines push the metaphorical function of dining perhaps to its furthest point, and the film's exploration of, and assault on, etiquette and 'good eating' proves an expressive means to interrogate wider social phenomena. In the first and longest of the film's dinnertime pranks, Marie I invites herself to sit with Marie II and the latter's date, and promptly wages war on virtually all the conventions of the dining table. She grotesquely over-eats, and eats messily with her fingers, taking large mouthfuls and smearing her lips with cream. The traditional ordering of courses is not only disregarded but apparently reversed, as Marie I begins with cakes and ends with a full-size chicken.[20]

The assault on codes of correct dining is fused with the assault on gendered codes of behaviour. In such scenes Chytilová is identifying the obviously arbitrary and culturally acquired customs of dining (such as the order of courses) with other, more intensive though equally 'artificial' systems of convention that regulate the lives of individuals. Marie I's behaviour here also defies the conventions of 'correct' feminine deportment. She behaves in a forthright, assertive manner, sitting down to dine without being invited and asking 'impertinent' questions of this older man ('have you any kids?'). As if her demonstration of gluttony were not proof enough, she breezily admits to a hearty appetite ('I really love to eat'), while, conversely, ascribing the man's refusal of dessert to a typically 'feminine' concern for appearance: 'Are you on a diet?' Such misbehaviour is set in pointed, instructive contrast with the ideal feminine seemliness embodied, parodically of course, by Marie I, who picks, nibbles and sips in a manner both coquettish and coy. The girls' contrasts in behaviour 'lay bare', and indict, a patriarchal code of conduct that impels women to render themselves as sex objects yet simultaneously forbids them from expressing autonomous desires.

The film can be seen, perhaps above all, as an examination of various kinds of codes, from the multiform, intersecting codes that govern behaviour (codes of dining, codes of courtship, the codes that regulate gendered and social identity) to the aesthetic codes that inform filmic practice and the construction of narratives. If the work of art comprises a deployment and arrangement of codes, then *Daisies* glories in disarrangement and disarray, mismatching and misuse: adopting the words of the film's closing caption and extending its use of culinary metaphor, *Daisies* constitutes a 'trampled-on salad' or, in English parlance, a dog's dinner of a film. Yet through this very spectacle of aesthetic vandalism we are able to observe all the more clearly those collective codes that govern cinematic expression, those conventions that have been over-used into invisibility yet whose observance guarantees that crucial 'reality effect' of a film. As the Maries flaunt the conventions of dining and gendered behaviour, so Chytilová flaunts the rules of cinematic 'grammar'. During that first dinner date, for instance, she conveys the lapse of time through a series of jump-cuts (a technique still fairly new in 1966), rather than through the less 'obtrusive' devices of conventional realist cinema, such as dissolves or fadeouts. Furthermore, she tints each new shot into a different colour, a device that both calls attention to the cuts and is in itself virtually unprecedented in narrative cinema. In defiance of the more general convention that form must

---

20. Eagle, 'Dada and Structuralism in Chytilová's *Daisies*', in Matejka, *Cross Currents 10*, p. 228.

follow function, the film's profligate use of colour filtering appears unmotivated and 'meaningless', not to mention glaringly obtrusive; as Herbert Eagle observes, this device is even punningly alluded to in a line from this scene, when Marie I asks her 'host', 'Do these cigarettes have filters?'[21] Chytilová foregrounds cinematic conventions not only through defiance but also through mocking adherence. After the girls announce their 'project' in the film's second scene, Marie II slaps Marie I hard across the face and, in the next shot, Marie I falls back not onto the hard floor of the bath-house, but into an overgrown field of daisies. She emerges from the lush undergrowth rubbing her cheek, and finds herself now in vivid colour and dressed in a white slip. Despite its glaring illogicality, the cut is seamlessly matched: thus Chytilová, like Buñuel and Dalí in their Surrealist classic *Un Chien Andalou* (1925), retains here a formal adherence to classical syntax, hollowing out 'realist' technique from within. As a device that sews together different moments in time and often disparate spaces into an apparently unified whole, there is nothing 'natural' in the traditional cut. In its very jarring quality this cut is, in Shklovsky's terminology, 'typical', exposing the classical cut as a stylistic device by dramatically heightening it.

Identity is itself unmasked as a collection of codes, or, to use the theatrical metaphor inherent in the concept of the 'performative', as a rendition of preconceived roles. The beach-house setting in which we first greet the film's protagonists can also be seen as a stage; the girls' creaking limbs suggest this might be the stage of the puppet theatre, whose performers do not 'exist' outside the character types imposed on them. Chytilová's distanced, emphatically anti-realist introduction of her heroines was discussed earlier as a means of announcing a lack of interest in conventional characterization. Yet the aesthetic agenda is also a philosophical, and political, one: the characters' one-dimensionality, the film's anti-psychological performances and writing style, serve not only to foreground the fact that we are watching actors perform in a film, but also to assert the performative basis of social and sexual identities. Chytilová then reinforces this point, and demonstrates its subversive potential, through the characters' parodic over-investment in traditional images of femininity. Identity is rigorously externalized, transformed into a composite of visual, verbal and behavioural signs: 'I am a virgin', Marie I announces at the beginning of the film, but the film offers only her declamation, her white slip and her kitschy crown of daisies as testament to that. The clothes maketh the (wo)man: dress codes do not so much reveal personality as create it. At the same time, Chytilová's ironic deployment of conventional linguistic and visual tropes for women at their most idealized and virginal (daisies, butterflies) stresses the cultural determination of gender

---

21. Ibid.

Figure 4.3 A banquet for two. *Daisies* (*Sedmikrásky*, Věra Chytilová, 1966) ©Ateliéry Bonton Zlín, reproduced courtesy of Second Run DVD.

identities. Bliss Cua Lim describes the Maries as doll-like ('*panna*', the word Marie I uses for virgin, has the secondary meaning of 'doll') in their embodiment of a grotesquely exaggerated, artificial image of an ideal femininity: 'Woman' as social construct rather than biological entity. Cua Lim links these representations with the subversive deployment of the doll motif in feminist literature, and with Judith Butler's theoretical writings on the 'performative'. For Butler, the parodic representation of a particular gender identity is subversive as it points to the way such identities are themselves already parodic, imitative; indeed, '[t]he parodic repetition of the original ... reveals the original to be nothing other than a parody of the *idea* of the natural and the original'.[22] The garish mask reveals the absence of a true face.

Performance, in its broadest sense, permeates the world of *Daisies*. Sometimes the 'performance' of real life even threatens to usurp a staged performance, as in the nightclub scene, where the girls' spontaneous larks deflect attention from the cabaret entertainment. Yet, as the girls' actions reiterate Chytilová's own subversive project within the diegetic world of the film, their various 'pranks' must themselves be seen as attempts to stage the self as performance, as imitations in

22. Judith Butler, quoted in Bliss Cua Lim, 'Dolls in Fragments: *Daisies* as Feminist Allegory', *Camera Obscura*, Vol. 16, No. 2, 2001, p. 60.

search of an original. To this extent the protagonists are 'in' on the film's central philosophical insight: indeed Cua Lim considers the girls' behaviour throughout the film as a 'knowing deployment of [the] signs' of Woman.[23] The final banquet scene, for instance, comprises a slapdash melange of parodically assumed roles, the overwrought theatricality of this feast standing in contrast to the secrecy and surreptitiousness with which the powerful usually commit their enormities (for Georges Bataille, the wretchedness of the bourgeoisie, as, presumably, of its 'red' surrogates, consists in the fact that it can only enjoy its expenditures behind closed doors). The girls' performance here conflates a number of iconic, indeed clichéd, images of patriarchally defined female identity, including the stripper, the fashion model, the virgin bride, and finally, in the act of punishment, the witch. The characters trample over or 'spoil' traditional feminine roles, mediating them parodically through the hackneyed representations of popular culture. The girls even swing from the chandelier in a re-enactment of a particularly tired cliché from 'Hollywood film orgies'.[24]

Just as the sweet and savoury dishes are mashed together, so the girls also subject these wildly conflicting representations of femininity to a kind of semiotic mashing, thus foregrounding the contradictory nature of patriarchal injunctions. Moreover, the character types and behavioural patterns represented here, not least greed and coarse sybaritism, are manifestly 'bourgeois': clearly the social and sexual identities that the girls inscribe in their performance are not those of the 'new man', but are drawn from stock. In fact the scene makes for an iconography of 'decadent' capitalist culture, with its evocations of Hollywood, the fashion parade and the striptease as well as its rock and roll soundtrack: the clichés of Western decadence may be closer to state socialist reality than the clichés of Eastern asceticism. On the other hand, the denaturalization of this behaviour suggests that the persistence of such retrogressive models of identity is not inevitable, and that alternative models are possible. Here, ironically enough, Chytilová's film reveals itself as more 'socialist' than Socialist Realism, as more apposite for a materialist, progressive politics than Socialist Realism's appropriation of nineteenth-century Realist aesthetics. Was not the Soviets' original commitment to the 'new man' founded on that same conception of the mutability of the self, of human 'nature' as dynamic and historical rather than stable and eternal, that Chytilová's anti-illusionist aesthetic asserts? It is worth pointing out here that the practitioners of 1960s Brechtian counter-cinema considered the officially sanctioned art of the Communist countries to be as much the embodiment of 'bourgeois' aesthetics as anything produced in the West: Godard's militant-era 'western' *Le Vent d'est* (1970, co-directed with Jean-Pierre Gorin) bluntly equates 'Brezhnev–Mosfilm' and 'Nixon–Paramount'.

---

23. Lim, ibid.
24. Hames, *The Czechoslovak New Wave*, p. 220.

If the aesthetics of estrangement serve to de-naturalize reality, then the effect of traditional realism is, conversely, to make reality appear natural, immutable, normal. Realist convention serves, furthermore, to naturalize ideology itself, presenting an inevitably biased, politically coded vision as though it were an objective description of the world and passing off values as self-evident facts. Realism achieves these effects by effacing the mechanics of signification: technique is disguised, subdued, rather than 'laid bare'. Writing in relation to cinema, Martin Walsh describes realism, or 'bourgeois illusionism', as 'a system of representation whose fundamental intent is to make the audience suspend its disbelief and enter the world of the film as if it were the real world';[25] 'the materiality of language, the work of signification, is repressed from view in favour of the dominance of the signified. Language is thus conceived of as a transparent means to knowledge of the world beyond, through the window.'[26] Another irony here is that traditional realism can be seen as deeply duplicitous for failing to respect the truth of the signifier, for presenting the unnatural as natural and the ideological as impartial. By contrast, a 'formalist' aesthetics attains its own realism in revealing the truth of the inauthentic, in preoccupying itself not only with 'the reflection of reality' but also with 'the reality of reflection' (to paraphrase one of the students in Godard's *La Chinoise* (1967)). It would be a mistake to regard the deconstructive aesthetic practices of a film such as *Daisies* merely as disinterested formal play, for the 'naturalizing' discourse of realism plays a significant political role in legitimizing and thus shoring up the status quo. Rudolf E. Kuenzli argues that this was one of the central insights of Dada, and that the movement's political project was enacted through its aesthetic practice of semiotic disordering:

> In deconstructing the cultural sign system through their own sign productions the Dadaists attempted to convince their audience of the arbitrary nature of signs, and thereby to liberate them from the prison of their murderous social order. Through a deconstruction of the semantic function of the sign system the Dadaists hoped to disrupt and change the way in which society saw the world.[27]

For Kuenzli, the immediate impetus for Dada's cultural project was the role played by official culture in rallying the public to war:

---

25. Martin Walsh, '*Rome Open City; The Rise to Power of Louis XIV*: Re-evaluating Rossellini', *Jump Cut*, No. 15, 1977, p. 13.
26. Ibid., p. 15.
27. Rudolf E. Kuenzli, 'The Semiotics of Dada Poetry', in Stephen C. Foster and Rudolf E. Kuenzli (eds), *Dada Spectrum: The Dialectics of Revolt* (Madison: Coda Press, 1979), p. 56.

During the First World War the social sign systems were much more intensely ideologically coded than during peace time. Journalists, poets, artists, philosophers, teachers in conjunction with all the available mass media created an enthusiasm for the war and, as Hugo Ball put it, 'passed off this civilised carnage as a triumph of European intelligence.' Moreover, the constant and repeated glorification of war and death for the fatherland remained largely unchallenged due to a well-functioning system of censorship which suppressed any direct critique of the war culture.[28]

An obvious parallel can be found here with the Czechoslovak regime of the 1950s, which also censored all dissenting voices and promoted an aesthetic whose apparent stylistic neutrality belies its own intensive ideological coding. As with Dada and other avant-garde movements, the terms of Chytilová's polemic with authority are to a large degree linguistic or discursive, yet these terms indicate less the abandonment of politics than the understanding that aesthetic issues are inevitably also political ones. Chytilová wittily alerts us to the film's critique of official discourse by dressing up her heroines in newspapers during their moment of 'reform'. Josef Škvorecký interprets the newspaper outfits as a symbol of 'proper convictions'[29], yet they also stand in for the insidious naturalizing discourse to which Chytilová's film opposes itself: after all, news-speak, and state socialist news-speak at that, represents the epitome of an ideologically manipulative discourse that conceals its partiality beneath an 'objective', impersonal style.

As we have seen, Chytilová's editing practices fragment the film's diegetic world, revealing as illusory that impression of spatial and temporal continuity that is part of classical cinema's reality effect. Cinema might be considered to have an inherent ontological superiority over other media by virtue of the truth claims of its photographic apparatus, a point of view most famously propounded by André Bazin. Thus film more naturally and thereby more insidiously suggests a window on the world than, say, literature (indeed the metaphor itself is irresistibly cinematic, what with the easy alignment of window-frame and camera-frame). Yet Chytilová sullies even the literal transparency of the image, obtrusively mediating the photographed 'reality' by means of filters and cinematographer Jaroslav Kučera's experiments with colour solarization; during the periodic train journeys, the latter technique transforms the image into a beautiful, abstract blur. Equally striking are the intermittent montages of objects (leaves, apples, sawdust), or more precisely of images of objects: these are in fact the pictures the girls themselves have cut out of magazines, and thus the self-contained interludes comprise images of

---

28. Ibid., pp. 55–56.
29. Škvorecký, *All the Bright Young Men and Women*, p. 109.

images. Moreover, in their half-suggestion of motion, these sequences also resemble crude pieces of animation, and thereby point to the illusory nature of that most basic and taken-for-granted 'convention' of cinema, the appearance of movement. As in Borowczyk and Lenica's *Dom* (1957), the very alternation of still frames, an aspect of cinematic artifice that is usually imperceptible, achieves its own plastic presence.

Yet not only does *Daisies* dissipate the effect of raw reality through flagrant visual manipulation, it also indulges in a grotesque heightening of narrative conventions. The film has seldom been considered as cultural parody, yet its 'story' facetiously recycles two well-worn tropes from Socialist Realist narratives, that of the protagonist's return to the countryside and to 'the people' as a form of salvation, and that of voluntary reform whereby a negative or 'parasitic' character decides to become socially useful. The use of the former trope can even be seen as a case of self-parody: Škvorecký rebukes Chytilová's screenplay for her early film *Ceiling* for reiterating a tired 'socialist-realistic "philosophy"' that 'evaluate[s] human efforts according to the governmental tariff of "social usefulness"'.[30] Škvorecký takes particular objection to the film's conclusion, in which the film's heroine, a fashion model and medical student, abandons her shallow lifestyle for 'simple country people': this 'kitsch' bears 'an obvious ideological resemblance to the then fashionable "return to the people for cathartic purposes"'.[31] (It must be said that the realized film of *Ceiling* is somewhat subtler than this suggests, not least because Chytilová abandoned the crudely redemptive ending in which the protagonist 'starts a new life by returning to the study of human maladies'.)[32] Yet here both tropes are vigorously parodied and ultimately subverted. During the girls' voyage into the country, they are greeted by the bizarre image of a group of near-identically dressed male workers riding bicycles, to the accompaniment of a twee music box soundtrack. Effenberger is particularly critical of this sequence, arguing that, 'where conflict should have occurred, there resounds a surprising banality and an almost Zhdanovite instrumentality'.[33] Yet Chytilová's concern here is less with social reality than with cultural representation; far from indulging in 'banalities', Chytilová in fact estranges the representation of an idyllic, politically correct pastoralism so that the artificial conventionality of such images stands revealed.

The scenes of punishment and reform are more openly parodic in their use of distancing, deliberately over-explanatory dialogue: 'We're crying for help';

30. Ibid., p. 100.
31. Ibid.
32. Ibid.
33. Effenberger, 'Obraz člověka v českém filmu', *Film a doba*, p. 350. The term 'Zhdanovite' refers to Andrei Zhdanov, the Soviet official responsible for the theoretical formulation and entrenchment of Socialist Realism in the 1930s.

'We'll be happy because we're hard-working'; 'We'll be hard-working and everything will be clean'. Of course, the latter scenes can also be seen as a more general parody of conventional codes of narrative closure, which insist that amends be made for wrongdoings, and that the bad be punished or reformed. Effenberger fails to notice that the reiteration of these Socialist Realist tropes is also a betrayal of their politically instructive function. This return to the 'authenticity' of soil and toil yields neither revelation nor catharsis, and prompts only another existential crisis for the protagonists: the girls are not embraced but ignored by these faceless 'simple' folk. As we have seen, the act of reform actually reforms nothing. Indeed in these revoltingly reconstituted dishes we find an apt metaphor for Chytilová's narrative and formal practice, which at once adheres to conventions and grotesquely deforms them.

The Aesthetic Self

As has hopefully been evident throughout this chapter, the practices of denaturalization and deformation in *Daisies* do more than simply critique patriarchal society or the evils of state Communism: they also challenge humanist notions of an authentic, unified, stable identity. The film's overwrought aesthetic language serves to 'aestheticize' the self, revealing identity as the sum of the discourses that shape it, influence it and finally reinforce it. The protagonists lack any 'depth' whether as fictitious individuals or as screen entities. Neither of the two main performers was a professional actor, and neither is called upon to create that illusion of fully-fledged subjectivity that, ironically, a professional actor is best equipped to provide. Here Chytilová turns on its head the celebrated New Wave practice (influential on realist filmmakers such as Ken Loach) of using non-professional actors as a token of a greater 'authenticity';[34] Chytilová herself abides by this practice in her early work. At a visual level, Chytilová's insistence on the plasticity and manipulability of the filmed image establishes a similar sense of depthlessness by rendering screen as surface. In its anti-humanist aesthetics *Daisies* is one of the most radically challenging and philosophically original of all the Czech films of the 1960s. Chytilová's following film, *The Fruit of Paradise*, was described by one critic as 'a film for the next decade', though one could argue that even the lapse of years has not brought either this film or *Daisies* full critical understanding or appreciation: perhaps only the recent pieces by Hanáková and Cua Lim have done justice to the implications of *Daisies*.

The subversive value of the Czechoslovak New Wave (as of other East European film movements of the 1960s) is sometimes staked on its revelation

---

34. 'Non-professional protagonists … fulfilled young filmmakers' pressing need of truthful artistic accounts.' (*Přádná, Škapová and Cieslar, Démanty všednosti*, p. 161).

Figure 4.4 Production still from *Daisies* (*Sedmikrásky*, Věra Chytilová, 1966) ©Ateliéry Bonton Zlín, reproduced courtesy of Second Run DVD.

of an 'authentic' human subject, previously hidden from view by the ideologized distortions of Socialist Realist representation. Thus, such characters as Miloš Forman's Black Peter (from *Black Peter*) or Jaromil Jireš's Slávek (from *The Cry*) are claimed as symptomatic of an average, imperfect and unschematized 'real life'. Yet *Daisies*, as we have seen, problematizes that very idea of authenticity, revealing social identities as constructs and attacking the notion of a coherent, unique self. Even the way the protagonists refer to themselves reinforces the assault on traditional ideas about identity. The preponderance of the first-person plural pronoun throughout the film can be seen as a refutation of individual uniqueness: the 'I' of the spontaneous, unique individual becomes the 'We' of socially constituted identity. Marie I's declaration that 'We are really both so happy' (*'My jsme přece obě tak šťastná'*), which ungrammatically yokes together a plural pronoun (*'my'*) and a singular feminine adjective (*'šťastná'*), asserts the social basis of identity even more forcefully, while the grammatical mismatch conveys the confusions and incoherences of the self.

Does this representation of identity mark an impasse for the radical, even revolutionary, ambitions that the film and Chytilová otherwise espouse? How can Stalinism, patriarchy or consumer capitalism distort or deform a self that is, fundamentally, not there? It is perhaps on that very absence of self that the film founds a normative dimension of its own, proposing a model of identity based on the recognition and valorization of fluidity. The negation of an essential being is seized on in its positive guise, as a newfound license to construct or play with one's identity. While the fluid, nebulous or insubstantial quality of the self is occasionally implied to be a source of despair or existential anxiety, at an aesthetic level the instability of the characters inspires a wild exhilaration. If the fluidity of the self is expressed through variations in design and artistic style, then that is because identity itself is shown to possess an 'aesthetic' or artificial quality. This proto-Foucauldian 'aesthetics of the self' is embraced by the protagonists themselves, who forever change names and costumes, and rearrange the décor of their apartment around different motifs (leaves, magazine illustrations, written and typed names), each suggestive of distinct feminine personas or traits (nature, consumerism, coquetry).[35] The individual arrangements are telling in their own right (the décor of indoor leaves and lawn is particularly suggestive in its striking reinvention of nature as artifice), while the device as a whole at once asserts the detachability and exteriority of our 'natural' characteristics and re-envisages the self as something perpetually unstable, subject to the ceaseless re-establishment of new themes or ensembles.

Of course, what persists is the body itself, the given reality of desire and affect. When, during their excursion in the countryside, the girls discover the husks of the corn they had been eating, they find in these husks tangible proof of their existence. On one level this moment is an ironic commentary on the way female self-actualization, in a society that identifies work with masculinity, must be relegated to the sphere of consumption, but at another level the scene suggests the recourse to the body, to 'appetite', for a sense of something authentic, immutable and irrefutable in our existence. (This is as much of the authentic self as the Socialist Realist quest for 'authenticity' is permitted to uncover.) Indeed the only consistent aspect of the girls' character throughout all their transformations is an insatiable appetite that may be interpreted as the persistent demands of the primary drives. If there is no stable or essential female self, there is nonetheless a recalcitrant female desire with which to combat social constraints. The motifs of food and eating provide a means for Chytilová to represent drives as drives, shorn of any sublimatory sentimentality. In this way the film is able to contrast desire as a social phenomenon, invested with ideological terms, and desire as a psychosomatic, pre-cultural phenomenon, best symbolized by the straightforward materiality of hunger. The piano-playing suitor played by Jan Klusák attempts to woo Marie I with his music and his high-flown, yet implicitly diminishing, romantic effusions: 'Like some message from another world … And certainly you're earthly, even though you're like a goddess.' (Even the butterflies Klusák's character collects constitute a patriarchal figure of ideal femininity, offering a similar combination of ethereal delicacy and 'earthly' naturalness.) Marie I, unimpressed by such

---

35. Alec McHoul and Wendy Grace, *A Foucault Primer: Discourse, Power and the Subject* (London: UCL Press, 1995), p. 124.

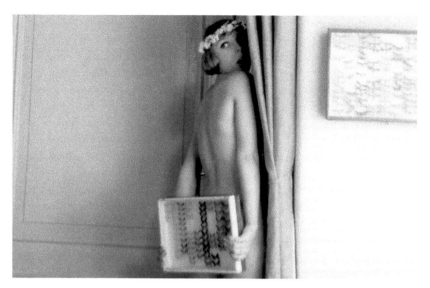

Figure 4.5 *Daisies* (*Sedmikrásky*, Věra Chytilová, 1966) ©Ateliéry Bonton Zlín, reproduced courtesy of Second Run DVD.

insidious sophistication, responds by asking if he has any jam. The distinction between ideology and corporeality is expressed even more bluntly when Marie I asks her friend, 'Why do they say 'I love you'? … Why don't they say, for example, 'egg'?'

Lest the film's aesthetics appear overly self-reflexive, too insistent upon the absence of reality within signification, it should be noted that Chytilová's avant-garde-inflected formal language (unlike, say, the punishing aesthetics of Straub-Huillet or Dziga Vertov Group-era Godard) also possesses an affective dimension and could thereby be seen to express something of the subject's own inner 'reality'. The film's various formal devices, such as its splashily deployed colour filters and its photographic experiments, may serve to foreground the constructed nature of discourse, but at the same time we must not discount our own sensual response to these devices, that level of stimulation that usually goes unmentioned in film analysis if only because it is, in a strict sense, inarticulable. According to poststructuralist textual theory, the embodied individual emerges at precisely that point where signification cannot go, at the beyond point of meaning. Julia Kristeva's theory of 'semiotic' discourse examines the way instinctual drives are invested in aspects of aesthetic form, such as rhythm, sound and, significantly for *Daisies*, colour. In an essay on Giotto's paintings Kristeva argues that colours have their own instinctual affectivity, indeed writing that 'it is through color – colors – that the subject escapes its alienation within a code (representational, ideological, symbolic, and so forth) that it, as a conscious subject, accepts'.[36] Colour is even seen to have a close relation to infancy, with Kristeva asserting that colour perception precedes 'centred vision', i.e. 'the identification of objects, including one's own image (the "self" perceived at the mirror stage ...)'.[37] Kristeva acknowledges that the 'chromatic apparatus' may be made subject to systems of signification, yet *Daisies'* bright and obtrusive filtered colours are unsubordinated to any symbolic function and stand independent of the represented objects: they are poured over the images with abandon. This 'undisciplined' alternation of colours can be seen to inscribe the protagonists' infantile tendencies and libidinal compulsions at a formal level.

The transition from the idyllic Garden of Eden setting of the film's second scene to the dreary 'real' world of the following scene could be interpreted as a 'Fall' from the plenitude of infancy into the emptiness of symbolic structures: indeed the view from the window of the girls' flat reveals only a deserted street, with a brief burst of brass band music suggesting a taunting reminder of lost fullness. Yet whatever these early scenes suggest, the remainder of the film asserts more a sense of plenitude and infantile pleasure than the lack and despair illustrated in, say, Pavel Juráček's films. That early evocation of loss might even represent the legacy of Juráček's own involvement with the film. (The Garden of Eden scene can, incidentally, be seen as a reference to the Dadaist Hugo Ball's conception of an infantile 'Adamic' language concerned with the material properties of sound and rhythm.) The gendered opposition that pertains throughout the film between feminine desire, play and illogicality on the one hand and masculine or 'phallic' power, law and reason on the other (in one memorable scene the girls blithely 'castrate' various phallus-shaped foods) can of course be read in terms of Lacan's essentially abstract association of the symbolic order and the law with paternal authority and Kristeva's corresponding assignation of semiosis to the maternal realm. Yet some commentators (such as Hanáková and Eagle) have read the film's aesthetics and its protagonists' behaviour as exemplifying a *jouissance* or pleasure that is more precisely or literally feminine. By the terms of this reading the heroines' transcendence of the strictures of law and logic ensues from a unique, specifically feminine psychic and libidinal economy. In fact the style of Chytilová's film goes some way towards epitomizing Hélène Cixous's account of '*écriture féminine*', which envisages 'liberated' female writing as an 'overflowing' of 'luminous torrents', an 'invention' of 'new desires', a 'bursting' with different forms.[38]

36. Julia Kristeva, 'Giotto's Joy', *Desire in Language*, edited by Léon S. Roudiez and translated by Alice Jardine, Thomas A. Gora and Léon S. Roudiez (Oxford: Blackwell, 1980), p. 220.

37. Ibid., p. 225.

38. Hélène Cixous, quoted in Raman Selden and Peter Widdowson, *A Reader's Guide to Contemporary Literary Theory* (Hertfordshire: Harvester Wheatsheaf, 1993), p. 227.

While of course linked specifically to women, Cixous's valorization of contradiction, plurality and fluidity shares something with other psychoanalytic theories and literary explorations of the unconscious: a sense of desire as fluid and manifold, of the unconscious not as an internally coherent 'secret self' but as a terrain itself irreparably split. Arguably these ideas have been central to the representations of both Dada and Surrealism: Hal Foster has described the Surrealist unconscious as a disruptive force that is itself rent asunder by conflicting drives. Considered in these terms the presence of libidinal or instinctual urges, however persistent and irrefutable, hardly provides significant grounds for existential reassurance, or the belief in a stable self. *Daisies* can be seen as pursuing some of the radical or anti-humanist implications of Surrealist investigations, for some of the film's images of fragmentation and disassembly are easily read in terms of the plural nature of desire. In one scene the girls move from rolling each around on their bed to literally cutting each other to pieces. As if keen to partake in this frenzy of fragmentation, the film image itself breaks up into shards, so that the whole thing resembles a moving human collage. In a climactic move from the anti-humanist to the literally inhuman, the scene finally succumbs entirely to the abstraction of writhing lines, the non-representationality of pure semiosis. As with other aspects of *Daisies*, that joyous rendering of broken bodies as crazy-paved mosaic is remarkable not only for its aesthetic and technical accomplishment, but also for its representation of the fragmentations of the self in positive, valorizing and even ecstatic terms.

The latter part of this chapter has suggested how *Daisies* celebrates play, fluidity and multiplicity and upholds a non-essentialist vision of the self. Prior to that it emphasized how the film encourages different interpretations, its heavy use of reference and parody, and its foregrounding of its own status as text. In many ways, then, *Daisies* could be considered, for better or worse, as proto-postmodern, a suggestion that should not be so surprising given the film's acknowledged affinities with Dada: the spirit of postmodernism has itself been described as Dadaist.[39] Marianne DeKoven has argued, persuasively, that the most advanced cultural products of the 1960s represent a point of transition between the modern and the postmodern.[40] While DeKoven herself relates this claim mainly to the analysis of American culture, it surely has a much wider validity, Chytilová's early work comprising a case in point. Chytilová's public stance is generally that of an artist concerned, in exemplarily modernist fashion, with the pursuit and revelation of truth, and that concern is expressed in the films themselves, although more consistently in *The Fruit*

---

39. See Steven Connor, *Postmodernist Culture: An Introduction to Theories of the Contemporary* (Oxford: Blackwell, 1989), pp. 110–11, p. 192.

40. Marianne DeKoven, *Utopia Limited: The Sixties and the Emergence of the Postmodern* (Durham; London: Duke University Press, 2004).

of Paradise than in *Daisies* (like the later film, however, *Daisies* does allude to the Biblical Tree of Knowledge). The notion of objective, definite or univalent truths is of course an object of suspicion for postmodernism, even though it may be difficult for any work of art, including postmodern ones, not to encode some kind of truth content. Perhaps the most important 'truth' that postmodern texts have to offer is that of the relativity or contingency of all perspectives, as well as the 'truth' of textuality itself, of the text's constructed status and its mediated vision of the world. From that perspective, the assertion of both these 'truths' in *Daisies*, through the promotion of multiple meanings on the one hand and the insistence on the process of enunciation on the other, comprises the film's ultimate 'realism'.

Along with claims to the truthful, postmodernism also problematizes claims to the new, even if the assertion of groundbreaking newness constitutes a disavowed claim of postmodern culture itself.[41] It would be difficult to avoid the conclusion that *Daisies* does offer something radically new, for the cinema and the Czech cinema in particular, and that the film's technical innovations comprise a means of impudently insisting on that novelty. Alongside those technical and photographic effects, and the references to what were then excitingly new and vital artistic movements (such as Pop Art and Happenings), the newness of *Daisies* consists in its articulation of what was virtually a new aesthetic for mainstream cinema, one that stresses the visibly assembled, the inauthentic and the *détourned*. The spirit of that aesthetic is even inscribed directly, in the form of the beautiful costumes that the Maries construct from wood shavings and metal scraps, and opposed to an implicitly conservative or malign 'classical' culture (the piano-playing suitor's 'poetic' speech, the orchestral performance hidden away in the building where the banquet is to be held). There is perhaps a tension between the attack on the single, unique author implicit in the film's deployment of borrowed or collective 'codes', and the very singularity, uniqueness and indeed oddity of the film's innovations. It is worth noting, however, that those innovations were to a large extent forged collectively. The input of Chytilová's collaborators cannot be overemphasized, particularly that of cinematographer Kučera and screenwriter-art-director-costume-designer Krumbachová, the latter of whom, as Peter Hames suggests, probably supplied many of the film's artistic references.[42] I may myself have proven guilty of an auteurist bias in implicitly identifying Chytilová as the 'creator' of a work that was (at least as Krumbachová describes it)[43] produced through intense collaboration.

41. Connor, *Postmodern Culture*, pp. 239–40.
42. Hames, *The Czechoslovak New Wave*, p. 195.
43. Ester Krumbachová, in Liehm, *The Politics of Culture*, p. 126.

CHAPTER 5

Flights From History: Otherness, Politics and Folk Avant-Gardism in Juraj Jakubisko's *The Deserter and the Nomads* (1968) and *Birds, Orphans and Fools* (1969)

From Folk to Avant-Garde to Proto-Postmodern

'I, Juraj Jakubisko, a Slovak film director, will tell you about those who wanted to be mad.' Those words, with which the opening voiceover commentary to *Birds, Orphans and Fools* begins, accompany Jakubisko's trademark charging camera as it pursues a group of children dressed in colourful folk costumes and holding aloft a large sheet. On that sheet the shadow of the film crew is clearly visible. Jakubisko does not recite his commentary himself, but 'speaks' through, first, the voice of a young child and then through that of an adult woman. Though Jakubisko had already completed two features before he made *Birds, Orphans and Fools*, this prologue sequence ideally introduces, in microcosm, a number of the key characteristics of Jakubisko's cinema, and some of the distinctive qualities of the 'Slovak New Wave' itself. Clearly intimated here is the preoccupation with a multiform Other: this prologue presents a veritable panoply of Otherness, with the circling and tracking camera revealing joyous crowds of children and mentally handicapped people, transvestite nuns, and of course the ubiquitous Slovak folk apparel. The display of 'exotic' alterities is hardly uncommon in 1960s art cinema, but Jakubisko, somewhat more unusually, is keen to define his relationship to such Otherness in terms of sympathy and identification, as that recasting of the authorial voice in infantile and feminine registers indicates. The very words of that opening commentary point both to *Birds, Orphans and Fools*' exploration of the specific Otherness of madness and to the slippery, ludic and ambivalent nature of Jakubisko's cinema as a whole, flirting as this text does with a 'mad' or illogical discourse of cryptic assertion and contradiction: 'The world is nice, although not completely, unhappy but not really unhappy, crazy and full of love, and just the opposite. Everything changes, nothing ends without a beginning.' Perhaps most striking of all though in this prologue is the blatant, almost artless self-reflexivity, achieved not only through the spoken commentary but also through the display of technical equipment and the photograph of Jakubisko with his cast and crew that closes the sequence. Self-reflexive gestures proliferate in a near-compulsive manner in the films of Jakubisko and his New Wave compatriot Elo Havetta, serving to foreground the constructed (and thus partial) status of these films. If the admission of textuality appears attached here to a particular subjectivity ('I, Juraj Jakubisko'), it is a subjectivity that is neither unified nor stable, but rather plural, fluid and inauthentic: Jakubisko speaks literally as another in *Birds, Orphans and Fools*' voiceover, and in shifting voices or personas.

As my account of this brief, dense sequence might suggest, the Slovak New Wave films are among the most aesthetically radical, the most avant-garde, works of the 1960s Czechoslovak cinema. Jakubisko's own development as a filmmaker during the late 1960s is quite remarkable, representing in accelerated form and arguably exceeding the standard trajectory of the international New Waves. That development is all the more remarkable for having been accomplished in Jakubisko's own terms, and inspired by aesthetic sources often quite distinct from those of the other New Waves, including the Czech one. Within two years, Jakubisko passes from the black-and-white quasi-realism, existential examinations and individual heroics (or anti-heroics) of *Christ's Years* (*Kristove roky*, 1967), through to the blood-red baroque and panoramic horror of *The Deserter and the Nomads* and the countercultural implosions of *Birds, Orphans and Fools*. Havetta's emergence two years after Jakubisko's debut is striking for a different reason, his first feature, *Party in the Botanical Garden* (*Slávnosť v botanickej záhrade*, 1969), presenting a distinctive and fully-formed aesthetic that seems both (sometimes within one and the same device) wildly advanced and disarmingly naïve, highly sophisticated and enamoured of a kind of patched-together amateurism. The apparently avant-garde, international or 'modern' qualities of *Party in the Botanical Garden* or the mature films of Jakubisko coexist alongside a pronounced interest in folk culture, in the 'primitive' and exotically local. Such a coexistence might be seen in terms of contradiction or tension, yet the former qualities as often derive from the latter interests as supplement them. For instance the plentiful, 'poetic' violence of *Deserter and the Nomads* is rooted, Jakubisko suggests, both in folk art and in the rural Slovak's typical intimacy with slaughter and butchery, yet it also seems akin to the blithe, stylised, 'not blood but red' violence of Godard or Alejandro Jodorowsky (Jakubisko has asserted, along

Godardian lines, that 'blood is predominantly a colour').[1] One of the most thrilling things about *Birds, Orphans and Fools*, in particular, is its dense tangle of obscure folk elements and such familiar and universal cultural icons as the MGM logo, Mao Zedong and Shakespeare's *Hamlet*: exemplary in that regard is a scene where Yorick, the film's protagonist, performs a windswept folk jig on the bonnet of an American Cadillac.

That very melding or commingling of the local and the international, the traditional and the modern, suggests the play with hybridity in these films, one way in which they look forward to the aesthetics of postmodernism. The last chapter cautiously identified a proto-postmodernist aspect in Chytilová's *Daisies*, but in these Slovak films, and particularly those of Jakubisko (on whom the bulk of this chapter will concentrate), that dimension is more prevalent and multifaceted. What this chapter will reveal, in its focus on such themes as Otherness, subjectivity and possibilities of revolutionary change, is how Jakubisko's cinema invokes modernist ideas and utopian fantasies while also intimating a (political and aesthetic) position that is more modest and pragmatic (or more cynical and despairing, depending on one's view of postmodernism and of the films themselves). Tropes native to Surrealism or the counterculture undergo more contemporary modulations, and the evocation of the cultural-revolutionary fervour and revivified avant-gardism of the 1960s shades into the bleak, ironized dissection of that decade's dreams. It must be noted that, unlike some of the other films explored in this study, Jakubisko's work never reached back in any explicit or systematic way to Surrealist and avant-garde traditions, Slovak or otherwise (the most direct evocation of the Surrealist movement in any of Jakubisko's films is the still photograph of Dalí interjected into the rich visual tapestry of *Birds, Orphans and Fools*, though this image is one of many diverse cultural references, and Dalí is arguably as much an icon of popular culture as of Surrealism). Unlike Jaromil Jireš, Jiří Menzel or the Slovak director Štefan Uher, who adapted Dominik Tatarka's 1944 Surrealist novel *The Miraculous Virgin* (*Panna zázračnica*) into an eponymous 1966 film, Jakubisko never derived any of his films from literary works of the avant-garde. At the same time, the links between Jakubisko's cinema and a Surrealist or avant-garde sensibility should be fairly evident.

In and of themselves, such qualities of Jakubisko's work as his experimental visual style, the clearly critical or oppositional stance of his films and his interest in subjectivity, love, madness and the utopian would amply justify his place in a study such as this. Yet Jakubisko's use of motifs and techniques from

---

1. Juraj Jakubisko, interviewed in Antonín J. Liehm, *Closely Watched Films: The Czechoslovak Experience* (White Plains: International Arts and Science, 1974), p. 359; Jakubisko, quoted in Jan Jaroš, *Juraj Jakubisko* (Prague: Československý filmový ústav, 1989), p. 10.

folk culture and peasant art can be connected with the Surrealists' and interwar avant-gardes' interest in naïve painting, *art brut* and 'primitive' cultures. If Jakubisko or Havetta seem less interested in representing Slovakia's rich avant-garde heritage than the Czech filmmakers do in representing their own avant-garde, we should recall that the original Slovak Surrealists were themselves markedly influenced by, in Peter Petro's words, 'the beautiful folk tales and songs of the Slovak countryside', the 'world of folklore' with its 'miraculous' and magical qualities.[2] It is then possible, if paradoxical, to suggest that Jakubisko and Havetta's films evoke something of the flavour of the Slovak avant-garde in their very reach beyond modernity.

The use of folk and traditional influences, deriving as those elements do from a particular national context and even from particular regions of Slovakia, also anticipates, again paradoxically, the postmodernist assertion of cultural specificity, of the 'local-particular' as against the universalist assumptions and totalizing projects of modernism.[3] That concern for the local is perhaps most explicit in Havetta's work, especially *Party in the Botanical Garden*, whose central character is, in a sense, the life and local mythology of the town of Babindol (a town based on Havetta's own hometown, the Western Slovakian village of Veľké Vozokany). Yet Jakubisko has asserted the specifically Eastern Slovakian sensibility of his work, evident, apparently, in a 'temperamental', undefeatably joyous quality[4] (admittedly the Western Slovaks of Havetta's films are scarcely less temperamental and joyful, even if their joy is tested by less severe tribulations than in those of Jakubisko). One could even claim that the very obscurity or indecipherability that characterizes Jakubisko's treatment of folk motifs attests to the unavoidable reality of cultural difference, the existence of particularized regional myths or symbolic systems and their inscrutable separateness. But one could also claim that those symbols are thereby detached from their real meaning within their native context, and recuperated for international art cinema in their manifestation as 'avant-garde' floating signifiers. Furthermore, those markers of the local are, as I have suggested, mixed with obviously international elements and, even in *Party*, the bucolic appeal of this locale is qualified by the sense that the particular, the local, is also the small and insignificant, especially when embodied in such 'marginal' places as Babindol: Gašpar, the closest thing to a main human protagonist in the film, is smitten by thoughts of travelling the world, and remarks at one point, to the lover he will desert, that '[t]he world is vast ..., and our Babindol is like a dot left by a fly'.

2. Peter Petro, 'Slovak Surrealist Poetry: The Movement and its Rediscovery', *Canadian Slavonic Papers* (Volume 20, No. 2, June 1978), p. 240.
3. Marianne DeKoven, *Utopia Limited*, p. 16.
4. Jakubisko, in Liehm, *Closely Watched Films*, p. 357.

Figure 5.1 Gašpar (Jiří Sýkora) leaves Babindol. *Party in the Botanical Garden* (*Slávnosť v botanickej záhrade*, Elo Havetta, 1969) Author: Vladimír Vavrek, source: Photoarchive Slovak Film Institute (©).

In addition to that qualified assertion of the local and specific, these films also share with postmodernism their interest in making visible various forms of Otherness. The films of both Jakubisko and Havetta present a broad cast of 'Others', including peasants, gypsies, children, the elderly and the mad (did not intellectuals and artists, protagonists in *Christ's Years* and *Birds, Orphans and Fools*, also represent a kind of Otherness in Communist Czechoslovakia?). Otherness, of course, is typically defined as such in relation to a normative Western modernity, to a model of identity or system of values that is 'rational', 'civilized', white, bourgeois, male, and so on. Postmodern culture concerns itself with rediscovering the hitherto repressed, silenced 'general Other of modernity', just as the condition of postmodernity marks the Other's re-emergence into 'subjectivity, audibility, agency'.[5] (We should note that Linda Hutcheon, writing of postmodern fiction, substitutes the term 'difference' for 'otherness', the former term intended to reflect postmodernism's commitment to particularity and its refutation of the idea of a monolithic Other).[6] The exploration and valorization of Otherness in these films is

5.   DeKoven, op. cit.
6.   Linda Hutcheon, *A Poetics of Postmodernism: History, Theory, Fiction* (London; New York: Routledge, 1988), p. 6.

something shared not only with postmodernism, but also with Dada and Surrealism, both of which movements, as 'deviant' products of modernity, celebrated such manifestations of Otherness as childhood, the 'primitive', the 'feminine', madness and hysteria. Yet the celebration of, or identification with, the Other can take dubious forms, as is notably the case with the historical avant-gardes: the sustained discussion of *Birds, Orphans and Fools* later on in this chapter will highlight the film's critical engagement with the Surrealist (as well as countercultural) infatuation with madness.

It is in a sense highly apt that explorations of Otherness should be staged on this particular regional territory, for Slovak national identity itself represents a kind of Otherness, at least as far as the Czechs are concerned. According to Ladislav Holý, among the Czechs a favoured image of the Slovak is that of 'an exotic Other living in a traditional and picturesque mountain village', while Slovakia itself is frequently constructed as 'an exotic and unspoiled wild country epitomised by the rocky mountains of the High Tatra, slivovitz, and ethnic dishes made of sheep cheese'.[7] These images, to which many Slovak writers and artists have themselves contributed, have enabled a kind of mild and relatively benign internal Orientalism and perpetuated the belief among the Czechs that 'if it were not for their own civilising efforts, the Slovaks would still be walking around with their bellybuttons exposed'.[8] From such perspectives the differences between the Czech lands and Slovakia are easily reducible to clear-cut oppositions between Czech 'culture' and Slovak 'nature', historical modernity and ahistorical ruralism[9] (for Eugen Steiner, the Czech view of Slovakia as 'a region without history' derives from the lack of common history between the two nations).[10] While Jakubisko and Havetta's work in many ways manifests a specifically Slovak identity, and while both filmmakers proudly and unapologetically uphold some of the more obviously 'exotic', 'wild' or 'primitive' aspects this identity entails, it should be noted that Jakubisko, at least, has always simultaneously manifested a strong sense of closeness, affinity and common cause with the Czechs (Jakubisko's training at FAMU in Prague has no doubt played some part in forming this attitude). Internally, this is evident in, say, the allusions to the Warsaw Pact invasion of Czechoslovakia and the 'New Wave' in, respectively, *The Deserter and the Nomads* and *Birds, Orphans and Fools*, and the casting of Czech actor Jiří Sýkora in the lead roles of both *Birds, Orphans* and *Christ's Years*.

The postmodernist emphasis on Otherness and marginality is conceived less as a means of establishing a new hierarchy of value than as a way of

---

7.   Ladislav Holý, *The Little Czech and the Great Czech Nation*, p. 103.
8.   Ibid.
9.   Ibid.
10. Eugen Steiner, *The Slovak Dilemma* (Cambridge: Cambridge University Press, 1973),
     p. 18.

displacing that very system of meaning, of problematizing the binary distinctions that oppose Same to Other, centre to margins.[11] As Mark Pegrum has argued, postmodernism is in this respect anticipated by both Dada and Bakhtinian carnival. These earlier movements fight on two cultural fronts, on the one hand valorizing or embodying a shocking Otherness (the Otherness of irrationality or the grotesque body, for instance) but on the other hand mixing together apparently opposed or incompatible elements in an attempt to 'collapse binary structures and ... open polarities to interchange'.[12] The notion of carnival is something generally applicable to the work of both Jakubisko and Havetta, not least because carnival celebrations (along with such obviously carnivalesque phenomena as ribaldry, 'low' and scatological humour, and plebeian or peasant culture) appear in both directors' work. Yet the carnivalesque sensibility also manifests itself as that 'heterodox merging' of qualities, the hybridization of apparent binary opposites.[13] We have already shown how these films stylistically merge the local with the international, the native with the foreign, the traditional and amateur with the avant-garde and progressive; we might also mention the mixing of high and low cultures (Bergmanesque allegory jostles with slapstick and toilet gags in *The Deserter and the Nomads*), the natural and the artificial, beauty and ugliness, even life and death. Equally suggestive of that hybridizing impulse are those surrealistic, peculiarly permeable buildings in which the protagonists of *Birds, Orphans and Fools* and *See You in Hell, My Friends!* make their homes: of course these ambiguous spaces are hardly apt to make their occupants feel at home, situating them as they do on the border between inside and outside. These spaces also attest to the carnivalesque rejection of closure for openness, that sense of the easy flow between one condition and another, as through apertures of the body.[14] One could then claim that these films are marked by the same double emphasis as carnival and Dada: while the marginalized Otherness of folk culture or Slovak peasant life is vigorously celebrated, Jakubisko and Havetta are not content to leave such Otherness pure and uncontaminated, to let the boundaries dividing margins from centre go unchallenged. The assertion of hybridity can even be seen as an implicit challenge to the characterization of the Czech and Slovak regions themselves in the binarized terms of 'culture' and 'nature', historical and eternal.

As these hybridities attest, Jakubisko and Havetta are too sophisticated to let their celebration of folk festivities and rural life drift into a proclamation of pastoral innocence. This is evident also in the subtle undermining of those

---

11. Mark A. Pegrum, *Challenging Modernity: Dada between Modern and Postmodern* (Oxford; New York: Berghahn, 2000), p. 168.
12. Ibid.
13. Peter Stallybrass and Allon White, quoted in Pegrum, p. 167.
14. Pegrum, p. 169.

ideas of authenticity or essence that these contexts might otherwise suggest. To take *Party in the Botanical Garden* as a case in point, the film's plentiful imagery of lush fields and sun-dappled leaves, its rich display of extroverted and untamed rural eccentricities and its implied counterpoint between the simple village and the great cities and monuments of the wider world (as shown in Gašpar's postcards) might easily render this setting a bounteous repository of the authentic and natural, of vitality and wholeness. Much of the film's action revolves around the re-enactment of that miracle on which, according to legend, the village of Babindol was originally founded: the emergence of wine from the ground, a motif suggestive of the spurting forth of the life substance, of the literal bounties of native soil. Yet the miracle's re-enactment is of course a fake, a spectacle mechanically produced by the Wellesian figure of Pierre. The culmination of the local festivities, under Pierre's supervision, in a ramshackle yet magical theatrical display (complete with P.A. system and incongruous film crew), and the fact that Pierre is himself an itinerant Frenchman rather than a Slovak or a native of this village, carry further overtones of performance and imitation, of the inauthentic or non-essential. The emphasis on performance and artifice in Havetta, as well as in Jakubisko, of course also serves that tendency towards self-reflexivity and the foregrounding of the enunciative process that was mentioned earlier.

For all its sophisticated qualifications, the vision of *Party in the Botanical Garden* still retains much of the idyllic. While Havetta's apparent representative within the film may ultimately leave Babindol to fulfil his desire for worldly experience, the director's own artistic return offers a loving, even enchanted tribute to his hometown. Even the culminating 'miracle' is not entirely inauthentic, for that fraudulent re-eruption of earthly luxury does spark something suggestive of Bacchanalian frenzy as well as freak acts of nature (fire and then, miraculously enough, sudden savage rain). In another scene, a 'real' miracle blithely takes place in the form of an abrupt night-time sunrise. Yet in its exposure of day-for-night trickery, this miracle is arguably as much a joke at the expense of cinema's own higher-tech fraudulence. *Party*'s vision is fundamentally lyrical and, in the broad sense, comic. The wider world is somewhat bracketed here, existing at a remove and in an idealized form (the magical presence of Pierre, Gašpar's daydreams of travel). Jakubisko's work offers a more obvious dialectic of microcosm and macrocosm, of the local habitat and the larger arena of political and world-historical forces (Havetta's second and final film *Wild Lilies* (*L'alie poľné*, 1972) does, it must be said, deal elliptically with the First World War). Another kind of opposition that abounds in Jakubisko's films, sometimes related to yet not completely identifiable with that first dialectic, is that between the historical and the mythic-folkloric, the barbaric and the idyllic, between real evils and the valorized qualities, identities and environments that we have discussed, which hereto come to offer tentative, ambiguous, compromised glimpses of the utopian. The analysis of such oppositions, of the greater success or failure of one or the other term, will in fact comprise much of the work of the remainder of this chapter. As binary oppositions or distinct concepts themselves, some of those terms must retain much of their distinctness in order that a critical perspective be brought to bear within these films (such oppositions must at least remain distinct in our discussion, if we are to make critical or political uses of these works). Yet even these terms are also sometimes made subject to merging or blending, as when bloody revolutions are shown to contain a grisly *jouissance* and when folk sources help to recast history in the mould of myth.

The Deserter and the Nomads: A Dance of Death on the Stage(s) of History

It has already been mentioned that one of the stock images or stereotypes of Slovakia is of a land without history, timeless and unchanging in its pastoral way of life. While these Slovak New Wave films provide more than a glimpse of traditional, presumably long-enduring customs, festivities and myths, their vision is seldom unhistorical. Even *Party in the Botanical Garden*, apparently set in a sealed-off world of antiquated or ageless ruralism, can be seen subtly to inscribe an historical dimension within its own development. The film begins with the origins of cinema itself, in the form of an explicit homage to the Lumiére brothers' *L'Arrivée d'un train à La Ciotat* (1896), and ends with the television monitors of the modern film crew, and with the presence of Havetta himself, yelling his directions: history is thus present metonymically as the history or technological development of film.[15] (At the same time that opening allusion, to a single-shot depiction of an oncoming train that famously (if apocryphally) sent its initial spectators running away in terror, comprises another representation of cinema in its illusionistic, tricking guise, and aligns Havetta's film with the early days of the travelling cinematograph, in other words with such modest popular entertainment as the film itself depicts.) Jakubisko's films, hardly so subtle in that regard, are saturated in bloody history, the narrative of *Deserter and the Nomads* collapsing world history into a series of global wars and leaping from one event, one catastrophe, to the next as though propelled by the same energy as Jakubisko's dizzying camerawork. While the irrational or Dionysian seems often in Jakubisko's work to represent a healthy respite from, or a subversion of, an oppressive modernity, the distinction between 'primitive' folk traditions and a 'rational'

---

15. Jana Dudková, 'Elo Havetta: *The Gala in the Botanical Garden* (*Slávnosť v botanickej záhrade)*', *KinoKultura*, 2005 (http://www.kinokultura.com/specials/3/slavnost. shtml) (retrieved 1 February 2009).

modernity is not as clear-cut as it may appear: indeed twentieth-century conflict is revealed in *The Deserter and the Nomads* as an arena of barbarism. There is no mitigating sense of progress, of any advance into enlightened peace, though 'progress' or 'enlightenment' might themselves be key culprits in this horror: the fruits of civilization are at least shown to play little positive role in ameliorating humanity's lot.

The literal temporal progression of the film's three episodes is undercut by a grim logic of repetition, this being foregrounded by the repeated use of the same motifs and even actors (the Bolshevik revolutionary of the first episode already, tellingly, appears with the same leering, malevolent face as the Soviet captain of the second). The only meaningful development is in the increase in the efficiency and scale of killing from one episode to the next, with each fresh cycle of violence and destruction drawing in a greater crop of victims. After episodes dealing with the First and Second World Wars, Jakubisko moves beyond real history to depict the culmination of that logic of 'rationalized' violence in the apocalypse of nuclear war. Life on earth has now been destroyed, except, it seems, for the young nurse Nevěsta and the hordes of terrified, half-mad old people who take shelter, naked or swaddled in blankets, in underground bunkers. This final episode is then a cruel parody of a triumphant climax of history, for the ascent of civilization is presented not only as humanity's twilight but also in terms of a senile insanity or grotesque infantilism. The world outside is peaceful because everybody has been killed or driven underground, and pastoral because civilization has obliterated itself.

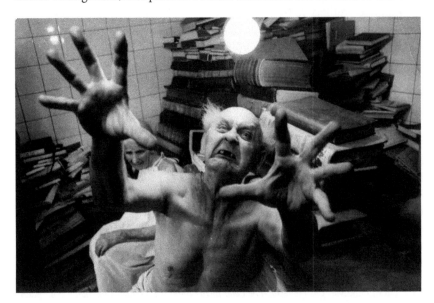

Figure 5.2 The final section of *The Deserter and the Nomads* (*Zbehovia a pútnici*, Juraj Jakubisko, 1968) ©Slovak Film Institute, reproduced courtesy of Jakubisko Film.

This pessimistic, absurd, non-redemptive approach towards history and society helps distinguish Jakubisko's work from the films made by Godard or Rocha during the same period, films that might seem similar in many ways but whose doctrinaire zeal and faith in the existence of progressive or liberatory historical agents are quite alien to Jakubisko's cinema. The disillusion that was pervasive during, and is synonymous with, the end of the 1960s was perhaps experienced most acutely in Czechoslovakia, where the Warsaw Pact invasion arguably stamped out former dreams more abruptly and surely than any other phenomenon (we might except the overthrow of Chile's Allende government, that other great experiment in socialist democracy, a few years later). Jakubisko was in fact the only Czechoslovak filmmaker of this period to incorporate the invasion directly into his feature work, an incorporation that he enacts not through mere reconstruction but as actuality: real images of the invasion tear through the stylized world of *The Deserter and the Nomads*, a convulsive impingement on the narrative's unabashed artifice.

As Dina Iordanova notes, *Deserter* and *Birds, Orphans and Fools* have been interpreted as Jakubisko's 'reaction to the crushing of the Prague Spring'.[16] Jakubisko had already begun shooting *Deserter* by the time of the invasion (he tells a story about how, during filming, one of the tanks drove unexpectedly into shot), so one cannot entirely attribute the film's bleak view or its jaundiced eye on communism and revolution to the events of August (these events may, however, have confirmed or strengthened those views, reiterated as they are, with different degrees of emphasis, in Jakubisko's subsequent films). Nonetheless, that direct evocation of the invasion can be seen as exploiting the emblematic status of that incident: its power as an image of the death of hopes for a truly emancipatory socialism, of the failure of 1960s radical-political modernity, of a general loss of optimism or idealism. Of course, this footage, intercut as it is with sequences dealing with the Red Army's presence in Slovakia at the end of the Second World War, also reinforces none too subtly the idea of that earlier Soviet intervention as something other than a liberation (this idea is already clear enough in the depiction of a boorish group of Soviet soldiers 'occupying' a farm and abusing its inhabitants). Again uniquely among the New Wave films, *Birds, Orphans and Fools* refers directly to the destruction of the New Wave itself, an event which Jakubisko represents in the form of a huge pile of burning film strips. 'The New Wave!', Yorick yells with ironic joy after the film is set alight. But this reference alludes in turn to the destruction of the reform socialism that at once tolerated these films and shared their liberal values. The clowning that precedes this conflagration, where the characters imitate the logos of Mosfilm, Rank, MGM and Columbia Pictures (sole or signature film studios of the USSR, UK and USA respectively), can be seen, by contrast, to

16. Dina Iordanova, *Cinema of the Other Europe: The Industry and Artistry of East Central European Film* (London; New York: Wallflower, 2003), p. 58.

allude to the established, unvanquishable forms of political organization and their chief representatives-enforcers.

For many commentators, postmodernism originates in the aftermath of the failed revolutions of the 1960s. Perry Anderson, in accord with both Alex Callinicos and Terry Eagleton, suggests that the 'immediate sources of postmodernism' lie in the Left's 'experience of defeat' at the end of that decade, in the comprehensive 'snuffing out' of the 1960s' 'political dreams' (Anderson of course includes the Prague Spring, 'the boldest of all Communist reform experiments', among those lost dreams).[17] A negative view of such developments would regard the postmodern age as a point of political impasse, marked by fatalistic passivity, self-absorbed quietism and complicity or affinity with established (late capitalist) power. For its more sympathetic commentators, postmodernism constitutes a rejection of oppressive, totalizing 'grand narratives' of history and global emancipatory projects in favour of localized political interventions, partial or internal forms of resistance and the affirmation of discrete 'language games' and particular identities. Jakubisko's films, and *The Deserter and the Nomads* most explicitly, share that postmodernist dismissal, in whatever terms it may be characterized, of notions of global emancipation or of a society progressing towards peace and justice. In this respect Jakubisko's outlook can equally be compared with that of the 'pre-modern' peasant who encounters the ubiquitous figure of Death at the end of the first episode: Death, asked what he is looking for, replies, 'Happiness', and the old man guffaws.

More specifically, the three narratives of *Deserter* could be aligned with postmodernist attacks on the crimes or failures of modernity. After all, the film's many horrors are all ultimately perpetrated by some form or other of political or intellectual modernity, whether bourgeois imperialism (the First World War), Communism (portrayed as malign and oppressive even in its initial, spontaneous outbreak), or scientific and technological development (the nuclear war). Progress in the twentieth century, it is implied, has brought not only technical advance and its array of new machineries, but also the mechanization of human beings themselves, the mass production of violence. The second episode's opening caption contrasts the former stimuli of human passions with a new, coolly mechanized killing: 'When people kill each other out of hatred, it is terrible; it will be far more terrible when they learn to murder mechanically.' Scientific rationality has come to serve irrational and evil ends, and enables the perpetration of violence on a previously unimaginable scale. Jakubisko's critique of modernity both looks forward to postmodernism and connects back to Dada and Surrealism, movements that, despite themselves being products of modernity, were also often sceptical about the benefits of science or the supposed superiority of Enlightenment reason. Near

---

17. Perry Anderson, *The Origins of Postmodernity* (London; New York: Verso, 1989), p. 91.

Figure 5.3 Death (Augustín Kubán) in *The Deserter and the Nomads* (*Zbehovia a pútnici*, Juraj Jakubisko, 1968) ©Slovak Film Institute, reproduced courtesy of Jakubisko Film.

the end of *Deserter*, Death realizes that he has no part to play in this world of manmade devastation. The redundancy of the allegorical figure within this post-nuclear landscape can be seen to signify the culmination of enlightenment or scientific 'progress' and the consequent eradication of all mythologies and 'irrational' beliefs. (Death's more active functioning in the previous two stories can, by the terms of this reading, serve to suggest the residual irrationalities of those earlier points in history.) The deserted windmill in which Death and Nevěsta make their home, an obvious allusion to Cervantes' *Don Quixote* (1605), stands as the sole commemoration of a world of pre-Enlightenment superstition and romance. The explicit reason for Death's redundancy here is that mankind is quite capable of doing its own killing: in a perverse twist on the Feuerbach thesis about religious alienation, Death now realizes that the murderous abilities (or inclinations) he believed to be his alone are within the power of human beings themselves. The mythological being is left to look in awe at humanity's now God-like capacity for mass annihilation.

The vision presented in *The Deserter and the Nomads* might thus seem entirely negative, pessimistic and horrifying. One could of course claim that the film's apocalyptic climax is intended to be cautionary. Jan Kučera, reviewing *Deserter* in 1969, argues that the film is not 'hopeless' and that its 'verve' attests to a 'deep faith in the progressive forces of humanity'[18] (Kučera's language is

---

18. Jan Kučera, 'O lidech a smrti', *Film a doba*, No. 9, 1969, p. 475.

typical of the Czech Marxist humanist rhetoric of the period). Yet there is little suggestion here of a progressive political agency that might offer a different course of development or an alternative to the existing configurations of oppressive, fundamentally irrational power. While the film is not without representatives of goodness or innocence, its more benign figures are generally powerless, persecuted, martyred individuals like Nevěsta (who is ultimately murdered by an old man believed to be God), the gypsy Kálmán (the hunted military deserter of the first episode), the egg-seller accused of espionage in the second episode and the various children who get caught up, helplessly, in the vortex of revolution and battle. According to Kučera, the very last image of the film, depicting the turning sails of the aforementioned windmill, suggests 'the persistence of human works, and even of human Quixote-ism'.[19] Maybe so, but the idea of such a continuation is small comfort indeed, given these circumstances and the horrors we have already witnessed. Moreover, that literary allusion might be seen to attest rather to the 'quixotic' futility of all attempts at social change.

Yet while the claims of negativity and horror are in large part accurate as an assessment of *Deserter*'s content, even of its explicit themes or ideas, such claims do not do justice to the sensory experience of the film. In fact the bleakness of the film's content is offset by the vitality and exuberance of its form. The notion of the dance of death has been evoked more than once in commentaries on Jakubisko and *Deserter*: Antonín Liehm remarks that Jakubisko's heroes 'dance a merry jig of revolution and war', and for Peter Mihalovič *Deserter* depicts 'an insane dance of death from which there is no escape'.[20] Such terms are unusually apt in this case, capturing at once the film's joyous, carnivalesque mode of expression and the violent content that this style encodes. The conclusion of the first section speaks for the film as a whole in its marriage of libidinal exuberance and ugly history: the bodies of executed deserters Kálmán and the Bolshevik revolutionary Martin are laid beside each other on a bed, but the surrounding dances cause them to rock in a manner suggestive of sexual congress. It is as though the erotic, affirmative, life-sustaining impulses, dominated or mostly squeezed out by opposing tendencies (murder, destruction, the collective death wish) within the narrative itself, are forced to spill over into form, the resources of colour, movement, rhythm and design. As Jakubisko himself suggests, what the film depicts is at once 'inhuman' and 'beautiful', 'as beautiful as a ballad, as folk art – and as inhuman as every death in war'.[21] Other commentators have seen the

---

19. Ibid., p. 470.
20. Liehm, *Closely Watched Films*, p. 354; Peter Mihalovič '*Zběhové a poutníci/ Deserters and Pilgrims*' [review], *44th Karlovy Vary International Film Festival* (http://www.kviff. com/en/film-archive-detail/20030192-deserters-and-pilgrims/) (retrieved 5 February 2009).
21. Jakubisko, quoted in Jaroš, p. 11.

film's 'poetic cruelty'[22] as itself reflecting the inspiration of folk art. Once again, what strikes us here as a merging or synthesis of moral ugliness and aesthetic beauty, of life-affirming vitality and violent extinction, can be seen in terms of the carnivalesque mixing of opposites. Yet the film's poetic qualities might also reveal an aspiration towards the sublimation of violence. Folk art might already represent such a sublimation, though we could suggest that Jakubisko's aesthetic transfigures the narrative material in yet another way. According to Jan Jaroš, Jakubisko looks on the film's 'catastrophes' as on 'something that has now passed into the realm of folkloric reworking, that has been remoulded into horrifying ballads, reflecting experiences which, while heavy going, are now beyond living memory'.[23] Through the stylization of folk sources and avant-garde techniques, and the presence of obviously allegorical elements such as the figure of Death, the reality-rooted material is transformed into something resembling modern myth, a softening of history into fable that may permit a degree of distance in relation to these disturbing events (the footage of the 1968 invasion, on the other hand, preserves the raw shock and pain of a recent blow).

The coexistence of horror and pleasure, dystopian and utopian qualities, that characterizes the relationship between content and form also pertains, though in a grossly unequal ratio, to the content itself. Gypsies and peasants conduct their festivities at the weddings of the wealthy and powerful, their merry dances thronged by moustachioed hussars and the ever-watchful military commanders. Anarchy and repression momentarily coexist: as life-affirming collectivity usurps the domains of power, so the exponents of violence and hierarchical order infest the joyous celebrations. (Sometimes the merging of these qualities is even more direct, as when the sadistic and proto-dictatorial Martin performs a rousing folk song at a lively and boozy party, and when, in a particularly bizarre moment during the pursuit of Kálmán, the Austro-Hungarian commanders are shown rolling around on the ground with female partners.) Jakubisko here dispels as illusory the idea of some pure, undivided locus of happiness. Such a bucolic purity is shown to be sorely lacking when Kálmán, returning to his native village to seek sanctuary there, finds that war and revolution have caught up with him and contaminated this place too. What the film reveals instead is a kind of constrained libidinal effusion, complicit with power but still somehow effortlessly denying its logic and values. While these effusions are, needless to say, staged in circumstances very different from those of consumer capitalism, they might even be considered as a form of proto-postmodernist 'resistance from within': a partial, contained subversion of the dominant values, rooted in the local-particular and exemplified by or imaged through the internal Othernesses of

22. Jaroš, p. 12.
23. Ibid.

gypsy and peasant culture. Another point of reference here is, of course, Bakhtinian carnival, with its temporary loosening of restraints and collapsing of social hierarchies. As an affront to assumptions of human universality, the vivid display of Otherness in these festivities is matched by Kálmán's own rationale for his desertion: he admits of little closeness to 'whites' and cares nothing for the objectives or outcome of 'their war'.

Such 'alternatives' as then exist to the realities of war and oppression are really possibilities of transient and partial escape: into revelry and song, love and sex. Yet even Kálmán's romantic refuge with his lover Lila seems haunted by intimations of death: Lila's mention of a 'love as big as death' unwittingly suggests the ambiguous status of love as at once strong enough to withstand death and obscurely related to or shadowed by it. The would-be Edenic idyll created by Death and Nevěsta in the final, post-apocalyptic episode (this coupling also expresses the intertwining of love and death, for Nevěsta appears earlier on in the film as a bride, and the word *nevěsta* means 'bride') is an even more pitiful respite, and suggests a grim parody of the Sixties counterculture. Upon reaching the windmill, Nevěsta declares that she and Death have found paradise without even looking for it. But this 'paradise', like the final section of the film as a whole, is revealed as a cruel inversion of the utopian. Nevěsta becomes consumed by forebodings of imminent death, before denying the existence of death altogether and plunging headlong into hallucination and spirituality. The windmill itself is revealed to be infested by bats. Death's dressing up in hippie apparel and his gyrating and bopping to music offer a grotesque mockery of countercultural aspirations, rendering them a literal 'dance of death'. These scenes are at once absurd, poignant, capricious and portentous; their almost crassly parodic quality suggests a somewhat derisive attitude towards Sixties cultural upheaval. Yet these scenes also represent the germs of the more nuanced and sustained exploration of Sixties-style utopianism and alternative living in *Birds, Orphans and Fools*. It should be noted however that *Birds, Orphans* also concerns the impasse of revolutionary ambitions, even if its dissection of failure is more complex and ambivalent: the view of history hammered home throughout *Deserter* forms part of the background, indeed seems virtually a given, in the later film. Both films thus comprise a continuum with one another, offering variations on the same themes and essentially the same ideas, and by means of a similar blend of bleakness and exuberance. What makes *Birds, Orphans* of even greater interest to us is that, in this film, Jakubisko's enduring preoccupations – notably the assertion of the link between subversion and Otherness – take on not only a more countercultural dimension but also a more classically Surrealist one.

Birds, Orphans and Fools: Flights of Fancy, or Surrealist Escapes

The original Slovak title of *The Deserter and the Nomads* is *Zbehovia a pútnici*, or *Deserters and Pilgrims*, a title that could be seen to juxtapose the rejection of certain values, ideologies or political configurations (desertion) with the embrace of new faiths and destinations (pilgrimage). Yet as we have seen, the pilgrimages of that film are ultimately forms of temporary escape, and its apparent shrines mere occasions for ecstatic, partial forgetting. *Birds, Orphans and Fools* is more enamoured than the earlier film of the 1960s' articles of faith, though even here the folk-hippie furnishings and avant-garde ambience do not represent the microcosm of a new world, but only – and at best – a refuge or enclave for another band of anxious pilgrims. The film's protagonists are Yorick, Marta and Andrej, who form an initially idyllic *Jules-et-Jim*-style *ménage à trois* (though as Godard, rather than Truffaut, might have imagined it). Orphaned literally and, in a sense, figuratively, the characters turn their backs on a violent and senseless world in which they have no place, and determine to become 'fools'. What then are these apparent orphans if not the children of Death and Nevěsta from Jakubisko's previous film, born under the shadow of the atomic bomb and at the foot of Quixote's windmill?

Figure 5.4 Marta (Magda Vášáryová), Yorick (Jiří Sýkora) and Andrej (Philippe Avron) in *Birds, Orphans and Fools* (*Vtáčkovia, siroty a blázni*, Juraj Jakubisko, 1969) Author: Vladimír Vavrek, source: Photoarchive Slovak Film Institute (©).

One of the most obvious ways in which *Birds, Orphans and Fools* manifests its affinities with a Sixties, countercultural or New Left sensibility is in its representation, and indeed its conception, of revolution. The film's treatment of revolution is much more sympathetic than was *Deserter's*, and this is evident not least in the choice of more obviously liberatory embodiments: the Bolsheviks of the earlier film are replaced by representatives of such uncontroversially noble endeavours as the Slovak National Uprising of 1944 and the First World War-era drive for Czechoslovak independence. The sanctified figure of Milan Štefánik, a Slovak general and politician instrumental (along with Masaryk and Edvard Beneš) in the creation of the 1918 Czechoslovak state, is particularly central here, although the film's attitude towards this Slovak national martyr is far from conventionally reverent. The single reference to Mao (with Yorick urging a handicapped child to eat her porridge for 'Mao's red star') could simply be jocular, throwaway or ironic, but a certain sympathy for cultural revolution, Chinese- as well as Haight-Ashbury-style, would of course tie in with the film's evocation of the New Left and its debts to Godard (*Birds, Orphans* is Jakubisko's most Godardian film, and the only one in which he deploys Godard-style direct-to-camera address; moreover, the Godard film that *Birds, Orphans* arguably recalls most directly is the very explicitly Maoist *La Chinoise* (1967), another portrait of a group of young, idealistic but isolated revolutionaries). Yet if revolutionaries are not excoriated here, as the Bolsheviks were in *Deserters*, they are often imbued with a certain sense of absurdity or impotence (and the horrific failures of Maoist revolution are of course more than evident in retrospect): a gun-toting Slovak Partisan runs alongside Yorick's car, apparently convinced the fascists have not yet been vanquished, and an incongruous band of guerrillas fall down 'dead' in a street skirmish, only to get up again. Yet these images could equally be seen as attesting to the commonality and continuity of revolutionary attempts throughout history, the resilient throb of the emancipatory urge. (The anachronistic figure of the Partisan is also a youthful Slovak's comment on the rigid, stultifying nostalgia for canonized liberations of the past.)

The inclusion of Štefánik among the revolutionary images is perhaps more significant or ambiguous than has been suggested. Štefánik died, 'under unclear circumstances',[24] in a plane crash in 1919, and was posthumously mythologized as 'an ardent Slovak nationalist' who, if he had lived, 'would have promoted Slovak autonomy and opposed a centralized Czech-dominated government'.[25] It is easy then to see how the myth of Štefánik might be appropriated for the assertion of local difference and the promotion of particular, regional interests,

---

24. Martin Kaňuch, '*Vtáčkovia, siroty a blázni/Birds, Orphans and Fools*', in Hames, *The Cinema of Central Europe*, p. 169.

25. Richard C. Frucht, *Eastern Europe: An Introduction to the People, Lands and Culture* (Santa Barbara: ABC-CLIO, 2005), p. 312.

in other words for a more postmodern vision of political intervention. (Of course, from this perspective Štefánik's fate also comprises a narrative of failure, no less than the more 'modernist' versions of revolution; the irreverence shown towards Štefánik in the film is among other things an attack on the consoling belief in 'heroes'.) On the other hand, one of the explicitly progressive aspects of the protagonists' alliance is their incipiently utopian transcendence of ethnic or religious differences. Andrej overcomes his initial antipathy to the Jewish Marta, a distaste founded on the fact that Jews killed his parents. Indeed, with the remark 'Our parents killed each other', Yorick distinguishes the bitter and murderous nationalisms and ethnic squabbles of the previous generation from the fraternal and internationalist attitudes of the young (this remark also echoes Jakubisko's own concern to demonstrate that 'the traditional Czech/Slovak antagonisms were always linked to older people and not shared by his own generation').[26] The reference to parents also roots the notion of revolution in generational difference, which was frequently perceived as the basis of the 1960s upheavals in culture and mores, as well as politics. Considered in these terms the characters' symbolic 'orphanhood' is as much a kind of cultural and social patricide.

It is in fact the quintessentially Sixties 'revolution' in lifestyles that is explored most explicitly and fully throughout the film. Dressing in weird apparel that suggests equal parts Slovak goatherd and Carnaby Street freak, the protagonists attempt to embody the ethos and values of the counterculture: 'free love', sharing, play and casual creativity, the abandonment of work or remunerative activity (one subtle sign that the idyll has come to its end is Andrej's attainment of paid employment as a photographer). A key facet of Sixties radicalism was the link it established between politics and the spheres of subjectivity and lifestyle, a link best expressed by the well-worn New Left-feminist slogan 'the personal is political'. In the words of Marianne DeKoven, the Sixties 'modernist politics of the self ... radiates out from the exemplary subject to a potentially transformed society and culture'.[27] DeKoven roots this politics in the 'romantic tradition of adequation of transformed self with transformed world';[28] that tradition is also clearly incarnated in the Surrealism of Breton, which committed itself to both imaginative liberation and revolutionary political upheaval and famously combined the injunctions of Marx ('transform the world') and Rimbaud ('change life').[29] Yet the politics of the self comprises a point of transition from modern to postmodern, shifting during the 1960s 'into a postmodern politics that coincides with and is

26. Hames, *The Czechoslovak New Wave*, p. 213.
27. DeKoven, *Utopia Limited*, p. 190.
28. Ibid., p. 255.
29. Breton, *Manifestoes of Surrealism*, p. 241.

contained by formations of subjectivity'.[30] As we shall see later, *Birds, Orphans and Fools* can itself be seen to depict a concern for subjectivity, for the cultivation of lifestyle and the imagination, that comes at the expense of social or political engagement and is essentially consolatory. Once the film is considered from this angle, its relationship to two of its chief cultural sources, the utopian movements of the Sixties counterculture and (Bretonian) Surrealism, appears as far from straightforward.

What can also be seen as proto-postmodern is the protagonists' fondness for dressing up, for stylized or poetic declamation and exuberant performance (two infectious sequences of play and posing, both set to a jaunty piano score, comprise virtual self-contained 'numbers'). These concerns might be seen to intimate a postmodern understanding of subjectivity as 'performative', as fluid and non-essential, indeed the sum of its performances (that principle is arguably already latent within or implied by the Sixties countercultural imperative of transforming the self). The expression of fluidity through references to gender-bending is a particularly and strikingly forward-looking aspect of the film. In an early scene, Yorick attends what is clearly a gay party, where he is surrounded by men in make-up and androgynous pre-adolescent boys, and where he himself appears in a Jaggeresque combination of lipstick and sailor suit. Even Marta, with her cropped hair and masculine dress, is believed by Yorick to be a boy when he first encounters her (he must, he remarks, have been very drunk to sleep with a woman). These comfortable, casual references to androgyny and homosexuality, if hardly extensive (though a homo-erotic bond between Yorick and Andrej is not so subtly implied throughout the film), are groundbreaking and almost unique in the Czechoslovak cinema of the time.

The embrace of 'foolishness', the most radical aspect of the protagonists' lifestyle experiment, connects back to a long tradition of the valorization of madness that runs through romanticism, various modernisms and avant-gardes, and, perhaps most obviously of all, Surrealism. It is with such mental Otherness that *Birds, Orphans and Fools* is most concerned: the peasant and gypsy Others of *Deserter* are less prominent, or absent, here (childhood, or childishness, is important though, and mentally handicapped children swarm through the film, unambiguous mascots or envoys of Otherness). The view of madness or irrationality as something positive, a condition one should seek somehow to emulate or even to attain, was not only adopted by Surrealism and the avant-garde but was also part of the radical 1960s cultural and political landscape that Jakubisko's film evokes. That view was expressed most rigorously in the writings of the British psychiatrist R.D. Laing, a founder of the anti-psychiatry movement of the 1960s and 1970s. In *The Politics of*

---

30. DeKoven, p. 190.

Experience (1967), his most widely read work, Laing states his position starkly: the mad person can be a 'hierophant of the sacred', and madness may be 'break-through' as well as 'breakdown', 'liberation and renewal as well as enslavement and existential death'.[31]

For the tradition of which Laing's work partakes, madness is associated with innocence and authenticity, and thus counterposed to the alienation of the 'normal', conventionally rational self. In the immediacy of its access to a realm of fantasy and its capacity to forge striking new imaginative or linguistic connections, mental illness is portrayed as a rich source of visionary revelation and poetic inspiration; the mad person's immunity to the precepts of 'normality' and tradition (whether in terms of linguistic and artistic conventions, morality or social behaviour) makes him or her a choice figurehead for the more calculated resistance of convention.[32] (The parallel should be evident between the avant-garde's fascination with madness and its embrace of folk art, a phenomenon situated outside 'rational' modernity and a dominant or hegemonic set of cultural traditions.) We should note that madness, broadly speaking, is a constant point of reference in postmodernism too: this theme thus represents another quality held in common, or rather another scene of the transition from modern to postmodern, as the terms in which the postmodern valorizes madness are quite different (authenticity and innocence, for instance, are in general no longer feasible for postmodernism). Not only does postmodern discourse approach madness as its explicit object (as in Foucault's *Madness and Civilisation: A History of Insanity in the Age of Reason* (*Folie et déraison: histoire de la folie à l'âge classique*, 1961), a 'strong defence of the voice of unreason'),[33] it also defends, and often inscribes within its own forms, such associated qualities as illogic (or 'paralogic'), fragmentation and contradiction.

As the discussion of *The Deserter and the Nomads* has already revealed, rationality is hardly an object of enthusiasm in Jakubisko's work: on the one hand, 'civilized' reason is shown to be incapable of guarding against the outbreak of barbarism, and on the other, the horrors of *Deserter* are at least in part attributable to a particular form or application of rationality. (Yorick, in *Birds, Orphans*, remarks that his parents were killed 'by those who are said to be ... sane'.) Yet *Birds, Orphans and Fools*, which turns its focus from tyrannical reason to resistant unreason, is by no means an unambiguous celebration of 'foolishness', and the film might even be seen as problematizing or subverting

---

31. R.D. Laing, *The Politics of Experience and The Bird of Paradise* (Harmondsworth: Penguin, 1967), pp. 109–10.

32. See J.H. Matthews, *Surrealism, Insanity, and Poetry* (Syracuse: Syracuse University Press, 1982), Hal Foster, 'Blinded Insights: On the Modernist Reception of the Art of the Mentally Ill', *October* 97, Summer 2001, pp. 3–30.

33. Pegrum, *Challenging Modernity*, p. 131.

those ideas about madness on which the avant-garde and countercultural celebrations were founded. One might suggest, for instance, that mental illness is embraced or upheld in the film less because it is 'revelatory of an innocent vision' than because it promises the comfort of ignorance, because, indeed, it represents the very denial of vision in its disturbing guise. Yorick, it is implied, was himself raised in an institution for mentally handicapped children; as Peter Hames points out, he envies these children 'their happiness and ignorance of the true nature of the world'.[34] In a scene where the protagonists visit such an institution, the sympathetic nurse who shows them round remarks that 'These kids will never become people.' Presented in such terms, mental illness represents debility rather than any special potency, the lack of insight or vision rather than their abundance. Jakubisko himself has characterized that less extreme 'foolishness' that the protagonists embrace as a form of willed obliviousness towards the world, a means of taking 'the load off [one's] conscience' and a denial of 'commitment'.[35]

Yet such a reading of the protagonists' project belies the complexities of the film, and perhaps the confused or ambivalent impulses of the characters themselves. The sense of blinded vision or narcissistic obliviousness jostles with the idea of compulsive observation, as the protagonists alternate between a posture of retreat from the world and the intense need to explore and document it. Photography is a key motif: Andrej is a professional photographer and takes pictures throughout the film (his handiwork is usually displayed onscreen); Marta, fittingly enough in an address to the camera, claims that she is comprehensively 'photographing' the world and its evils with her eyes, in an attempt to absorb and thereby eliminate it. This conceit could be seen as metaphorically asserting the subversive power of representation and thus as implying the value of intellectual engagement with the world; it also suggests that the protagonists' self-induced madness might itself represent the instructive 'absorption' or imitation of the grotesque absurdities of society.

The representation of madness is in fact also made subject to that central ambivalence, the oscillation between escapist and 'documentarist' tendencies. The incorporation of mentally handicapped children and adults into the film's self-reflexive prologue, blurring the boundaries between the film crew and the institution inmates, entreats us to read these individuals (alongside the infantile and 'feminine' personas that literally assume Jakubisko's voice) as directorial representatives, alter egos of the artist figure and models to be lauded for their exemplary 'clear vision' (according to Martin Kaňuch, for this film Jakubisko 'allowed mentally handicapped children to join his crew and handle the camera').[36] References to the cultural iconography of madness also sometimes

---

34. Hames, *The Czechoslovak New Wave*, p. 218.
35. Jakubisko, quoted in ibid.; Jakubisko in Liehm, *Closely Watched Films*, p. 359.
36. Kaňuch, in Hames, *The Cinema of Central Europe*, p. 168.

point in this direction. Yorick re-christens Marta 'Sibyl', an allusion that refers back to the identification of madness with prophecy and preternatural insight, the telling of truths in a cryptic tongue. (Jakubisko's fragmentary and sometimes perplexing cinematic discourse, coded as 'feminine' in the film's prologue, could itself be considered 'sibylline'.) Most importantly, the name Yorick, which is of course the name of the dead jester in *Hamlet* (and is also, significantly, a diminutive of Jakubisko's own first name, Juraj), alludes to the tradition, copiously evoked in Shakespeare, of the jester or 'holy fool' who offers satirical commentary and privileged insight. But these allusions might be seen as implying yet another tension, this time between the urge to protest and a hermetic seclusion or non-engagement. Yorick's elderly landlord plummets to earth wearing a makeshift parachute that bears the slogan 'The word is the weapon of the powerless'. That slogan suggests the idea of language, of expression, as incendiary communication. Yet the language of madness might be considered as radically uncommunicative, politically redundant in its privacy or incoherence: the message fails, as the messenger falls.

For all those tensions and ambiguities, it is undeniable that the film powerfully articulates the feeling that escape constitutes the only feasible and bearable response to a world of horror. Surrealism and the counterculture yoked madness and subjectivity to political revolution and an ebullient utopianism; in many ways Jakubisko's film links these things with a posture of despair or resignation. To the extent that history is again presented here as an irredeemable cycle of violence and oppression, Jakubisko reinforces the validity of the sense that 'foolishness' can only ever represent an indulgence, a retreat, a minimal and marginal breach of the prevailing logic. At one point Yorick offers an eloquent rationale for his 'project':

> Everything which is subject to the law of eternal changes, to the law of power, everything beside yourself, is vanity. So return into yourself. If they have demolished your house, start to build it again – but in your soul … Build a house inside, live in it and you'll find happiness. They will call you a fool. But don't pay attention, if you are fine. You are fine because you are free. You are free because you are a fool.

This passage is rich with meanings, all of which, however, suggest an essentially defeatist or quietistic stance towards the world and ascribe a function to the inner life that is consolatory rather than revolutionary. The description of the external world of history and politics as 'vanity', an obvious echo of the Book of Ecclesiastes, can be seen to proffer a vision of life as something absurd, senseless, cruel and mad, a vision thus running contrary to a modernist conception of history in terms of progress and constant improvement. Vanity is perhaps also what inheres in the attempt to change that reality. In itself, that

Figure 5.5 *Birds, Orphans and Fools* (*Vtáčkovia, siroty a blázni*, Juraj Jakubisko, 1969)
Author: Vladimír Vavrek, source: Photoarchive Slovak Film Institute (©).

vision would be a sufficient injunction to will the world out of existence, yet the reference to vanity has the additional meaning that the exterior world is insubstantial, ephemeral and illusory[37] (the fact that Yorick wears a monk's cowl while making this speech suggests how Jakubisko's use of allusion is always both serious and playful). In contrast to the world's inessentiality, the self or 'soul' is substantial and real: at least those houses built in the soul are less likely to be demolished than real houses. The injunction that we build such houses represents the insistence that we should compensate for material deprivations and sufferings with the riches of the inner life, and also implies that the surest barriers against the world are internal rather than external. We attain freedom in foolishness either because our dependence on the outer world for our happiness is relinquished, or because, as already suggested, that world now ceases to trouble our consciousness. Madness, as a 'drug for life'[38] (in Jakubisko's description), is at once hallucinogen and painkiller.

These remarks, apparently supportive of a reorientation towards subjectivity, lifestyle and even spiritual values, could be linked with postmodernism and perhaps also New Age tendencies (the suggestion of an insubstantial or illusory outer world seems particular attuned to the latter). The turn towards self-

---

37.   David Noel Freedman, Allen C. Myers, Astrid B. Beck (eds), *Eerdmans Dictionary of the Bible* (Grand Rapids: William B. Eerdmans Publishing Co, 2000), p. 367.

38.   Jakubisko in Liehm, *Closely Watched Films*, p. 359.

cultivation and spirituality is often and easily seen as 'the fallen progeny of the Sixties',[39] the substitution of an attempted (and failed) transformation of the world with the transformation of the self. As has already been noted, the suggestion here of such a turn inwards is presented with some sympathy, and while Yorick's notion of building a house in one's soul might evoke, from a contemporary perspective, the hackneyed language of New Age self-help, at the point of the film's making his sentiments are still fresh, and this account generally retains a poignancy and lyrical vitality. If the self is to be a site for the building of houses, the real house in which the protagonists live all too readily offers a model of the inner self, especially of the Surrealist, imaginatively liberated kind. A rough-edged, folk-art approximation of Magritte or Escher, this dream domain gives concrete form to an imagination believed to represent sanctuary. Yet the house's outlandish or Surreal sense of permeability is itself problematic: while that permeability suggests both the postmodernist refusal of binary distinctions and that breakdown of boundaries between Self and Other that is, for Laing, part of the experience of madness, it could also be seen to affirm the impossibility of erecting an absolute barrier between self and world.

The antics of *Birds, Orphans and Fools* lack the collective character of the festivities in *The Deserter and the Nomads*, and what might most forcefully indicate that the 'mad' lifestyle is more an escape than a prelude to revolution is the absence of any broader affiliations or significant communal engagements. In *See You in Hell, My Friends!*, Jakubisko's subsequent film and a virtual retread of *Birds, Orphans*, the protagonists break out of the seclusion of their hippie-ish idyll in order to redistribute money to the poor. But the quixotic attempt to extend the 'revolution' outwards and upwards, into the realms of political or economic organization, is exceptional, and of course fails miserably (the would-be beneficiaries prove hostile, and the protagonists are pursued, in a Keystone Cops-style chase, by policemen and war-whooping priests). If Yorick, in *Birds, Orphans*, identifies with a political figure such as Štefánik (he even pretends at one point that he is Štefánik's son), then this is perhaps to imply that such figures are themselves fools, and that political intervention comprises the ultimate foolishness: conversely, the will to be a fool is (as Jakubisko himself argues) all too rational given the nature of this world.[40] And yet, for all that political gestures seem futile and that the film's protagonists appear to reject engagement, Yorick's antics do prove provocative or threatening to the authorities, for he is arrested and thrown into prison for no apparent reason other than his unconventional dress and clownish behaviour. Of course, the world of the late 1960s (and especially that part of it controlled by neo-Stalinist bureaucracies) was very different from that of today, lacking both the endless multiplicity of 'lifestyle choices' and the knowledge of just

---

39.   DeKoven, *Utopia Limited*, p. 255.
40.   Jakubisko, quoted in Hames, *The Czechoslovak New Wave*, p. 218.

how easily those choices and their subversive implications could be recontained by the system. In that context such a conspicuous example of alternative living does represent a 'political' gesture of sorts, even if it is a minuscule and ultimately futile one.

The futility of attempts to enact change within the wider political arena is perhaps implicit from the outset, yet the attempt to construct a new lifestyle even on an individual basis fails dramatically too. The protagonists' *ménage à trois*, which derives at once from the embrace of free love and from Yorick's commitment to 'sharing' Marta, selflessly, with his friend, is complicated by Yorick's sexual jealousy. Andrej and Marta eventually become a conventional couple, eased into this by the absence of the imprisoned Yorick, and Andrej starts to have his photographs published. If the attempt to change the world is utopian (in the more pejorative sense), the attempt to change one's identity and cultural values perhaps also has a utopian dimension, not least because the reality one seeks to escape is already, inevitably, part of oneself: Yorick remarks at one point that in attempting to flee the world, he has really been fleeing himself. Yorick's final murderous act, ironically given that it is in part a reaction to the very failure of his ideals, suggests how the commitment to a new mode of life has not vanquished an all too worldly capacity for violence. Shortly before she and her unborn child are killed by Yorick, Marta comments that Yorick has 'lost the courage' to sustain his madness. However, again ironically, Yorick's horrific reaction to the failure of his project suggests something like an emergent psychosis, the onset of a form of madness seldom emphasized among the Surrealist and countercultural eulogies to irrationality, 'inner voyages' and the casting off of social inhibitions. At the same time this violence evokes the dark excesses of the counterculture itself at the heady turn of the 1960s (Marta's grotesque murder recalls, no doubt purely coincidentally, the Sharon Tate murder of the same year). Thus, despite its emerging from an environment and perspective far afield of California or Paris, *Birds, Orphans and Fools* joins that list of contemporaneous films (a list including Arthur Penn's *Alice's Restaurant* (1969), Dennis Hopper's *Easy Rider* (1969), the Maysles brothers' *Gimme Shelter* (1970), Jacques Rivette's *Out 1: noli me tangere* (1971) and Jean Eustache's *The Mother and the Whore* (*La Maman et la putain*, 1974)) that somehow stay true to the counterculture while lamenting its impossibility.

Poor Yorick, unable truly to separate himself from the world, finally enacts his literal exemption from it. This grotesque suicide, which has Yorick attempting at once to strangle, immolate and drown himself, evokes political martyrdoms both conscious and retroactive: the self-immolation has obvious echoes of Jan Palach's suicide-protest against the Warsaw Pact invasion (though Jakubisko has since claimed that this reference was unintentional), as well as the iconic images of the burning Buddhist monks of South Vietnam, while a statue of Štefánik, attached to a rope around Yorick's neck, is used both to choke and sink him. Once again there is an apparent tension here, for the elaborately ritualistic, referentially over-egged nature of the suicide suggests a communicative and thus purposeful act, even though the suicide itself represents the acknowledgement of failure and futility. Moreover, there is no one around, barring the viewer, to witness this suicide: it suggests, like much else in Jakubisko's cinema, an excess of gesture over function, the divorce of signification from effect (Jakubisko's early films, which were all immediately banned, were themselves signals or performances sent into the void, hence perhaps a certain melancholy sympathy for fruitless gestures). The conceit of Yorick's being dragged down by Štefánik's statue reminds us of the generally downward direction that things take in the film, and constitutes the most vivid expression of the impossibility of flight. Standing at once for the flight from the world's cruel and oppressive logic and the flight of fancy or fantasy (if not the Deleuzian line of flight), the motif of flight is a recurrent one throughout the film, yet flight, literal or figurative, is never really achieved: the real birds in the film are more often shown confined, captured or endangered than in flight, the landlord plummets to the ground, and Štefánik, one of the film's constant reference points, had his plane shot down. To this extent *Birds, Orphans and Fools* is a bleaker work than *Party in the Botanical Garden*, a film equally Icarian in its concerns but one in which the transcendent bliss of sexual love enables people to defy gravity.

Yet despite the explicit pessimism present in how the film's events actually transpire, it is hard to see *Birds, Orphans and Fools* as entirely pessimistic or unremittingly bleak. For whatever reason the savage violence of the ending never quite registers as strongly as it should do (at least for this possibly jaded viewer), and the film never seems to summon itself in the memory as an especially bleak or dark work. While Jakubisko's announcement in the opening voiceover that '[t]his story has a tragic end' could be seen as a way of showing how that ending is predestined, latent within the protagonists' project from the start, it arguably also defuses the shock of those events. (It may be worth noting that, in the very last moments of the film, birds are glimpsed flying over the river in which Yorick has drowned: mordant irony or subtle message of hope?) Moreover, the earlier adventures of the three friends provoke an elation that is not easily extinguished. The film's exuberance is not simply a matter of formal flamboyance (as it was, to a large extent, in *Deserter*) but also of a sense of love, joy and comradeship. That earlier *joie de vivre* prompts a spirit of support or encouragement, at least the desire that things might somehow work out, if not as revolutionary change (which is more or less ruled out here) then as that postmodern 'utopia limited' of alternative living or transformed subjectivity. In addition, we should take heed of the film's prologue, which not only contains an obscurely optimistic dimension ('there's no end without a beginning'), but also insists that we be wary of absolute or totalizing judgements, that apparently solid interpretations may prove reversible: to cite those opening words, Jakubisko's world is violent and cruel, though not, perhaps, completely, and a message of apparent hopelessness might turn out to affirm just the opposite.

The mix of exuberant life and grisly death in Jakubisko's films is apt because, at a deeper level, the films are at once expectant and funereal, brimming with a vivid, fresh life and marked by deathly foreboding. The mix of folk influences, avant-garde aesthetics, affective counterpoint and eclectic reference herald a bold new direction for the New Wave at the same time as the films intimate, implicitly or explicitly, the New Wave's burial or terminus. If there is anything that should symbolize the end of that hiatus, and the resumption of Jakubisko's radical remoulding of New Wave aesthetics, it is the 1990 completion of *See You in Hell, My Friends!*, a film which Jakubisko began in 1970 but which the authorities prevented him from then completing. The jubilance of the end of cultural repression is illustrated directly, when the protagonists of the latter film are released from the confining, purgatorial 'red ark' that clearly represents the totalizing Communist regime: as Jakubisko's film is itself recovered from decreed non-existence, so the New Wave is, supposedly, brought back from the dead. Perhaps the aesthetic experiments will continue, and perhaps, whatever the flaws and horrors of global capitalism, it will be easier now to live the 'utopia limited' of alternative lifestyles. But the promise of such a continuation, at least as far as Jakubisko's work itself is concerned, proved somewhat false: the familiar aesthetics – just like *See You in Hell*'s aged performers when compared with images of their younger selves from the same film – seem tired and ravaged in the later work, while the playful nudity and embrace of free love in *Birds, Orphans and Fools* have turned into the vulgarized sexuality of the recent *Post coitum* (2004). Yet Jakubisko's early films are as striking and fresh as they ever were, and while their Surrealist stylings and countercultural concerns are redolent of a specific time and atmosphere, such qualities as their political cynicism and their revelation and (qualified) valorization of Otherness also make them relevant in a contemporary context.

CHAPTER 6

Back to Utopia: Returns of the Repressed in Jaromil Jireš's *Valerie and Her Week of Wonders* (1970)

Nezval, Normalization and the Meaning of the Gothic

Jaromil Jireš's *Valerie and Her Week of Wonders* is adapted from a 1935 novel by Vítězslav Nezval, a writer whose transformation from bohemian experimentalist to exemplary literary representative of Stalinism, while not unique, seems as abrupt and remarkable as the shape-shifting of *Valerie*'s protagonists. The greatest poet of the Czech interwar avant-garde, Nezval founded the Czech Surrealist Group in 1934, only to try and disband it four years later in a display of his allegiance to Communist cultural and political orthodoxy. After February 1948, Nezval established himself as, in Alfred French's words, the 'official poet of the regime',[1] embracing Socialist Realism and composing such works of quasi-propaganda as *Stalin* (1949), written on the occasion of the Soviet leader's birthday, and *Song of Peace* (*Zpěv míru*, 1950). Although he regained some of the lyricism and iconoclasm of his earlier work in the last few years of his life, this 'national artist' (as he was designated in 1953) would remain, long after his death in 1958, one of the most lauded figures in Czech letters. *Valerie and Her Week of Wonders*, however, is unmistakably the work of the early, avant-garde Nezval. Guiseppe Dierna even calls this novel '[p]erhaps the most surrealistic of all Nezval's fiction'.[2] With its perverse eroticism and fantastic, mystifying narrative, this avant-garde variation on the traditions of Gothic melodrama and the fairy tale represents everything that is, from an official point of view, most objectionable: a 1980 Czech monograph on Nezval excises *Valerie* from a bibliography of his

1. French, *Czech Writers and Politics: 1945–1969*, p. 102.
2. Guiseppe Dierna, 'On Valerie, Nezval, Max Ernst, and Collages: Variations on a Theme', translated by Jed Slast, in Vítězslav Nezval, *Valerie and Her Week of Wonders*, translated by David Short (Prague: Twisted Spoon, 2005), p. 199.

works altogether.[3] Discussing Jireš's film adaptation, Josef Škvorecký recalls with relish the critical contortions necessary for such Party mouthpieces as the notorious Jan Kliment, a critic duty-bound both to condemn the film and somehow absolve Nezval of any blame for its 'faults'. Predictably, Kliment attacked the film as 'too erotic and totally incomprehensible'; at the same time, as Škvorecký explains, Kliment

> masterfully by-passed the treacherous shoals of the fact that the novel was written by the great Communist, Nezval, by pointing out that 'the revered poet wrote the book at a time when he was overcoming the feeling of loneliness … in the year when he visited the Soviet Union. This greatly affected him.'[4]

The attempt to ascribe the novel to personal melancholy suggests the association, typical for Communist authorities and their cultural representatives, between modernist art (especially Surrealism) and psychic or emotional disorders, morbidity and sickness. These comments also imply, ludicrously, that this novel represents a mere aberration within an otherwise, by official standards, unblemished literary career. It can be surmised that one reason for Jireš's decision to adapt this particular book was precisely to undermine the stolid official construct of an artistically and ideologically acceptable Nezval and to restore rightful attention to the suppressed avant-garde period of the poet's career.

Despite Kliment's absurd dismissal of this book and the general neglect that it has suffered until very recently, the novel may be seen as one of the most significant works in Nezval's artistic development. Written only a year after the Czech group's founding, it is a quintessential example of Nezval's Surrealist period and represents an uncommonly successful incorporation of Surrealist preoccupations into narrative form. The book's neglect among critics, even those sympathetic to both Nezval and Surrealism, is perhaps due on the one hand to the belated publication (*Valerie* was not published until 1945) that deprived it of its rightful context of reception and a sense of its true place in the Surrealist chronology, and on the other to its conspicuous plundering of the tropes of Gothic fiction and the romantic novelette, genres traditionally considered lowbrow, sub-literary, even morally suspect. As Nezval reveals in the novel's preface, *Valerie* is a tribute to the 'old tales' and 'romantic books' that entranced him in his youth, and a sense of self-aware homage is evident in Nezval's mimicry of the novelette's formal conventions, from the contrivance of the self-contained, incident-packed chapters, each with their own shocking climax, to the inclusion of

---

3.   Miroslav Macháček, *Vítězslav Nezval* (Prague: Horizont, 1980).
4.   Škvorecký, *All the Bright Young Men and Women*, p. 190.

accompanying illustrations (although these frequently enigmatic images, actually pre-existent illustrations culled from a selection of children's stories, also represent as much a subversion of this tradition as the seemingly irrelevant and non-descript photographs that accompany André Breton's great Surrealist novel *Nadja*).[5] Yet this is not simply a matter of stylistic pastiche, nor merely one of childhood nostalgia (in any case hardly an innocent quantity in the work of a Surrealist). The damned terrain of horror and melodrama was a key source of inspiration for the Czech Surrealists, as it had been for the French group. Only in 'folk' books, Nezval asserts in 1936, does 'the miracle of the imagination' still hold good: the mysterious and marvellous thus border the 'laughable and valueless'.[6] In the Gothic tradition, perhaps above all, are to be found those subversive qualities which Surrealist interventions into the genre would bring provocatively to the surface. For Karel Teige, 'the romantic fondness for phantoms and scenes of horror' provides a means of 'disturbing the moral order', as such morbid poetry resists the bourgeois equation of 'Beauty' with 'Good'.[7] Teige's comments indicate, if only implicitly, his appreciation of the psychoanalytic significance of such horrors, their ability to illuminate those repressed infantile wishes and perverse desires that contravene bourgeois propriety. It is not by chance that the Czech avant-garde's newfound passion for macabre fantasy, replacing the carefree Poetist passions of circuses and slapstick comedy, coincided with its acceptance of Surrealism, an edifice built on Freudian foundations.

On the other hand, various critics have suggested that the turn towards morbid, Gothic imagery amongst the Czech avant-garde in the mid-1930s is an oblique reflection of the looming spectres of Nazism and Stalinism, and the constancy of such imagery has distinguished the Czechs from Surrealist movements in countries that have not endured decades of occupation and totalitarian rule. From this perspective it is interesting to reflect on a possible source of the 'feeling of loneliness' which, according to Jan Kliment, prompted Nezval to write *Valerie*. Kliment observes that this feeling arose in the year when Nezval 'visited the Soviet Union', and indeed the date of *Valerie's* completion comes only a year after the 1934 Soviet Writers' Congress, held in Moscow, in which Nezval participated. His experience at the Congress was, to say the least, frustrating: Alfred French writes, 'Nezval found with dismay that his remarks were misrepresented in the Soviet press, and his long defence of

5.   Vítězslav Nezval, *Valerie a týden divů* (Prague: Odeon, 1970), p. 7; Dierna, 'On Valerie, Nezval, Max Ernst, and Collages', in Nezval, *Valerie and Her Week of Wonders*, p. 200.

6.   Nezval, quoted in František Dryje, 'The Force of Imagination', translated by Valerie Mason, in Hames, *Dark Alchemy*, p. 149; Nezval, *Valerie a týden divů*, p. 7.

7.   Teige, quoted in Dierna, 'On Valerie, Nezval, Max Ernst, and Collages', in Nezval, *Valerie and Her Week of Wonders*, pp. 202–3.

Figure 6.1 Valerie (Jaroslava Schallerová) in *Valerie and Her Week of Wonders* (*Valerie a týden divů*, Jaromil Jireš, 1970) ©Ateliéry Bonton Zlín, reproduced courtesy of Second Run DVD.

surrealism was totally omitted from the report on the conference.'[8] Nezval had evidently hoped for a spirit of openness and tolerance on the part of the Soviets, a closure of intellectual ranks increasingly desirable in the context of emerging fascism. The Congress offered only confirmation of the regime's new dogmatism. At the risk of unverifiable speculation, it is easy, in the light of Kliment's unwitting and, for him, unfortunate connection, to interpret Nezval's 'loneliness' as his sense of isolation from his orthodox colleagues in Moscow, or even, his later conversion or capitulation notwithstanding, as his alienation from the increasing repressiveness of Soviet Communism. And if the vampires and villains, rape and treachery, of Nezval's Gothic novel can be seen as a response to revolutionary disappointment and fears for future liberty at home and abroad, then what of Jireš's film? Jireš, himself an apparently sincere, even credulous, Communist Party member, made *Valerie* shortly after the crushing of Prague Spring liberalization by the Warsaw Pact tanks, and during the first stages of Normalization.[9] Jireš has claimed that film was a long-cherished project, yet this still leaves us free to speculate on his reasons for making *Valerie* precisely when he did.

However, it would be mistaken to read either the novel or the film simply as a dark, demoralized reflection of current or incipient repression. Nezval's novel is a lyrical and characteristically playful work that ultimately appeals to a Bretonian (and Poetist) principle of utopian synthesis. As we must remember, it was the postwar Czech Surrealists who explicitly renounced an active utopianism: while this later incarnation of the movement never abandoned, and arguably intensified, the moral purpose of Surrealism, its perspective was 'miserabilist', pessimistic, fixated on the twisted-mirror irrationality of a politically enslaving present. In retaining, indeed enhancing, the lyricism and utopianism of Nezval's novel, Jireš thus aligns himself more closely with the pre-war, classic traditions of Surrealism than with the movement's living current. This is not to imply that the film is, conversely, an academic exercise in 'dead' Surrealism, a museum exhibit of an extinct artistic genre: as will be argued throughout this chapter, the film's utopianism seems to feed off the radical culture of the Sixties, in Czechoslovakia and elsewhere, as much as off memories of the interwar years. Far from merely being a matter of ersatz

---

8. Alfred French, *The Poets of Prague* (London: Oxford University Press, 1969), p. 107.
9. From Pavel Juráček's diary, 1965: "Jarda [*sic*] Jireš goes around Prague and insists that *Bloudění* was not at all banned for ideological reasons … [A]bout all the banned and scrutinised films [Jireš] indulgently and on the whole dedicatedly insists that they are banned and scrutinised for some sort of practical reason; they say he does not know of any case where someone would today start something against culture from a Party or power-related position. However to show himself as a fighter, he set out recently to the Castle to see Novotný, with the intention to explain to him that things are happening which should not be happening.' (Juráček, *Deník 1959–1974*, p. 350).

elements, transposed directly from Nezval's novel, Surrealism, and Poetism, are integral to the film's own formal practices, the uniquely cinematic processes by which meaning is created, or withheld. Like many of the most interesting film adaptations, Jireš's *Valerie* is arguably as much an interpretation and extension of its source, a reading of the novel's 'latent content'. It is no more an innocently nostalgic revisiting of an 'old book' than was Nezval's original, with Jireš emphasizing the novel's most troubling and subversive aspects and tailoring its world to the political and cultural struggles of the present. If the film is not a work of 'pure' Surrealism by the standards of Effenberger or Švankmajer, it nonetheless fulfils the demand that Surrealism always be contemporary in its concerns and oppositional in its viewpoint.

Freudian Certainties: Fantasy as Phantasy

In the preface to his novel, Nezval writes of his 'love' for the 'mystery of old tales, superstitions and romantic books', which 'flitted before my eyes and which declined to entrust to me their content'.[10] What is the nature of this mystery, that secret content that entrances the juvenile reader even as it remains obscure? And how does Nezval's revisionist homage to these old books bring that content to light? As I stated earlier, the Czech avant-garde's interest in Gothic horror accompanied, and perhaps even partially conditioned, its redenomination as the Czech Surrealist Group, a transformation that indicates a serious engagement with psychoanalysis not present in Poetism. For Nezval himself, the appeal of the Gothic or romance genre clearly derives in part from its evocation of childhood, not only because, as *Valerie*'s preface implies, such stories informed the imaginative landscape of Nezval's own infancy, but also, in general terms, by means of the genre's dependence on the 'outmoded'. As well as frequently adopting archaic styles of narration and presentation (Nezval recalls those books 'written with Gothic script'), romances commonly locate their stories in the past (even in contemporary incarnations of the genre, such as the Gothic horror film), or against an historic backdrop of ancient cemeteries and crumbling castles (Breton's 'romantic ruins').[11] In an essay on F.W. Murnau's *Nosferatu* (1922), the most celebrated example of Gothic horror in cinema, Nezval writes of the presence of 'obsolete objects ... capable of touching our memories and our dreams'.[12] The outmoded can provide a vehicle for utopian projection in its suggestion of a historically distinct 'structure of feeling' – Nezval does not recommend

10. Nezval, *Valerie a týden divů*, p. 7.
11. Breton, *Manifestoes of Surrealism*, p. 16.
12. Nezval, quoted in Dierna, 'On Valerie, Nezval, Max Ernst, and Collages', in Nezval, *Valerie and Her Week of Wonders*, p. 205.

his 'black novel' for those 'afraid to look beyond the boundaries of "today"'[13] – but, equally importantly, it can evoke the lost paradise of early childhood: those pre-modern, 'artisanal' objects over which Nezval enthuses are directly inscribed with the body, 'related in the psychic register to the maternal',[14] to the plenitude of the infant's original relationship with its mother. While the outmoded has a relatively subdued presence in Nezval's novel itself (although we should note the fetishistic use of such outmoded objects as Valerie's oil lamp), Jireš's film comprises a musty treasure trove of sensuous antiques, from the rich décor of Valerie's house, with its elaborate furnishings, dolls and religious woodcuts, to the immense found object of Slavonice, the exquisitely preserved mediaeval town in which the film was shot.

The intimate connection between Gothic fantasy and psychoanalytic phenomena should hardly be a surprising one. After all, the English Gothic tradition finds its greatest German equivalent in the fantasies of E.T.A. Hoffmann, whose story 'The Sandman' (1816) helped Freud formulate his well-known definition of the 'uncanny'; this concept, as we shall see, has a specific relevance for *Valerie* as both novel and film. A psychoanalytic approach can be easily and fruitfully applied not only to the explicit, and perverse, sexuality of the genre's more notorious examples (such as Matthew Gregory Lewis's *The Monk* (1796), an important model for Nezval's work), but also to the genre's characteristic motifs, even to its very architecture: the innumerable underground passageways, crypts, vaults and generally tortuous, enigmatic spaces with which Gothic literature presents us suggest the secret, subterranean dimensions of the Freudian self, whether or not these locations comprise the literal scene of sexual transgressions or dreamlike encounters. The Surrealist nature of Nezval's novel amounts primarily to his attempt to make the psychoanalytic significance of these generic tropes explicit, to denude the Gothic of its illusory innocence. The story is framed by an explicitly sexual premise: seventeen-year-old Valerie's first period (her age is changed, wisely, to thirteen in the film). That first delicate spider's thread of blood,[15] heralding the blossoming of a previously latent sexuality, serves to situate Valerie on the threshold between childhood and adulthood. The overtly and anxiously sexual aspects intermittent throughout these daydreams could be seen as announcing the beginnings of adult sexual awareness, and betraying Valerie's sense of incipient womanhood: 'childish' daydreaming thus intimates the accession to adulthood and 'maturity'. As this chapter will show, both the novel and Jireš's film offer an examination of what it means to become an adult, an exposure of the shortcomings of 'maturity' and an affirmation of that which is usually castigated as childish.

---

13. Nezval, *Valerie a týden divů*, p. 7.
14. Foster, *Compulsive Beauty*, p. 164.
15. Nezval, *Valerie a týden divů*, p. 13.

If indeed we interpret the novel's action as a series of dreams or phantasies, much of its narrative appears as a highly 'realistic' approximation of the family romances that, according to Freud, occupy a large part of the imaginative life of children and adolescents.[16] These fantastic scenarios devised around 'the topic of family relations' originate in the child's critical attitude towards its parents:

> the child's imagination becomes engaged in the task of getting free from the parents of whom he now has a low opinion and of replacing them by others, who, as a rule, are of higher social standing.[17]

As a form of imaginative escape from one's parents rooted in the need ultimately to liberate oneself from their authority, the family romance can be seen as rehearsing the individual's attainment of mature independence.[18] The evocation of that psychic 'genre' thus further establishes Valerie's place at the border between childhood and adulthood. Yet the preponderance of regal or well-born young heroes and heroines in romances, Gothic stories and fairy tales would suggest that the traces of family romance are already endemic to these traditions; as Freud himself argued, in such stock narratives as that of the foundling ultimately revealed to be of royal blood, the links with childhood imagining are even stronger. Nezval's novel itself comprises a long, tantalizing riddle about parentage: was Valerie's real father the universally renowned, handsome and charismatic bishop; Tchoř the vampiric property owner and magistrate (whose own identity is forever in flux); or a humble forester? Here, however, the issue is never satisfactorily resolved, with every new, seemingly definitive account of Valerie's family history proffered only to be contradicted by the next. The narrative itself simulates the shifts, discrepancies and loose ends of primal phantasy, as though the professional storyteller had surrendered control to his pubertal heroine. Of course, this is key to the distinction between Nezval's novel and other, less self-conscious romances. Depriving his Gothic stock-in-trades of fiction's coherence or finesse, Nezval exposes the childhood psycho-dramas at the heart of the well-worn generic tropes. Valerie's dream scenarios are presented in all their bare-faced psychic expedience, 'authored' first and foremost by the needs and wishes that determine them.

Freud observes that many children, upon the attainment of sexual knowledge during adolescence, imagine erotic situations that involve their

---

16. The term 'phantasy' specifically refers to the activities and products of the Freudian primary process and thus distinguishes itself from the broader concept 'fantasy'.

17. Sigmund Freud, 'Family Romances', in *The Freud Reader*, edited by Peter Gay (London: Vintage, 1995), p. 299.

18. Ibid., p. 298; Margaret R. Higonnet, *Borderwork: Feminist Engagements with Comparative Literature* (Cornell: Cornell University Press, 1994), p. 169.

mothers, including situations of 'secret infidelity' and 'secret love-affairs'.[19] These phantasies are explained as a form of imaginary 'revenge' for those children who had been 'punished by their parents for sexual naughtiness'.[20] Nezval's story renders such feats of imaginative transformation as literal transformations, and suggests the real motivations behind the improbable events: it is such juvenile vengeance that transforms Valerie's stern, puritanical grandmother, the central 'maternal' figure in Valerie's existence and the story's psychic scheme, into the lustful Elsa. Similarly, as Tanya Krzywińska notes, the continuous and, in narrative terms, unsatisfying fluctuation of Orlík between the roles of brother, half-brother and potential suitor to Valerie simulates the tricks and subterfuges of incestuous phantasy: the relationship of brother to sister is, in Krzywińska's words, 'subject to disavowal' and the obfuscation of Nezval's narrative, just as the 'young phantasy-builder' fictively erases the bonds of kinship with a coveted sibling and thereby, temporarily, sanctions a forbidden desire.[21]

The topography of the Gothic genre is comparably 'psychoanalysed'. Beneath the bourgeois domain of Valerie's household there is revealed a suite of rooms and vaults, baroquely decorated and, in typical Gothic fashion, initially accessed via an underground passageway. These underground regions are the haunts, quite literally, of Tchoř, the story's troublingly ambiguous monster and villain who offers both the threat and promise of an initiation into dark secrets. These regions are explicitly identified from the beginning as the locus of repressed sexual desires, as Tchoř's lair initially provides the vantage point from which Valerie witnesses her grandmother's erotically charged self-abasement in front of Father Gracian, her sometime lover. As well as revealing the secret erotic, indeed sadomasochistic, desires of outwardly respectable characters, this spectacle also comprises the first of the story's several, barely disguised stagings of the Freudian 'primal scene', the infant's phantasy of witnessing its parents copulating. Only in the most sensational examples of the Gothic genre, such as *The Monk*, are the associations between spatial and psychic depths, literal and figurative darkness, secret hiding places and the secret self, as emphatic as they are here.

Nezval's knowing deployment of space also enables us to read the novel in terms of Freud's definition of the uncanny. Of course, the English word 'uncanny' is a translation from Freud's original term *unheimlich*, which literally means 'unhomely', 'unfamiliar'. It is from this literal meaning that the

---

19. Freud, 'Family Romances', in *The Freud Reader*, p. 299.
20. Ibid., p. 300.
21. Tanya Krzywińska, 'Transgression, transformation and titillation: Jaromil Jireš's *Valerie a týden divů* (*Valerie and Her Week of Wonders*, 1970)', *Kinoeye*, Vol. 3, Issue 9, 15 Sept 2003 (http://www.kinoeye.org/03/09/krzywinska09.php) (retrieved 12 January 2008); Freud, 'Family Romances', in *The Freud Reader*, p. 300.

concept's true significance derives: as Freud explained, '[t]he negative prefix *un-* is the indicator of repression', so that the uncanny really comprises what was once intimately familiar but has been 'made strange' by repression.[22] Freud concurs with Friedrich Schelling's description of the uncanny as 'something that should have remained hidden and has come into the open'.[23] Once familiar phenomena, from repressed infantile desires to the universal first 'home' of the maternal body, are re-encountered in uncanny apparitions and dreams. The dark 'kingdom' beneath Valerie's house, unknown to Valerie herself until Tchoř reveals it to her, literally represents the home made 'unhomely', the local and intimate made disturbingly unfamiliar by the antiquated décor and the sinister presence of Tchoř. The film's parent figures, representative of those who should be most familiar to us, are literally transformed into horrifying incarnations of dark desire. As with the exploration of family romance, the connection that has been made between the uncanny as a psychoanalytic category and the conventions of horror and Gothic fantasy is here established in advance. The erotic dimension, customarily 'converted into fear' through the workings of primary repression,[24] here peeps through the façade of horror: hence the refusal of that façade to take itself entirely seriously, that hint of feigned fright or camp masquerade accompanying moments of the greatest threat.

If Nezval's novel strikes us as a sustained exploration of phantasy and its mechanisms, variations and recurrences, it is nonetheless important, to paraphrase Freud's celebrated remarks to Salvador Dalí, to emphasize the presence here of the conscious as much as the unconscious. Breton's early technique of 'psychic automatism' has sometimes been misconstrued as the one 'authentic' form of Surrealist artistic production, as though the original Surrealists had sought in their endeavours nothing more – or less – than the unmediated channelling of the psyche. Yet this claim belies the high degree of artifice and calculation involved in many classic Surrealist literary and artistic works. Despite its apparently freewheeling narrative structure, this novel, as with the majority of Nezval's writings, is a work of immense formal and stylistic control (evident, for instance, in the self-consciously poetic language and convoluted syntax of the final chapter), which distributes phantasy scenarios and psychic traumas throughout the story in a manner that is knowing and flagrant. Nezval himself described the novel as a 'free, concretely irrational psychic collage of everything that belongs to the nether regions of

---

22. Sigmund Freud, 'The Uncanny', *The Uncanny*, translated by David McLintock (New York: Penguin, 2003), p. 151.
23. Friedrich Wilhelm Joseph von Schelling, cited in Freud, 'The Uncanny', *The Uncanny*, p. 148.
24. Ibid., p. 147.

our unconscious'.[25] The crucial part of this description is the phrase '*our* unconscious', indicating that *Valerie's* purpose is less literary self-analysis or 'psychobiography' than the depiction of transpersonal psychic conditions.[26]

The role of conscious intervention in the novel is worth pointing out because David Wilson, in the *Monthly Film Bulletin*, has attacked Jireš's film for offering a 'mere illustration of ordered disorder'.[27] Wilson objects that the film lacks the genuine spontaneity of dream consciousness and resembles rather 'a dream recalled in retrospect'.[28] That Wilson considers this a fault suggests that, for him, the film's very polish and artistry represent a betrayal of its Surrealist pretensions. Yet, as previously argued, by such criteria many classic Surrealist works, including Nezval's novel, would also have to be judged failures. In fact, in discussing either novel or film, it is less profitable to focus on the possible 'authenticity' of the depicted dreams than on the assumed general relevance of psychoanalytic concepts. It is this assumption, more than any insight into personal psychic fixations or traumas, that helps give Surrealist art its subversive power. The relative familiarity of a number of the film's dream symbols (feathers, apples, water), as well as the recurrent phallic and sexual imagery, suggest a concern to emphasize the paradigmatic quality of these phantasies.

Jireš respects the novel's carefully maintained ambiguity of time and place. Though the film's predominantly Art Nouveau décor might suggest some time around the turn of the century, this seems ultimately more a matter of strikingly coordinated visual design than of literal temporal location. The film is thus faithful to its fairy tale provenance, maintaining the air of an ethereal neverland neither modern nor anchored in any specific part of the past ('once upon a time', '*to bylo tenkrát*'), yet this temporal–geographical limbo also lends a universal, or mythic, quality to Valerie's phantasies: the fairy tale as fable of the id. The conclusion of both the novel and the film situates the protagonists in a natural world as ancient and eternal as the unconscious itself. In these respects Jireš's film was far more subversive in its immediate socio-political context than was the novel in its own context, at once subordinating the standard historical and class determinations of identity (though this is not to suggest that the film cannot be read in political terms) and giving implicit assent to Freudian theory and its generalizing claims. As previously shown,

25. Nezval, quoted in Dierna, 'On Valerie, Nezval, Max Ernst, and Collages', in Nezval, *Valerie and Her Week of Wonders*, p. 212.

26. Briony Fer, 'Surrealism, Myth and Psychoanalysis', in Briony Fer, David Batchelor and Paul Wood, *Realism, Rationalism, Surrealism: Art between the Wars* (New Haven; London: Yale University Press, 1993), p. 199.

27. David Wilson, '*Valerie and Her Week of Wonders*', *Monthly Film Bulletin*, 38, 448, May 1971, p. 105.

28. Ibid.

Soviet-style Communism was marked by a deep hostility towards Freudianism and psychoanalysis, which were attacked for their 'idealism', their preoccupation with sexuality in its most perverse manifestations, and their perceived incompatibility with the materialist basis of Marxism. Furthermore, at the very beginnings of Normalization, professional psychoanalytic activity itself, after a brief taste of legality during the years of the Prague Spring, was driven back underground. Remarkably, against such a background, Jireš does not simply retain the novel's psychoanalytic implications, but foregrounds and develops them.

A narrative that was already confusing and preposterous becomes virtually incoherent in Jireš's film. To make matters worse, the novel's lucid, linear style of narration is abandoned for an elliptical cinematic style that fully showcases Jireš's gift for suggestive montage. Nezval sought to reveal the oneiric in the generic, and, for all its Surrealist trappings, his novel is just about assimilable to the traditions of Gothic fantasy and novelettish romance on which it is modelled. Cinematically closer to mid-period Fellini than to Terence Fisher, Jireš's work is an unambiguous evocation of its heroine's psychic world and thereby difficult to enjoy as an 'innocent' horror film. The primary process, mercurial and illogical, here proves even less amenable to narrative conventions or the fantasy genre's broad enough standards of plausibility. In this sense, as in others, the film constitutes as much an interpretation as an adaptation of Nezval's work, presenting the book's already prominent Freudian themes in a more explicit, or indeed a 'desublimated', form. (Whether the film's greater thematic explicitness makes it a superior work to the novel is questionable, but it does make it a more oppositional and troubling work in its domestic context than it might have been.) Key to the film's more forthright character in this respect are the repeated shots of Valerie retiring to her bedroom to sleep; its very last image is of Valerie soundly asleep in a forest (the forest included as yet another Freudian image of female sexuality, and also perhaps as a reference to Baudelaire's 'forest of symbols', a phrase much cherished by the Surrealists). A kind of framing device, these shots suggest, without directly giving anything away, that the film's reality is essentially that of the imagination.

That interpretation is implicit in the film's editing strategies, its *mise-en-scene*, the strangely porous fabric of its diegetic 'reality'. Nezval's novel broadly respects the unities of time and space, its illogical character deriving primarily from its reliance on fantasy convention, on magic and the supernatural: the Gothic and folkloric staple of the vampire; the elixir that transforms Valerie's grandmother into the young and beautiful Elsa; and the bottle of magic potion that enables Valerie to feign death and to move about unseen, enveloped in a floating cloud of fog. By contrast, Jireš brazenly assaults the integrity of time and space throughout the film, with a series of dazzling inventions: Tchoř's periodic transformation into the beautiful, red-headed

Figure 6.2 Hedvika's wedding night. *Valerie and Her Week of Wonders* (*Valerie a týden divů*, Jaromil Jireš, 1970) ©Ateliéry Bonton Zlín.

young man who may or may not be Valerie's father; the crowded church sermon at which Valerie suddenly finds herself alone; and the final sequence, which resurrects the figures of Tchoř and Grandmother, both of whom, it seems, have already died. Along with real time, narrative chronology is scrambled by Jireš's associative editing strategy, which cites or repeats particular images out of their temporal context.

The novel's conceit of the cloud of fog is partially replaced by that of the preservative magic pearls, and partially abandoned. In the novel Valerie observes the farmer and Hedvika's grisly wedding night by floating, unseen, into the farmer's bedroom; in the film she manages to 'witness' the scene from the safety of her own bed, the uncanny events thus framed as a movie-vision projected into the empty dark of Valerie's room. Jireš's sequence is all the more effective for abandoning the naturalized illogic of generic fantasy, while the blithe disruption of spatial reality is itself authentically dream-like. The framing of the wedding night in this manner also foregrounds the event's fictive status, both in the sense of revealing it as Valerie's hypnagogic imagining and in the sense of exposing the primal scene as a fictive scenario 'staged' in the unconscious. At yet another level, the implicit film-within-a-film device can be seen as a self-reflexive comment on the cinema itself as an apparatus for eliciting desire. Film theorist Christian Metz directly invokes the idea of the primal scene 'to create an analogy between this specific production of a fantasy of origins and the psychic modalities of film spectatorship, and ... to define the matrix of vision and desire which connects cinema viewing with unconscious activity'.[29] As Metz argues, cinema stimulates desire and phantasy by means of its specific conditions of reception (darkness, solitude, etc), which situate the viewer in a comparable position to that of the unseen voyeur (the child's position in the primal scene phantasy), as well as to that of the

---

29. Robert Stam, Robert Burgoyne and Sandy Flitterman-Lewis, *New Vocabularies in Film Semiotics: Structuralism, Post-Structuralism and Beyond* (London; New York: Routledge, 1992), p. 164.

dreamer. Similarly conflating, as it were, primal scene and primal screen, Jireš exposes that provocation of desire that is intrinsic to the cinematic experience, whatever the nature of a film's overt content.

Avant-Garde Uncertainties: Refusal of Closure

Jireš supplies an unabashedly modernist addendum to the novel's neat conclusion, one that again reveals his commitment to a closer and more explicit approximation of psychic reality. At the end of the book, Nezval both resolves all antagonisms and provides, or at least seems to do so, a definitive answer to the book's central mystery: Tchoř is laid to rest as a weasel-skin trophy, Valerie's grandmother, on her deathbed, recounts the 'true' story of Valerie's parentage, and grandmother and mother are finally reconciled. This is itself only a half-hearted attempt at closure – what of the bishop previously identified as Valerie's father? – and even suggests a parody of fictional convention, with Grandmother's deathbed account virtually a scene from a hackneyed nineteenth-century novel. Jireš adopts this semblance of resolution, only, in the following scenes, to deny explicitly any possibility of closure. Phantasy charges confusedly onwards, resistant at once to impasse and unambiguous meaning, as tirelessly inventive as it is self-contradictory. Valerie's earrings magically reappear on the skin of the dead Tchoř, suggesting that the 'witching' of the unconscious continues. The appearance of Valerie's banished mother and handsome woodcutter father signifies not the re-establishment of family reality, but only another variation of family romance, a means for the gratifying psychic adventure to begin again. These, at first sight, benign figures exchange between themselves a darkly conspiratorial look that recalls Tchoř and Elsa and their secret pact; Valerie's mother even greets her daughter with a long, alarmingly un-maternal kiss: these characters comprise yet further additions to phantasy's cast of licentious intriguers. Despite the apparent reconciliation, the grandmother attempts to strangle the mother, a moment that not only plunges the film into further conflict, but also suggests two dream figures, both diversely representative of the maternal and both, significantly, played by the same actress, jostling for a lead role in Valerie's psychic melodrama.[30]

---

30. While Valerie's grandmother can be seen as one of the story's few 'real' characters, existing outside Valerie's dream world, her representation throughout the story is also heavily invested with elements of phantasy, and not only in her guise as Elsa: her tortuous deathbed narrative, in which she presents herself as Tchoř's jealous lover, seems a particularly clear instance of the family romance at play. Furthermore, the vampire fangs revealed at the moment of her apparent death narrow the distance between this 'realistic' figure and the obviously and purely imaginary Elsa.

In these scenes the film comes closest to attaining the status of the 'open text', resisting unitary meaning and enabling any number of different interpretations. Of course, from a Lacanian perspective this tendency towards polyvalence is crucial to the accurate representation of phantasy, as, for Lacan and his followers, it is precisely that free 'textual' play that comprises the unconscious: as Terry Eagleton writes, Lacanian psychoanalysis conceives the unconscious as 'a bizarre "modernist" text which is almost unreadable and which will certainly never yield up its final secrets to interpretation'.[31] The critic Robin Wood describes the notion of the open text as a 'myth' and a means of 'critical abdication';[32] certainly, in the case of *Valerie*, there are a number of definite meanings that arise. If the film's polyvalent qualities recall dream discourse, there is also something of a Freudian attempt to wrest diagnosis from out of that murky, ambiguous discourse. The film's broad political stance, in overall orientation if not in specific details, is also fairly easy to discern. Thus the film cannot completely be reduced to a poststructuralist 'play of signifiers' without any ultimate meaning. At the same time, Jireš clearly is interested in retaining a certain mystery, and not only at a narrative but also at a symbolic level. For every one of the film's easily 'glossed' symbols there is another floating signifier, an indeterminate figure either mute or charged with a surfeit of meanings, depending on one's response. The film's key motif or fetish object, Valerie's endlessly lost and retrieved magic earrings, is exemplary in this regard, as is the failure of many of the characters to 'signify' a firmly defined identity. Jireš is as much concerned with the creative possibilities of interpretation as with treating the film's narrative as a psychoanalytic case study.

This open-ended approach to narrative and meaning is something we also find in the films of Juráček and Chytilová and, perhaps in its most extreme form, in the late *Nouvelle Vague* marathons made by Jacques Rivette in the late 1960s and early 1970s (*L'Amour fou* (1969), *Out 1: noli me tangere* (1971), *Céline and Julie Go Boating* (*Céline et Julie vont en bateau*, 1974)). As in the final scenes of *Out 1* and *Céline et Julie*, the ending of *Valerie* suggests to us the possibility of an endless perpetuation, variation or recycling of story: fiction presents itself here less as the fixed work of professionals than as a communal, ceaselessly malleable substance. The refusal of narrative and interpretive closure has of course since become a characteristic of postmodern culture, yet in this case it is worth considering to what extent such textual practices were informed by Sixties political idealism. After all Jireš's work, like the Rivette films, was made in the aftermath of the turmoils of 1968, events that had demonstrated, in Paris as in Prague, an uncommon degree of mutual effectivity between the

---

31. Eagleton, *Literary Theory*, p. 169.
32. Robin Wood, 'Narrative Pleasure: Two Films of Jacques Rivette', *Film Quarterly*, Vol. 35, No. 1, Autumn 1981, p. 2.

cultural and political spheres. Rivette himself argues, in a 1968 *Cahiers du cinéma* interview, that 'what is most important *politically* is the attitude the filmmaker takes with regard to all the aesthetic – or rather, so-called aesthetic – criteria which govern art'. A progressive aesthetics consists in re-imagining the role of the viewer, now 'no longer the comfortable viewer but someone who participates in common work – long, difficult, responsible work something like delivering a baby'.[33] To describe the kind of creative participation Rivette seeks from his viewers as 'serious work' might be making heavy weather of what is, in many senses, a cinema of play. Yet was not the reconciliation of work and play, necessity and gratification, precisely what Sixties libertarianism sought? Perhaps key to this politicized cinematic vanguardism is the idea of *process*: film not as finished product but as a process of making, and creating, meanings and readings, as a means of stimulating the viewer's own subjective (primary?) processes. Amidst the loose ends and enigmas of *Valerie's* conclusion, Orlík turns to the camera and raises a finger to his lips, an allusion to the essential secrecy or privacy of our interpretation. As Rivette indicates, process is also praxis: the 'comfortable' spectator–consumer becomes a creative, critical agent. Poetry *will* be made by all, as will politics. Such 'soft' avant-garde works as those of Jireš and Rivette have routinely been attacked, by popular pundits and cultural commissars alike, as implicitly elitist in their 'impenetrability', yet these films' textual strategies could be considered entirely consistent with an egalitarian, or communitarian, politics.

While the film's cultivation of uncertainty acts as a goad to the viewer's creativity, it also has serious epistemological implications. Against the grain of Freud's cast-iron diagnoses (although perhaps in the awed spirit with which the elderly Freud remarked on the mysteries of female sexuality),[34] the film finally asserts the resistance of things to conclusive explanation, the mysterious, unknowable character of both self and world. 'I know neither the world nor even myself',[35] Valerie laments in the novel's last chapter. From this perspective, the film's unreadable symbols and its ellipses and confusions might be seen less as inviting a plethora of interpretations than as asserting the limitations or deficiencies of knowledge. In visual terms, this latter reading is enforced through the literal partiality or imperfection of vision: a number of scenes are shot through high windows, veils and peepholes, as Jireš's camera adopts the viewpoint of an adolescent eavesdropping on a world of adult secrets. As

---

33. Jacques Rivette, in interview with Jacques Aumont, Jean-Louis Comolli, Jean Narboni and Sylvie Pierre, 'Time Overflowing', in Jim Hillier (ed.), *Cahiers du Cinéma: Volume 2* (London: Routledge and Kegan Paul, 1999), pp. 321–22.

34. See Freud's *The Question of Lay Analysis*, with its notorious phrase: 'after all, the sexual life of adult women is a "dark continent" for psychology'. (*The Question of Lay Analysis*, translated by James Strachey (New York; London: Norton, 1989), p. 38).

35. Nezval, *Valerie a týden divů*, p. 169.

Rosemary Jackson observes, problems of vision represent a recurrent theme of the fantastic, a literary mode generally concerned with undermining all claims of authoritatively grasping reality and with problematizing all coherent, 'monological' ways of interpreting it.[36] *Valerie* does not entirely comply with Jackson's precise definition of the fantastic, the 'romance' or fairy-tale genre on which film and novel draw, being arguably too remote and hermetic in its 'un-reality' to have the interrogative, reality-rupturing effect of fantasy. Nonetheless, like fantasy narratives, Jireš's can be seen to question the possibility of omniscient vision or definitive interpretation. For Jackson, it is such implicit epistemological scepticism, not a story's direct content, that makes a work of fantasy subversive. Needless to say, the subversive effect is all the greater in the context of neo-Stalinist society, committed to an ossified Marxism–Leninism as the one 'scientifically' correct, all-encompassing account of human life, and to the suppression of all opposing ideologies. Socialist Realism, as Stalinism's cultural representative, comprises a creed of iron certainty, and like its heroes is troubled by neither 'unanswerable questions' nor 'impenetrable secrets'.[37]

What has been described here as a conflict between Freudian symbols and Lacanian signifiers, between diagnoses and doubts, inscribes the conflict of tendencies within Surrealism or the avant-garde themselves. Czech avant-garde tradition has arguably always been more resistant to 'literary' meaning than, say, French Surrealism. Theodor Adorno once beheld a 'luxuriant multiplicity'[38] of meaning in Surrealist images and texts that prevented them from being tied down by psychoanalytic categories, yet many of Surrealism's most famous or 'representative' figures, including Max Ernst and Salvador Dalí, consciously devised their works around such categories.[39] Much 'classical' Surrealist art and literature is essentially illustrative, pursuing a stylistic transparency so as to inscribe all the more forcefully a direct or literary 'content' (such as Freudian ideas). By contrast, Karel Teige, in his 1924 manifesto 'Poetism', eschewed the presence of 'contents and plot' in art as a remnant of the past, a leftover from 'mediaeval times' when 'even legal codes were written in verse'.[40] As is evidenced by Devětsil's experiments with typography and its pursuit of new artistic forms

36. Rosemary Jackson, *Fantasy: The Literature of Subversion* (London: Routledge, 1981).
37. Abram Tertz [Andrei Sinyavsky], 'On Socialist Realism', *The Trial Begins and On Socialist Realism*, translated by Max Hayward and George Dennis (London: Harvill Press, 1960), p. 173.
38. Theodor Adorno, 'Looking Back on Surrealism', in Lawrence S. Rainey (ed.), *Modernism: An Anthology* (Oxford; New York: Blackwell, 2005), p. 1114.
39. Briony Fer, 'Surrealism, Myth and Psychoanalysis', in Fer, Batchelor and Wood, *Realism, Rationalism, Surrealism*, p. 199.
40. Karel Teige, 'Poetism', translated by Alexandra Büchler, in Eric Dluhosch and Rotislav Švácha (eds), *Karel Teige 1900–1951: L'Enfant Terrible of the Czech Modernist Avant-Garde* (Cambridge, MA: M.I.T. Press, 1999), p. 68.

that would synthesize the plastic and the literary (such as picture poems), Poetism emphasizes the material self-sufficiency of the signifier and encourages the play of associations at the expense of unitary meaning. Teige suggested that Poetist art should not attempt to communicate anything, but should rather comprise '[a] game of beautiful words, a combination of ideas, a web of images, if necessary without words'.[41] We should add that postwar Czech Surrealism, while less obviously relevant in regard to Jireš's film, emphasized the 'active', even 'creative' contribution of the spectator in the establishment of meaning and conceived the 'message' of a work as a 'mobile structure'.[42] Those postwar practitioners also examined the way decisive answers are rebuffed by senseless fact and dissolved in the mysteries of the material. That Jireš's film defies unambiguous signification should not necessarily be seen to reflect the external influences of poststructuralist theory or the *Nouvelle Vague* (though Jireš was certainly versed in the French cinema of the time): *Valerie's* formal practices also have precedents in prominent and long-standing traditions of the Czech avant-garde.

In the movement's very first manifesto, Teige proclaimed, with bravura paradox, that Poetism did not intend to be another 'ism'. In this refusal of any coherent philosophical system, Teige defies the doctrinal Surrealism of that time and even anticipates, embryonically, the notion of 'disintegratory systems' developed in a much more disillusioned climate by Effenberger's U.D.S. group. If both Teige and Nezval encumbered themselves with two particularly formidable 'isms' in Marxism–Leninism, Poetist art itself resisted any attempt at intellectual systematization, even of a Freudian kind. While classical Surrealism has often been described, exaggeratedly no doubt, as something of a cult, administered by the dictatorial and Pope-like (Stalin-like?) Breton, Poetism (à la carnival) proclaimed a spirit of 'gay relativity'.[43] Poetist art and theorizing instigates a kind of intellectual acrobatics, a skipping from one proposition to the next; in Teige's words, Poetism 'calls for the free mind of a juggler of ideas',[44] hence the recurrent iconography of circuses and funfairs. Perhaps it is the implication of such a Poetistic 'juggling' that is the most enduringly subversive aspect of a film like *Valerie*: in fact, it is worth bearing in mind over the course of this chapter that, while a number of 'radical' systems and theories that the film explores (Freudianism, Surrealism, Marcuse's theories, revisionist Marxism) have since been challenged or even consigned to the dustbin of intellectual history, the refutation of omniscient knowledge and system-building in formal terms is still threatening to the world's demagogues and dogmatists.

---

41. Ibid.
42. Král, *Le surréalisme en Tchécoslovaquie*, p. 52.
43. Mikhail Bakhtin, *Rabelais and His World*, translated by Heléne Iswolsky (Cambridge, MA: M.I.T. Press, 1968), p. 12.
44. Teige, 'Poetism', in Dluhosch and Švácha, *Karel Teige 1900–1951*, p. 68.

The Priest and the Poetist: Libertarian Allegory

The film's subversive qualities have been shown to lie, first, in its psychoanalytic themes and then in those narrative and formal practices that stress ambiguity and uncertainty. Yet does the film also have a more directly 'political' aspect? Andrew Horton claims to find a close correlation between Valerie's adventures and post-invasion Czechoslovakia:

> Shot only a few years after the Soviet tanks rolled into Prague, the film is filled with images of corrupting innocence, rape and the betrayal of youth by those who should be protecting it. These themes are perpetuated both in the story line and in the film's images: pure white clothes being stained with blood is a notable example ... Czech audiences could identify, at some deep level, with the correlation between the film's plot and the way they perceived their nation as being defiled and abused by a foreign aggressor.[45]

This parallel seems at once too crude and too specific. Yet the film can still be read as a political commentary, albeit in broader terms than those of mere anti-Communist or anti-Soviet critique. What connects this political dimension back to the film's psychoanalytic aspects is the idea that psychic and erotic liberation should be part and parcel of 'liberation' *per se*. The film's affirmation of liberation, and of the compatibility of all its constituent forms, suggests the influence not only of Surrealism but also of the counterculture and the New Left of the 1960s, with the latter influences perhaps dominant here. As suggested earlier, the contemporary Surrealism of Effenberger was dismissive of all utopianisms, perceiving any such commitments as either futile or potentially totalitarian. But whatever the film's distance from contemporary Surrealism in this respect, its critical stance towards society is clearly in the spirit of Surrealism old and new.

If anything in Nezval's original novel reveals the Marxist in the fantasist, it is the way 'evil' manifests itself throughout the story's world not only as the grotesque, supernatural wickedness characteristic of the fairy tale, but also as an institutionalized commonplace, a prevalent and unspectacular reality. The story's adult characters are defined by their rapacity and their exploitation of those younger and weaker than themselves. The relationships they establish with others revolve solely around exchange, dependence, and outright coercion: Valerie's grandmother, as Elsa, grants her former lover Tchoř, as Richard, the deeds to her house in exchange for the restoration of her youth and beauty; Tchoř maintains the assistance of Orlík through the continuous

---

45. Andrew Horton, 'Dreaming a Bad Reality', *Central Europe Review*, Vol. 1, No. 9, 23 August 1999 (http://www.ce-review.org/99/9/kinoeye9horton2.html) (retrieved 3 August 2007).

threat of torture; the missionary Gracian uses his spiritual authority to abuse sexually the black woman whom he 'converted' in Africa, and to attempt the same with Valerie; and the miserly landowner in effect 'buys' his bride, the beautiful but impoverished virgin Hedvika, with thoughts of wealth and property. The story can be seen as charting an initiation into adult realities that is as much political as sexual: the secrets upon which Valerie eavesdrops are not only variations of the primal scene, but also the exposed machinations of power. From this perspective, the transformation of a protective guardian into a bloodthirsty monster dramatizes Valerie's apprehension, in both senses, of the world beyond puberty, the dawning awareness of a cruel, exploitative social order.

The story's monstrous parent figures were discussed earlier in the Freudian terms of the uncanny. We may remember that, in manifestations of the uncanny, what was once familiar resurfaces in an estranged, often frightening, form. Yet another kind of estrangement, more Brechtian than Freudian, may also be at work here, with the mystified realities of exploitation revealed, paradoxically, through viscerally 'defamiliarized' representation. The motif of vampirism becomes a means to penetrate the destructive, parasitic core of social and sexual relationships, representing less a fantastic intrusion into this world than its distorted reflection or outgrowth. Hedvika is the prey equally of the vampire and of her wealthy, ageing groom, both of whom value her only in so far as her maidenhead is intact. She has been forced to sell her 'uncontaminated' beauty and youth, as workers are compelled to sell their labour, in exchange for material security. In the wedding-night scene, Elsa's vampire assault begins simultaneously with the landowner's preliminary caresses of his bride, and Jireš positions the two figures at either side of Hedvika's neck, a literal mirror-image of one another. Hedvika displays the whitened face and the trancelike manner of the vampire's slave *before* the actual sucking of blood; a close-up of red wine spilling over a white tablecloth after the wedding party has ended evokes, none too subtly, the spilt blood of both the vampire attack and the virgin marriage, suggesting an identity between both phenomena. The melancholy figure of the vampire's slave is an image of both the kept woman and the numbed, reified, socially manipulated individual. Once having been bitten, Hedvika finds herself 'possessed' literally as well as figuratively. The vampire's mark with which she is left constitutes a mark of ownership; analogous to the branding of cattle, it comments on Hedvika's status in her marriage, barely any higher than that of the farmer's livestock.

Does this have any relevance for the film's state socialist present? On the surface of things, the story's most negatively or mockingly presented characters comprise a rogues' gallery of classic reactionary villains: priests and the clergy, a wealthy farmer, and an avaricious property owner (Tchoř). Even Valerie's grandmother, with her large estate, seems to represent a patrician bourgeoisie.

Figure 6.3 Gracian (Jan Klusák) and monks in *Valerie and Her Week of Wonders* (*Valerie a týden divů*, Jaromil Jireš, 1970) ©Ateliéry Bonton Zlín, reproduced courtesy of Second Run DVD.

Perhaps the vampires signify no more than the bourgeois 'blood-suckers' Nezval mentions in his 1938 memoir *Prague Pedestrian* (*Pražský chodec*). Jireš's adaptation might seem at first sight to do no more than transfer faithfully the original's obvious anti-capitalist, anti-clerical tendencies, yet Jireš subtly enriches the novel's satirical content and broadens its focus. The farmer, for instance, plays a less significant role in the film than in the novel, which means both discarding Nezval's somewhat crude satire at the expense of miserly, bad-tempered 'kulaks' and diminishing this character's specificity. Visual intertextuality transforms polemic literalism into allegorical sophistication, a canny means of tailoring the novel's satire to present concerns. The remains of an opulent wedding feast at the farmer's house recalls the trashed Party banquet at the end of Chytilová's *Daisies*, while the dinner with which Grandmother welcomes Gracian takes place at an ornately prepared table beside a lake, in direct reference to Jan Němec's *The Party and the Guests*, a film which constituted a fairly direct (though minimally allegorical) attack on Communist totalitarianism. Gracian is played by Jan Klusák, who played Rudolf, the head of the secret police in Němec's film, and Klusák here adopts the same leering, grotesquely ingratiating mannerisms with which he played Rudolf.[46]

---

46. Hames, *The Czechoslovak New Wave*, p. 205.

The latter reference is particularly interesting, comprising another instance of using the Catholic Church as a veiled indictment of Communist repression. This tactic is also deployed, with varying degrees of explicitness, in such films as Jerzy Kawalerowicz's Polish *Mother Joan of the Angels* (*Matka Joanna od aniołów*, 1961) and Juraj Jakubisko's Slovak *See You in Hell, My Friends!*, though it is perhaps most appropriate in a Czech, post-invasion context. In view of the ruthless imposition of Catholicism on Bohemia after the Habsburgs' victory at the Battle of White Mountain in 1620, the Catholic religion has long carried connotations among the Czechs of an enforced, artificial presence. Czech viewers in 1970 could scarcely have ignored the parallels with a political, economic, and cultural system that was derived wholesale from a foreign model, forcibly established, and then restored to former orthodoxies through military occupation. At the same time, by fostering an identification between these apparently antithetical ideologies, Jireš asserts his opposition to all forms of repression. Ideologies, belief systems, the precise forms that power assumes or the instruments it adopts, reveal themselves as fluid and easily blurred: ascetic Catholicism borders lascivious paganism (Gracian's secret 'rosary' of animal teeth, the Sacramental wine mirrored by the drinking of blood), while Tchoř's dress alternates between the priest's cassock and the wig and hat of the magistrate.

As constable, bishop, property owner, possible father to Valerie, as well as a demon vested with supernatural powers, Tchoř constitutes an archetype of power, absorbing the various forms of authority (administrative, religious or ideological, economic, patriarchal) and revealing their oppressive commonality.[47] If the forms of power change, its malign essence does not, and Tchoř's deathlessness might suggest the persistence of cruel, subjugating power throughout history. Alternately, just as Tchoř's monstrosity periodically gives way to the benign face of the woodcutter, power might sometimes, Dubček style, assume a 'human face'. Yet the representation of Tchoř is more complex than this. At first sight Tchoř is the most puzzling character in the film, as he comprises at once a grim exponent of repressive order and a carnivalesque lord of misrule, a savage tyrant and Valerie's tempter into transgression. In fact, Tchoř serves as the film's primary representative of the unconscious, a patron of taboo art and psychic self-expression: the itinerant folk musicians play in his 'kingdom', and he is also seen lurking among the revellers at the wedding party, both disturbingly out of place and oddly apt. As in Freudian dream language, Tchoř seems to 'condense' in one figure the dual, contradictory aspects of Gothic subversion, the genre's insight into the depths of the psyche *and* its distorted reflection of malign political currents; he signifies the return of traumas at once psychic and historical.

---

47. Ibid., p. 203.

Highly relevant here is that Nezval's direct inspiration for Tchoř was Nosferatu the vampire from Murnau's Expressionist classic. Jireš has carefully preserved the association in making Tchoř a close physical approximation of the earlier screen villain. Moreover, Jireš's film itself, with its high degree of stylistic artifice, can be seen virtually as an Expressionist film in colour. These overt references back to the greatest movement of 1920s German cinema cannot but recall that movement's contemporaneity with the rise of National Socialism, as well as the contentious yet well-argued claims that the cultural movement anticipated or even paved the way for the political movement. That staunch anti-modernist Georg Lukács, for instance, argued that the irrationality unleashed and valorized by Expressionism (and by implication Surrealism) found its rancid culmination in Hitler: 'expressionism was undoubtedly one of the diverse bourgeois ideological currents that would result in fascism'.[48] Whether or not one accepts such claims of avant-garde culpability, the figure of Tchoř comprises a powerful reminder of the monsters brought forth in the sleep of reason, and in this sense he illustrates the dark side of the unconscious that Breton and Teige forever disavowed. Thus Jireš reminds us that violence and repression also draw on the irrational, and that the fascist tyrant is in many ways the negative inversion of the Surrealist sybarite: a manifesto of the postwar Czech Surrealists, written in the aftermath of Nazi and Communist horrors, speaks of 'Ubu Stalin and Maldoror Hitler'.[49] By conflating the dual 'readings' of the Gothic so directly and by making those readings so explicit, Jireš complicates what would otherwise have been too straightforward an identification of the irrational with the positive and progressive.

As we have seen, the film transcends the mere anti-Communist satire routinely expected of East European films. By refusing to aim its critique at a single, specific target, the film suggests the influence of the radical political analysis of the 1960s. Various representatives of the international New Left (the German–American Herbert Marcuse, the Yugoslavian 'Praxis' philosophers, the Czech Ivan Sviták) and cultural underground (hippies, Situationists, Surrealists) insist on the identity, or at least the common qualities, of the great political opponents of capitalism and state Communism, the similarities hidden behind the 'merely formal differences'.[50] In fact, the film's central moral and political schism occurs not in Cold War geographical terms (as in, say, Bořivoj Zeman's 1952 *The Proud Princess* (*Pyšná princeza*), with its blissful

48. Georg Lukács, quoted in Patrice Petro, 'From Lukács to Kracauer and Beyond: Social Film Histories and the German Cinema', *Cinema Journal*, Vol. 22, No. 3, Spring 1983, p. 47.

49. 'U.D.S.', in Alan, *Alternativní Kultura*, p. 530.

50. 'The Platform of Prague', in *Surrealism Against the Current*, edited and translated by Michael Richardson and Krzysztof Fijałkowski (London: Pluto Press, 2001), p. 59.

(Communist?) kingdom of song divided from a corrupt (capitalist?) land where singing is banned), but between generations. The film's young characters are, in contrast to their elders, generally loving, virtuous, resourceful and creative, and thereby suggest the possibility of an alternative social order based upon freedom, mutual cooperation and play. The film thus alludes to the youthful nature of the Sixties counterculture, and also perhaps to the role of youth in the developments of the Prague Spring. Writing of the 1966 student protests in Czechoslovakia, Z.A.B. Zeman describes the opposition between the young and what they saw as a morally compromised adulthood: 'Young people found it hard to understand the moral turpitude of their elders. They felt that something incredible, discreditable, was going on in the world of authority.'[51]

'Rational' maturity often proves synonymous with corruption: Valerie's 'childish' inability to understand the reasons for Hedvika's marriage to the farmer seems superior to her grandmother's coldly mercenary 'wisdom'. If Hedvika is condemned by the adult world to the status of commodity, object of exploitation and literal 'new blood', Valerie offers a tender, nurturing relationship of equals. Hedvika's spiritual recovery, her awakening from a thing-like passivity, is enacted through non-subjugative contact and the free expression of sexuality. While the film's adult characters use their powers, supernatural and otherwise, to enslave and destroy, the young characters use theirs to restore and protect: Orlík and Valerie are white magicians. The film's cooperative, libertarian values and its valorization of a 'radical gentleness'[52] clearly link it to the contemporary counterculture, an affiliation also reflected in Jireš's evocation of many of the most salient trappings of hippie culture: long hair, flower-bedecked youths, Orlík's acoustic guitar, sexual experimentation and 'free love', and even the suggestion of psychedelic drugs in the magic pearl which Valerie consumes in order to effect drastic shifts in her 'reality'. The embrace of an idyllic natural world at the end of the film also evokes a Woodstock-era pastoralism and nascent environmental concerns: the unspoilt adolescent heroine at one with the unspoilt natural landscape. Faithful to the spirit of both its source and its time, the film points up the essential affinity between avant-garde and counterculture, the extent to which the aesthetics, lifestyles and politics of the original Surrealists were re-embodied on a broader scale by the 1960s underground. J. Hoberman describes the counterculture as 'in many respects populari[s]ed, updated, mass-produced surrealism' and the more mystically inclined Surrealists as themselves 'virtual proto-hippies'.[53] As though reinforcing visually this compatibility of interwar

---

51. Zeman, *Prague Spring*, p. 79.
52. Raymond Durgnat, *WR: Mysteries of the Organism* (London: BFI, 1999), p. 14.
53. J. Hoberman and Jonathan Rosenbaum, *Midnight Movies* (New York: Harper and Row, 1983), p. 100.

dreamer and postwar tripper, the phantasmagorical imagery that recurs throughout *Valerie* seems pitched halfway between the carnivalesque iconography of Poetism and psychedelia.

The defining image of repressive social reality in the film is that of the priest, the missionary, and the dourly regimented lines of droning, monochrome clerics that cross Valerie's path. The defining image of libertarian resistance is that of the minstrel, the actor, the teeming, garish crowd of masked revellers, musicians and acrobats. Like much of the film's commentary, this opposition can be seen as having a broad political application. However, because the film's carnival figures so directly evoke Poetism, it is difficult not to interpret this opposition specifically as the conflict between Stalinist Communism and a liberal, bohemian yet generally Leftist avant-garde. Recalling Leszek Kołakowski's famous dichotomy between the Communist as jester and the Communist as priest, the acrobats suggest Teige's irreverent 'jugglers of ideas', while the dogmatic, hierarchical nature of Stalinism is well represented by the Catholic Church. Within this allegorical representation, art itself is privileged as the locus of progressive values and artistic activity as the model of a non-repressive social order. This is, of course, entirely consistent with Poetism, as Teige's 1924 manifesto defines the utopian society of the Communist future as precisely one that will permit the reconciliation of art and life, the entry of fantasy and creativity into common existence. Furthermore, as both Teige and the Frankfurt School concur, art itself, in its ideal manifestations, offers a vision of human liberation as it gives voice to the unconscious and to utopian imaginings. Marcuse, citing Adorno, writes:

> Art is perhaps the most visible 'return of the repressed' ... The artistic imagination shapes the 'unconscious memory' of the liberation that failed, of the promise that was betrayed. Under the rule of the performance principle, art opposes to institutionalized repression the 'image of man as free subject ...'[54]

The film thus celebrates those forms of art and cultural activity perceived by the Poetists, if not by the culturally more rarefied Frankfurt School, as most representative of this liberatory, psychically purgative function: the popular entertainments of folk celebrations, circuses and travelling theatres. The close bonds between popular or 'folk' art and sexual and political transgression are foregrounded in the character of Valerie's brother Orlík (notwithstanding Jireš's omission of any reference to the transvestite tendency that Orlík indulges in the novel, a witting or unwitting 'repression' of this challenge to socially constructed masculinity). Jireš's representation of Orlík is explicitly indebted to

---

54. Herbert Marcuse, *Eros and Civilization: A Philosophical Inquiry into Freud* (Boston: Beacon Press, 1966), p. 144.

Figure 6.4 Orlík (Petr Kopřiva) in *Valerie and Her Week of Wonders* (*Valerie a týden divů*, Jaromil Jireš, 1970) ©Ateliéry Bonton Zlín, reproduced courtesy of Second Run DVD.

Poetism's romantic iconography of popular culture and draws particularly on the tradition of spritelike artist-enchanters in Nezval's own work, from Straw Hubert to the eponymous hero of the 1927 poem 'Akrobat'. Orlík conflates the talents of artist, musician, acrobat and magician; with his theatrically whitened face and spectacles, he physically resembles a combination of intellectual and mime. He is as romantic as Pierrot and as playful as Harlequin, a synthesis that Karel Teige recognized in the persona of the circus clown.[55] While Orlík's restorative powers and manifold torments suggest the Nezvalian trope of the artist as redeemer ('this cosmic tumbler/he who dies for us each day/a death that's not death'),[56] he is ultimately less Christlike than Orphic (he is even seen playing a lute). Marcuse embraces Orpheus as a subversive 'culture-hero', a mythic icon for a non-repressive order: in a description that would equally suit Nezval and Jireš's creation, Marcuse writes that Orpheus's is 'the voice which does not command but sings; the gesture which offers and receives; the deed which is peace and ends the labor of conquest'.[57]

55. Karel Teige, *Svět, který se směje* (Prague: Odeon, 2004).
56 Vítězslav Nezval, 'Akrobat', in *Antilyrik and Other Poems*, translated by Jerome Rothenberg and Miloš Sovak (Los Angeles: Green Integer, 2001), pp. 137–38.
57. Marcuse, *Eros and Civilization*, pp. 161–62.

Jireš even recuperates the more vilified and commercial genres of popular culture (horror films, softcore pornography) on account of the furtive insights they offer into unconscious desire, and absorbs trappings from these genres into a broad iconography of cultural transgression. Jireš's film has itself often been regarded, especially in Britain and the USA, as horror-softcore schlock of an uncommonly elegant, or pretentious, kind, yet the synthesis of formalist highbrow and generic lowbrow (skirting the tasteful, classically plotted middlebrow) has many precedents in the Surrealist and avant-garde tradition (and, of course, also looks forward to postmodernist poetics). Freely appropriating from both 'high' and 'low' sources, Jireš renders Tchoř's underground kingdom a deviant conflation of ominous smoking cauldrons, Weimar nightlife and *fin de siècle* style; carnival mingles with Gothic horror, kitsch with 'high art'. Earlier Tchoř's lair was discussed as offering a spatial model of the unconscious, yet it is as much a comment on cultural policing as on psychic repression. This den of unseen iniquities is also a repository of marginalized and forbidden art, packed as this kingdom is with 'beautiful pictures' (as mentioned in Nezval's novel) and dusty old tomes. The various generic tropes and cultural echoes (including a young girl in a Victorian-style dress who suggests some debauched cousin of Lewis Carroll's Alice) themselves stand as the ciphers or spectres of that long tradition (or counter-tradition) of the fantastic, irrational and grotesque in which Surrealism, Poetism and the Gothic genre must be situated. As mentioned earlier, repressed elements, in Freudian theory, do not simply 'go away', but pursue their own active life 'underground', always threatening to resurface in the form of the uncanny. Despite the overtly repressive policies of state socialism, or indeed the homogenizing tendencies of the marketplace, the culturally transgressive reasserts itself again and again, in forms at once provocatively new and as old as the unconscious itself: thus the interwar avant-garde 'returns', uncannily enough, in the estranged form of the Sixties counterculture. Near the beginning of the film, Valerie watches as the lavishly carnivalesque wedding procession bursts forth from a tunnel into the brightly lit street: the sudden manifestation of this oneiric spectacle within the everyday serves as both an expression of the ceaseless return of the cultural repressed, and a tribute to that transition from the enforced obscurity of the 1950s into the all too brief light of the 1960s.

Back to Utopia: Surrealist Synthesis

Guiseppe Dierna argues that the structure of Nezval's original novel replicates the tripartite nature of Surrealist ontology, proceeding from 'reality', through 'unreality' or dream, to an ultimate 'surreality', a state comprising the dialectical resolution of the first two states. Arguably this description is already a simplification of the book, and at the most literal level it is simply inaccurate in regard to the film, for in the latter's final scenes Valerie succumbs to her dream world and Jireš to an oneiric illogic. Yet once we examine the meaning of the dream images themselves, the Surrealist principle of a synthesis or reconciliation of dream and world seems not at all inappropriate. In this sense we see revealed the normative function of the imagination identified by Teige and Sviták, the 'rational' dimension of phantasy. As an image of utopia, *Valerie*'s closing scene most obviously suggests a vision of 'liberation' in keeping with the Sixties sexual revolution, in other words a permanent and collective return of the repressed. Even in this aspect, the film is remarkable for offering a surprisingly rare affirmation of erotic utopianism. There are numerous examples of the dark side of instinctual liberation in 1960s and 1970s art cinema, yet the desublimatory vision of *Valerie*'s final scene is both libidinal and harmonious, lewd and innocent, the film's characters finally at one with themselves, with their natural environment and with each other. Chaste in graphic terms, these concluding images celebrate the heterodox, polymorphous and fluid: narrative logic along with social norms are violated in a ceaseless permutation or dance of desire. Jan Čuřík's camerawork, revelling in the autumnal blaze of leaves, the shimmering, lotus-decked waters and the preternatural beauty of the film's performers, helps render the scene a soothingly softcore recreation of the id. Once again, the film reveals affinities, consciously or not, with Marcuse's then widely publicized (if controversial) valorization of liberated Eros as an essentially wholesome phenomenon. Yet what is perhaps most noteworthy is that the film's representatives of authority, the priests and the other adult characters, are also included in this idyll. Religious figures cavort with musicians, actors and lustful servants; forbidding ceremonial blacks mingle with innocuous whites and the glowing hues of the natural world. This is a vision of revolution as reconciliation: between dream and reality, freedom and necessity, anarchy and order. The priest finally holds hands with the jester.

The centrality of such resolutions to Surrealism is well known, but the idea of a reconciliation between rational and irrational orders was also explored, and in more concrete and rigorous terms, by Karel Teige in his Poetist phase. In contrast to the vaguely expressed character of Bretonian resolutions, Teige (more theorist and ideologue than poet) gives a solid base to his dialectical project, sketching out his own social 'blueprint' of a 'future that is red'.[58] Teige conceives the resolution of the rational and the irrational, reality and dream, as a synthesis of Constructivist and Poetist cultures: the rationality of Constructivism presides over the sphere of necessity, over work and social planning, while Poetism attends to the stimulation of the senses and the

---

58. Breton, *Manifestoes of Surrealism*, p. 123; Teige, 'Poetism', in Dluhosch and Švácha, *Karel Teige 1900–1951*, p. 67.

cultivation of the imagination. In Teige's vision, Dionysian excess is integrated into the life of a happy, productive society. Teige's basis for this is a temporal allocation whereby 'man' will live 'as a working citizen' for six days of the week, but will 'live as a human being, as a poet', on the seventh.[59] At the same time, even Marcusean liberation involves some negotiation with reason, utopia comprising a truce between license and necessary repression: as Marcuse suggests, the 'repressive rationality' of old would be replaced by a new, 'libidinal rationality' (bizarre as the term sounds) that would ensure the cultivation of the 'sex instincts' in fundamentally benign forms.[60] The images of a newly indulgent authority can also be seen as an allusion to the promise of the Prague Spring, the liberalization movement that had been put paid to a year before the film's shooting. To pursue the specific analogy between the Communist establishment and the Catholic Church, religious faith is now revealed in its 'reformist' guise: repressive orthodoxy is transmuted into 'liberation theology'. Religious imagery persists, but this reflects the gentler aspects of Christian faith: as Peter Hames notes, the tableau of a group of youths gathered round a lamb and a baby clearly suggests a 'nativity scene'.[61] The Church thus emerges as the 'lamb' rather than the predatory 'lion', as represented by Father Gracian, who now lies imprisoned in a low cage.

Of course, as the film was being made, the wheels of Normalization were beginning to turn; the reversal of policies of liberalization, and the purges of those 'tainted' by reform, were already under way. Given the depressing

Figure 6.5 The final scene of *Valerie and Her Week of Wonders* (*Valerie a týden divů*, Jaromil Jireš, 1970) ©Ateliéry Bonton Zlín, reproduced courtesy of Second Run DVD.

---

59. Ibid.
60. Marcuse, *Eros and Civilization*, p. 16.
61. Hames, *The Czechoslovak New Wave*, p. 208.

political circumstances in which the film was made, one is tempted to ask whether the fantasy of the film's ending is less a case of utopian speculation than of nostalgia for vanquished possibilities: does this finale, which fades away to the mournful air of a flute, comprise only an elegy for lost hopes, the bedimmed constellation of 1960s radical idealisms? In the film's closing moments, the various characters encircle Valerie's bed and sing her a lullaby: 'When you awake/Don't reveal your secret'. Then these figures suddenly vanish, leaving Valerie alone and sleeping. This moment anticipates the dissipation of such visions in what Nezval elsewhere calls the 'filthy light' of waking reality.[62] Yet perhaps, as the lullaby suggests, secrets are best kept: perhaps utopian visions *are* best left consigned to the dream world, or its objective surrogate, the world of art. The film's final 'disappearing trick' in fact serves to underline the illusory nature of cinema, to foreground the fact that these characters are no more than entrancing yet nebulous images. Jireš's direct homage in this scene to the end of Federico Fellini's *8½* (*Otto e mezzo*, 1962), itself a self-reflexive film about filmmaking, is comparable to Orlík's reference at the end of the novel to 'beautiful old volumes full of magical engravings'[63] and further heightens our awareness of the fictive or aesthetic status of this liberatory new reality. Can art do no more than ameliorate an inadequate reality, indeed much in the manner of the family romance? Are the resolutions of stories more a compensation for the world than a means of changing it? The dying melody of the flute is hardly a clarion call to action. In 1924, the 'Proletarian' poet Josef Hora suggested that the work of Poetists such as Nezval, demonstrating 'a passionate longing for a happiness which the world lacks', ultimately served as 'light reading to soothe us into an enchanted dream'.[64] Jireš's film, whose finale is no less enchanting than any of Nezval's works, can itself be considered a political lullaby for a time of defeat.

The discourse of sexual and political 'liberation' has now disappeared from both the artistic avant-gardes and the wider culture. In that respect *Valerie and Her Week of Wonders* feels the most dated of all the texts examined here. Certainly it is more dated than the contemporaneous films of Juráček, with their unfulfilling quests of desire, or those of Švankmajer, with their beady-eyed appreciation of human (and often non-human) malevolence. Indeed *Valerie* is a film that now operates at a triple remove, given that its tale of a *fin de siècle* fantasy-world was conceived in the 1930s and then adapted in a manner that is profoundly of the late 1960s. The film's utopian spirit is qualified and problematized, as we have seen, yet it is there, saddened and aggrieved. Jireš's willingness to entertain political and sexual fairy tales takes on a poignant quality, even a defiant one, given the political circumstances in

62. Nezval, 'The Revolt of Madness', *Antilyrik and Other Poems*, p. 46.
63. Nezval, *Valerie a týden divů*, p. 168.
64. Josef Hora, quoted in French, *The Poets of Prague*, p. 49.

which the film was made. In this sense the film resembles Valerie herself at earlier points in the story, serene and unfazed in the midst of all kinds of implied horrors. Yet if the film seems to manifest a sweet-natured naïveté comparable to that of its heroine, in another sense its very datedness, its evocation of a particularly adventurous period in 'mainstream' European filmmaking, is synonymous with its progressive qualities. As an explicit study of sexual taboos focalized through the phantasies of a female adolescent, and as an experiment in polysemic discourse, the film still seems remarkably bold, demonstrating how Surrealist preoccupations and avant-garde aesthetics, when pursued in an uncompromising way, have retained their provocative power.

CHAPTER 7

Jan Švankmajer: Contemporary Czech Surrealism and the Renewal of Language

'Militant Surrealism'

Jan Švankmajer is the only major Czech filmmaker to have joined the Czech Surrealist Group, and on such grounds he has distinguished his work from the, in his view, superficial appropriations of Surrealism by the more 'mainstream' New Wave filmmakers. Does that privileged status necessitate excluding Švankmajer from a study focused primarily on the New Wave? As Švankmajer demonstrates in his own work, distinctions and boundaries exist to be interrogated, if not overthrown, and the strict differentiation between the Surrealist and the non-Surrealist (or ersatz Surrealist) can prove problematic. Michael Richardson questions whether there exists 'a pure surrealism and then various degrees of its adulteration', and asks how 'such a distinction' might be made.[1] Rather than rigidly separating Švankmajer's work from the New Wave films, it might be preferable to look to the cultural context, in both historical and temporally specific terms, that he shares with other Czech filmmakers. His films can, and should, be seen as one of the more extreme or committed products of an engagement with the avant-garde (in its classic and modern guises) that was widespread. Like a number of other filmmakers and artists, Švankmajer benefitted from the newfound acceptability and visibility of the experimental. A significant part of his artistic apprenticeship, his tenure at the avant-garde Semafor theatre, was an experience shared by New Wave directors Forman and Menzel, as well as by the self-professedly non-New Wave Juraj Herz. Of course, one might argue that Švankmajer is *a priori* excluded from the New Wave's company by virtue of the fact that he has worked predominantly in animation: with its playful qualities and infantile associations, animation is too often the ghettoized, abjected 'other' of 'respectable' live-action cinema. Yet

---

1.   Richardson, *Surrealism and Cinema*, p. 35.

this distinction, even supposing it should be taken seriously, should not compel us to set Švankmajer apart, as heterogeneity of means is part of the very nature of the New Wave. Furthermore it would be a simplification to describe Švankmajer only as an animator, as he tends to work at the very limits of that genre, incorporating real objects and live action elements and often emphasizing not the miraculously animate but the stubbornly inanimate.

The notion that Švankmajer's career can itself be divided up neatly into its Surrealist and pre-Surrealist phases proves as problematic as these other distinctions. Indeed, Švankmajer's conscious embrace of the Surrealist movement came later than might be assumed: he made his first 'intentionally' Surrealist short, *The Garden* (*Zahrada*), in 1968, after six other shorts and an accomplished theatre career, and he only joined the Surrealist Group in 1970, after a meeting with Effenberger, the group's then leader. Of course, the timing of Švankmajer's 'official' beginnings as a Surrealist – *The Garden* was shot not long after the Warsaw Pact invasion – cannot but encourage speculation about the political motivation and meaning of these decisions. Michael O'Pray argues that 'Švankmajer's decision to join [the] group brought to an end a brief but important period of "innocence" in his work', and suggests that the events of 1968 'were a major factor' in this 'loss of innocence'.[2] Certainly, the films from 1968 and 1969, *The Garden*, *The Flat* (*Byt*), *Picnic with Weissmann* (*Picnic mit Weissmann*) and *A Quiet Week in the House* (*Tichý týden v domě*), were the most obviously 'political' works Švankmajer had made up to that point, with the first three films offering dystopian fantasies on the themes of, respectively, dehumanization, entropy and destruction, and the fourth depicting a conformist who sabotages his own imaginative life. If O'Pray's assessment is correct, we could suggest that Švankmajer turned to the Surrealist Group as others turn to revolutionary political movements, adopting a group identity as a gesture of radical solidarity and embracing Surrealist methods as a strategy of calculated subversion. The ending of *The Flat* offers something of an allegory of Surrealism's subversive role under totalitarianism.

Figure 7.1 The end of *The Flat* (*Byt*, Jan Švankmajer, 1968) ©Kratký Film.

2.   Michael O'Pray, 'Jan Švankmajer: A Mannerist Surrealist', in Hames, *Dark Alchemy*, p. 48.

Trapped in a room full of rebellious and tormenting objects, the film's protagonist tries to escape by hacking down the door with an axe, but is confronted by an impenetrable wall, on which hundreds of names are scrawled. Upon close inspection, many of these names turn out to be those of Surrealists, past and present, iconic and obscure. The movement is thus directly identified with the attempt to forge an escape route, at once individual and collective, from the prison of contemporary society. The hero adds his own name to the wall, in a demonstration of solidarity or, as O'Pray puts it, 'communion' with his artistic comrades in dissent.

Yet if Švankmajer came to invest a new sense of purpose in his work during that pivotal year of 1968, it should be noted that, in aesthetic terms, there is little change between these consciously 'political' films and the ones made earlier (in fact there is a greater formal distinction between the films of the 1960s and early 1970s and those that Švankmajer made upon returning to filmmaking after seven years of enforced 'rest'). The forging of direct links with Surrealism represents a consolidation of tendencies already present in Švankmajer's work rather than any kind of 'revolutionary' artistic upheaval. It could be said that even when Švankmajer was drawing on influences other than Surrealism, he was utilizing the Surrealist impulses that had long been present in Czech culture. In fact, Švankmajer's oeuvre as a whole tends to reveal the affinities between a conscious Surrealism and Prague's local myths and cultural traditions (alchemy, black light theatre, the 'Mannerism' of the court painter Arcimboldo). There are few artists as intensely absorbed in the art and mythology of their native environment as Švankmajer, and to that extent his work illustrates how a transgressive, modernist sensibility can emerge, paradoxically, from a strong sense of cultural rootedness. There may be a more directly critical aspect to many of the consciously Surrealist films, but the other qualities that make Švankmajer's work provocative and oppositional are also present, if not in a fully developed form, in the 'innocent' early works. Švankmajer has insisted that all his films since 1968 have been conceived as political; no doubt this is true, but the political quality of Švankmajer's work is as much evident in its aesthetic organization as in the elements of direct critique that it offers.

Throughout this chapter it will be shown that Švankmajer's 'polemic' with his society largely concerns issues of communication and expression (artistic and otherwise), of language in its broadest sense, and even of different ways of relating to and interpreting the world. That polemic sometimes takes place at a thematic level, but it is more generally embodied in the formal articulation of Švankmajer's films. Unsurprisingly, it is a polemic heavily inflected by psychoanalytic ideas. The exploration of the relationship between particular forms of expression and the 'inner self' (whether defined as phantasy, desire or the libidinal drives) has long been a central aspect of Surrealism and of the avant-garde more generally. Of all the filmmakers explored here, Švankmajer has been the most interested (or the most successful) in forging a new kind of cinematic articulation that can 'speak' the body and capture the movements of unconscious thought. The fact that Švankmajer was forging this style in the films he made before his conversion to Surrealism aligns his work with the Surrealist project in a profound way right from the beginning. The centrality of language to Surrealism is evident in, for example, 'The Platform of Prague', the *de facto* manifesto of the resurrected Czech Surrealism of the 1960s (though one written in collaboration with the soon-to-be-disbanded French Surrealists). This 1968 document reiterates that Surrealism must oppose itself to both Stalinist Communism and Western capitalism: both camps are subsumed under a single denomination as 'the repressive system ... , whose differences really seem, whatever the political and institutional labels assumed, purely conventional'.[3] This viewpoint is echoed in Švankmajer's own assertion, made many years later, that Stalinism itself is nothing but an 'ulcer' produced by a fundamentally 'diseased' civilization.[4] Amongst its other malign practices, the international 'technocratic order' alienates the individual from his or her 'internal realm', something that it achieves through the misuse, the hollowing out, of language (we might construe this term as referring to signifying systems in general). Surrealism's true site of 'subversive' intervention is therefore the text itself, and the Surrealist's immediate emancipatory goal a 'liberation' of language that would divest signs of their 'utilitarian' character and enable them to reveal or encode desire:

> The repressive system monopolises language and restores it to mankind only when reduced to a utilitarian function or distorted to serve entertainment. People are thus deprived of the real powers of their own thought. They are forced ... to rely on cultural agents who offer them standardised patterns of thought that obviously conform to the proper functioning of the system ... The empty language people are thereby left with is unable to formulate the ardent images which could restore the imperious satisfaction of their true desires ... The role of surrealism is to tear language away from the repressive system and make it the instrument of desire. Thus, what is called surrealist 'art' has no other goal than to liberate words, or more generally the signs, from the codes of utility and entertainment, in order to restore them as bearers of revelation of subjective reality ...[5]

---

3.   'The Platform of Prague', in Richardson and Fijałkowski, *Surrealism Against the Current*, p. 59.
4.   'Interview with Jan Švankmajer', in Hames, *Dark Alchemy*, p. 118.
5.   'The Platform of Prague', op. cit.

We must not align the declarations of the 'Platform' too closely with Švankmajer's ideas and artistic approach. Nonetheless the term 'ardent images' is particularly apt for his work, as it implies the investment of libido within the processes of representation themselves, the construction not of images of desire but of desiring images. Furthermore, Švankmajer seems to have espoused the same ambition of forging a personal 'language', in this case a mode of audio-visual discourse, that is more than merely entertaining and more than merely functional. Utilitarian discourses or language systems (in visual terms, public information films or traffic signals would be exemplary) strive to reduce expression to a univalent, unambiguously denotational function, and it is to this form of signification that Švankmajer is resolutely opposed. Obviously the rejection of 'utilitarian' language can be linked to Švankmajer's attempt to divest ordinary objects of their utilitarian functions, to reveal them in their concrete specificity and wondrousness. As is equally true of the 'Platform of Prague', the wide-ranging assault on the principle of utility in Švankmajer's work (which includes an implicit critique of the way works of art themselves become the 'useful' instruments of those in power) is not a defence of art for art's sake, but a reorientation of need and use in terms of individual desires and compulsions. Švankmajer emphatically concurs with psychoanalysis and Surrealist orthodoxy that 'true desire' is retrogressive, directed back into early childhood, and thus to explore the relationship between language and desire in Švankmajer's work is largely to explore the relationship between language and infancy. In this sense Švankmajer's real enemy may be less the historically specific repressions of the present-day 'technocratic order' than the codified meanings and literalist logic of the adult world *per se*. It must be noted that the 'Platform of Prague', with its reference to a finally restored 'satisfaction' of desires, is rather more simplistic, more straightforwardly affirmative, in its call for personal 'liberation' than Švankmajer and his fellow postwar Czech Surrealists have generally been. The greater optimism of the 'Platform' may be attributed to the naively utopian libertarianism prevalent in 1968. The darkest images of Švankmajer's films suggest that absolute liberation might only unleash a new despotism.

Animation, Materiality and the Language of the Real

While Švankmajer's work often utilizes the subversive power of tradition, in other respects his films are profoundly anti-traditional, and nowhere is this more evident than in his approach to animation itself. Švankmajer's most celebrated and influential predecessors in Czech animation were Jiří Trnka and Karel Zeman, who best exemplified the 'schools' of the puppet film and the 'trick film' respectively. Švankmajer may share Trnka's interest in fantasy and Czech folklore, and Zeman's capacity for seamlessly blending animation with live action, yet in formal terms his work represents a fundamental break with both his major forebears. For Švankmajer, the key difference between his approach and the aesthetic 'systems' of Trnka and Zeman is that the latter 'worked with representational illusion', whereas he himself 'was attracted to brute reality':

> What interests me about an object or a cinematic setting is not its artistic eloquence but what it's made of, what affects it and in what circumstances, how it is altered by time, etc. This explains why from my earliest films on I have used the close-up which precisely searches out every 'scratch on the illusion'.[6]

Trnka's wish was for the viewer to forget the materials that constitute the representation, for the wood, paint and clay from which his puppets and sets were concocted to be magically subsumed into narrative and character. Yet in Švankmajer's work the textural reality of objects and settings gains priority over (or at least assumes equal importance to) what those objects or settings 'communicate'. Švankmajer's statements reveal a more complex conception of animation than had previously been developed, one that approximates the concern with the real properties of artistic materials in modern sculpture. Animation is generally considered synonymous with the enactment of illusions, but the violence with which Švankmajer brings his creations to life is also a means to reveal or emphasize the real nature of objects: the relentless smashing and breaking down of objects that occurs throughout his films enables us to see precisely how these objects are composed, the weakness or resilience of their material. The artificial but scrupulously synchronized sounds that Švankmajer dubs onto his films serve a similar purpose. The concern with 'brute reality' should not be seen to exclude a poetic quality; as we shall see, the poetic nature of Švankmajer's work simply has a different basis or source than in, say, Trnka's films. The physical reality of things remains inalienable, unmitigated by the leaps and manoeuvres of fantasy. Even at his most playful, Švankmajer adheres to the normal workings of objects: in the 1971 *Jabberwocky* (*Žvahlav aneb šatičky slaměného Huberta*), a pirouetting penknife only turns against its blade in one direction, and even self-constructing building blocks are easily knocked down.

If Švankmajer has any direct artistic predecessor, it is less any august figure from Czech animation than the eccentric father from Bruno Schulz's 1934 story collection *The Street of Crocodiles* (originally published as *Cinnamon Shops* (*Sklepy cynamonowe*)). In a celebrated episode, 'Treatise on Tailor's Dummies',

---

6.   Švankmajer, interviewed by Petr Král, 'Questions to Jan Švankmajer', translated by Jill McGreal, *Afterimage* 13, 1987, p. 22.

Figure 7.2 *Punch and Judy* (*Rakvičkárna*, Jan Švankmajer, 1966) ©Kratký Film, reproduced courtesy of the Czech National Film Archive.

Schulz's character, possibly deranged, possibly visionary, espouses a heretical principle of creation that emphasises 'matter' at the expense of 'life':

> 'Can you understand,' asked my father, 'the deep meaning of that weakness, that passion for coloured tissue, for papier-mâché, for distemper, for oakum and sawdust? This is … the proof of our love for matter as such, for its fluffiness or porosity, for its unique mystical consistency. Demiurge, that great master and artist, made matter invisible, made it disappear under the surface of life. We, on the contrary, love its creaking, its resistance, its clumsiness. We like to see behind each gesture, behind each move, its inertia, its heavy effort, its bearlike awkwardness.'[7]

This passage perfectly captures Švankmajer in his own 'demiurgic' guise: as a puppeteer Švankmajer is concerned as much with the grain of the body as with the soul. His puppets are always unnervingly poised between their role as players in a dramatic situation and their actual status as concrete objects,

---

7.   Bruno Schulz, *The Fictions of Bruno Schulz: The Street of Crocodiles and Sanatorium Under the Sign of the Hourglass*, translated by Celina Wieniewska (London: Picador, 1988), p. 41.

fascinating in their materiality. Like all other objects in Švankmajer's work, puppets are mutilated and destroyed in accordance with their real material properties: a wooden head may be splintered beneath a hammer or carved neatly in two with a sword. The close-up of a puppet's face does not, as in classical animated and live-action cinema, emphasize interior experience and encourage identification, but only reveals the static expression, the garishly painted features and the chipped, flaking surfaces: the 'scratches' that expose the illusion.

In Švankmajer's hands the puppet becomes an abject figure, not for the humiliations it suffers but for the way it disturbs 'natural' boundaries. According to Kristeva's psychoanalytic definition of the abject, a phenomenon is especially abject when it confuses the distinction between subject and object: the Švankmajerian puppet, at once recognizably humanoid and conspicuously composed of inanimate materials, is both subject and object, protagonist and prop. Švankmajer addresses this confusion directly in the 1969 *Don Juan* (*Don Šajn*), combining backstage glimpses of the marionettes in their 'lifeless' pre-performance state with the use of live actors dressed up in marionette costumes. The insistence on the materiality of the puppet is a means for Švankmajer to emphasise the puppet's fundamental alterity, its peculiar neither-living-nor-dead status. This emphasis can be linked back to classic Surrealism and its preoccupation with the disturbing qualities of mannequins, automatons and dolls. For Kristeva, the abject is uncanny because it intimates that condition of non-differentiation experienced in early infancy, but, like those earlier Surrealist humanoids, Švankmajer's puppets are also uncanny in the more orthodox Freudian sense of evoking infantile and atavistic uncertainties: these mobile yet lifeless creatures 'provoke a primordial confusion about the (in)animate and the (non)human'.[8]

Yet, most importantly, Švankmajer's assertion of the puppet's material status betrays his concern with the materiality of existence itself, with the world in all its tactile, voluptuous physicality. Such films as *J.S. Bach: Fantasy in G Minor* (*J.S. Bach: Fantasia g-moll*, 1965) and *A Game with Stones* (*Hra s kameny*, 1965) abandon anthropomorphic and dramatic elements altogether and devote themselves to the exploration of natural surfaces and textures. Surrealism is often seen as attempting to take us out of reality and into an ethereal realm of fantasies, but Švankmajer's brand of Surrealism more typically comprises a convulsive immersion in the minutiae of the real world. As Michael O'Pray suggests, Švankmajer's work attests to the fact that Surrealism is as much preoccupied with 'the shock or trauma of the real' as with the 'oozings of the unconscious'.[9] Švankmajer's choice of materials reveals

---

8. Foster, *Compulsive Beauty*, p. 128.
9. O'Pray, 'Surrealism, Fantasy and the Grotesque: The Cinema of Jan Švankmajer', in Donald, *Fantasy and the Cinema*, p. 262.

his passion for textures, even of a repulsive kind: smooth stone, porridge-like mush, and soft, thumb-patterned clay. In the Mad Hatter's tea party scene from Švankmajer's 1987 *Alice* (*Něco z Alenky*), what captivates is neither Carrollian wordplay nor the magical illusion of life, but an excess of jarring physical details: butter-smeared clocks, tea pouring through the hollow torso of the wooden Hatter, a creaking pushcart and a tattered March Hare futilely attempting to stitch a loose button eye back in place. Aided by rapid montage, extreme close-ups and realistic sound design, concrete reality here incites a kind of sensual delirium.

That process suggests how the affective, and also the imaginative, can develop out of the real and material. Švankmajer's work might impress us with its capacity to synthesize the fanciful and the corporeal, or as Vratislav Effenberger puts it to reconcile 'lyric pathos and raw reality',[10] yet for Švankmajer himself physical reality may be less an impediment to the imagination than its precondition. This idea seems to have been a central principle of Czech Surrealism in general; it is evident, for instance, in the Czech Surrealists' group activities focused around 'tactile experiments', where group members would touch the same hidden objects and then imaginatively extrapolate from those tactile sensations. The practice of alchemy, an enduring fixation of both the Surrealist movement and Švankmajer in particular, here reveals its metaphorical aptness to his work: the gold of poetry is wrought out of the basely material. Yet the interaction between the real and the imaginary is a two-way process, with poetry itself being transformed back into a material event. For Breton and the original Surrealists, the heart of Surrealism and the height of poetry was to be found in the meeting of incongruous realities; in the words of Vítězslav Nezval, Surrealism sets 'the star near the table; the glass hard by the piano and the angels; the door beside the ocean'.[11] Švankmajer treats what was here posited as merely an imagined, or linguistic, encounter in highly literal terms. Thus, such Surrealist encounters as Švankmajer offers in *A Quiet Week in the House* and *Dimensions of Dialogue* (*Možnosti dialogu*, 1983) – a clockwork chicken submerged under falling clay, a tongue put through a grinder, butter smeared over a shoe or a pencil-sharpener sharpening a tube of toothpaste – are as traumatic as they are poetic: the sublime poetic device that is Surrealist synthesis here proves messily material and often violent in its realization. The spirit of Bataillean materialism throws a spanner into the works of Bretonian idealism. While the visceral effect of these encounters partly illustrates the natural differences between literary and

---

10. Vratislav Effenberger, quoted in František Dryje, 'Formative Meetings', in Jan Švankmajer and Eva Švankmajerová, *Animus Anima Animation* (Prague: Slovart Publishers Ltd and Arbour Vitae – Foundation for Literature and Visual Arts, 1998), p. 12.

11. Vítězslav Nezval, quoted in Rothenberg and Sovak, 'Postface to Nezval's *Antilyrik*', in Nezval, *Antilyrik*, p. 153, n.1.

cinematic Surrealism, it should also be noted that Švankmajer exploits and intensifies the physicality, the superior tactility, of the film medium.

Like O'Pray, the modern art scholar Rosalind Krauss emphasizes the centrality of the real to the Surreal. Krauss even argues that the essence of Surrealism lies neither in the written nor the painted, but in the photographed (although Krauss has in mind mainly still photography). This claim, while bold, is less contentious than the assertion that the Surrealists seized on photography for its capacity to reveal reality 'as sign': 'it is precisely this experience of *reality as representation* that constitutes the notion of the Marvelous or of Convulsive Beauty – the key concepts of Surrealism'.[12] It might seem tempting to apply this observation to Švankmajer's work: as we shall see, Švankmajer seems to regard the world as a text waiting to be deciphered, and claims to be able to 'hear' the secret content of objects. Yet it would be inaccurate to suggest that Švankmajer's images or objects are enthusiastically or straightforwardly engaged in signification. These objects may evoke (and provoke), but they seldom 'signify': they are irreducibly the concrete entities they are, the 'meaning' of themselves. (Of course, these objects *are* signs in the sense that they are mere images of objects, not the objects themselves; yet as photographic representations, they are at least indexically related to the reality they evoke.) For example, the recurrent images of heavy stone walls and forbidding iron doors in *JS Bach* may be seen as indicating authoritarian entrapment or inaccessibility, but the materiality of those rough, keenly rendered textures ensures that the images exceed, in a sense discard, such meaning. Roger Cardinal writes: 'when Švankmajer shows us a rabbit with sawdust trickling from its belly (*Alice*), or a man drinking soup from a punctured spoon (… *The Flat* …), then it is that material aberration which he is most concerned to communicate, literally and emphatically'.[13] The process of interpreting a thing, allegorically or otherwise, benefits from a degree of distance: one must step back so as to be able to define an object, so as to see it in relation to other objects and bring rational processes to bear on it. Yet the interrogation of the real in Švankmajer's films is generally a close-up affair and one in which, courtesy of fast pacing and violent action, there is little opportunity for contemplation.

Krauss's comments on Surrealist photography are arguably inadequate not only for Švankmajer's work but also for postwar traditions of Czech Surrealist and post-Surrealist art in general. Photography again played an important role in such traditions, yet an artist such as Emila Medková, perhaps the major exponent of postwar Surrealist photography in Czechoslovakia, was as

12. Rosalind Krauss, 'The Photographic Conditions of Surrealism', *October*, Vol. 19, Winter 1981, p. 28.
13. Roger Cardinal, 'Thinking Through Things: The Presence of Ojects in the Early Films of Jan Švankmajer', in Hames, *Dark Alchemy*, pp. 87–88.

preoccupied by surface and substance as Švankmajer. Krzysztof Fijałkowski observes that the found signs that appear in Medková's photographs (graffiti, public notices) are pointedly stripped of their communicative purpose (according to Fijałkowski this is a comment on the blockage of authentic communication by totalitarianism).[14] Neither does Krauss's suggestion that the central principle Surrealism was that of 'representation' do justice to such quasi-abstract strains of plastic Surrealist-affiliated art as Explosionalism and Czech Informel (the latter an oft-unacknowledged influence on Švankmajer's early artworks). Informel artists conceived their aim more in terms of inscription than of representation, with the artwork defined not as text but as the material trace of a psychic or affective 'event', of that original mute 'something'.[15] In fact, such developments of the postwar avant-garde would be better interpreted by reference to another of Krauss's critical concepts, the Bataille-derived notion of the 'formless'.

According to Krauss, Surrealism both perceives reality as articulate in its capacity to represent, and presents reality as something literally 'articulated': fissures and gaps are introduced into the photographed scene, as though the seamless, formless mass of the world has been carved up into a set of discrete signs. Krauss cites Jacques Derrida's assertion that such gaps, enactments of 'spacing', provide 'the precondition for meaning as such'; signification emerges from the distinction or separation that is maintained between signs.[16] In this sense the 'presence' of the photographed reality is exchanged for the 'absence' at the heart of signification. Yet, as we have seen, it is precisely the 'presence' of reality, its material and substantial nature, with which Švankmajer is concerned; his images scrupulously preserve the 'traces' (in a concrete, indexical, rather than Derridean, sense) of once-present objects. Švankmajer is interested not in division or 'articulation' but in presenting reality in its original seamlessness and unity, even if, paradoxically, that 'original' condition must be recreated by illusionistic means. Of course, fissures and gaps are already central to cinematic technique in the form of the cut, and some Surrealist or Surrealist-influenced films (such as Chytilová's *Daisies*) have stressed the real rupture that the cut constitutes, emphasizing the temporal–spatial division that classical narrative cinema attempts to hide. Yet, while Švankmajer has often utilized montage to dazzling effect, especially in his early films, his continuity cuts are always scrupulously, indeed painstakingly, matched and never compromise the impression of a seamless reality. His work

14. Krzysztof Fijałkowski, 'Emila Medková: The Magic of Despair', *Tate Papers*, Autumn 2005 (http://www.tate.org.uk/research/tateresearch/tatepapers/05autumn/fijalkowski.htm) (retrieved 3 August 2008).

15. Mikuláš Medek, 'Text z katalogu výstavy v Teplicích 1963', in Ševčík, Morganová and Dušová, *České umění 1938–1989*, p. 242.

16. Rosalind Krauss, 'The Photographic Conditions of Surrealism', *October*, p. 22.

does not adopt a 'linguistic' strategy of differentiation but rather follows a logic of merging, melding and coagulating. This is evident in the materials that Švankmajer most frequently uses, in those viscous, porous, amorphous substances, and it is also present as a 'narrative' motif: in the first part of *Dimensions of Dialogue*, sets of objects are gradually broken down into an ever more indistinguishable mush, and in the second part two clay lovers literally merge together.

That sophisticated, 'proto-poststructuralist' understanding of language that Krauss discerns in Surrealism can also be glimpsed in Švankmajer's work, yet verbal signification is here less an object of emulation than one of critique. For a filmmaker who rarely used dialogue before he began making feature films in the late 1980s, Švankmajer is surprisingly preoccupied with the verbal model of communication, and several of his films can even be considered implicit polemics against language. As an attempt at ordering reality, language seems to represent for him another example of human vanity and the will to domination. The 1967 *Historia naturae (suita)*, though explicitly a critique of the taxonomizing practices of natural science, can be seen more generally as an assertion of the way reality inevitably escapes the categories, including linguistic ones, that we impose on it. Švankmajer ostensibly illustrates each of the established animal species; yet his illustrations strain against the limits of coherent categorization, with Švankmajer focusing on the more freakish variations of a particular genus (the scaly armadillo appears in the sequence on mammals) or offering his own hybrid concoctions (a fish skeleton flaps its fins like a bird, a human skull in the last section seems disturbingly simian). In addition, the heterogeneity of the artistic materials Švankmajer uses (paintings, lithographs, photographs, stop-motion-animated models, live-action) seems to refute or defy the rigidity of the various categories. Over all of this hangs the ludic spectre of the eccentric sixteenth-century ruler Rudolf II, subject of the film's dedication, whose well-known 'cabinets of curiosities' (in which disparate and exotic phenomena were bizarrely classified) reveal how arbitrary are our 'natural' categories of understanding. Between the various illustrations Švankmajer interposes a shot of a man's mouth eating a morsel of food, an image that both links understanding with domination and also alludes to that materiality, that base reality of drives and sensations, that precedes the acquisition of language. Finally the eater is himself reduced to an animated skull: the thinking, ordering subject stands revealed as a material, mortal being.

The skull returns as the dominant motif of *The Ossuary* (*Kostnice*, 1970), which was shot in the famous ossuary at Sedlec Monastery. Once again, Švankmajer is engaged in a commentary on language. The skulls and bones are arranged into a vast array of dazzling configurations that comprise both abstract patterns and representations of real objects (a chandelier, a monstrance). They are thus comparable to the phonemes, the combinable units, that make up any language system, a 'found' conceit suggestive of the Arcimboldo portraits much beloved of Švankmajer. The deathly nature of these skeletal forms could be seen to reassert the absence (or negativity) that underlies signification: the very 'articulation' of these forms required the deaths of those to whom the ossuary now constitutes a grisly memorial. Yet while the ossuary seems to comprise a morbid linguistic system unto itself, the actual words into which some configurations are arranged are, perversely but typically, rendered illegible.

If Švankmajer refuses to create a structured, 'literary' discourse out of these images, they nonetheless suggest a wide range of possible meanings and possess an immense affective and emotional power.[17] This power is offset, in the original version of the film, by the irascible, drearily factual spoken commentary of an unseen tour guide. Švankmajer intended this commentary to be 'pedestrian' and 'Party-line',[18] though it is difficult to imagine any form of spoken commentary that could approximate this spectacle. If reality seldom attains the status of writing, it is hardly to be written off. For Švankmajer the object world *does* constitute a kind of language, but a language of affects, emotions, memories, fantasies. What Švankmajer rejects, contrary to the tendencies identified by Krauss, is the verbal model of language, the domination of 'symbolic' or cognitive meaning at the expense of affective qualities, and the codification or fixing of meaning. Individual objects, whether skulls, wardrobes, dolls or stones, can mean many different things: indeed this is part of that treacherous quality that Švankmajer observes in objects.

As we have seen in relation to the work of other Czech filmmakers, the insistence on the plurality and privacy of meaning inevitably has a subversive quality, constituting a rejection of Socialist Realism's intensive polemical codification of its protagonists and narratives tropes. In so far as state power has already compromised verbal language by stamping its desired meanings on particular words (one facet of that debasement of language identified by 'The Platform of Prague'), Švankmajer's reliance on images and objects could be seen to reflect the search for a less codified, and thus less authoritarian, form of language or cultural expression. Yet, as will be argued throughout this chapter, Švankmajer's central aim in his approach to animation and filmmaking is to make us perceive the world as we did when we were infants. He strives to evoke and enliven that original wonder and responsiveness, that rich experience of a world teeming with new sensations, mysteries and imaginative incitements. Indeed the seamless vision of reality presented in Švankmajer's films is itself the condition of infancy, of that time prior to the imposition of verbal language.

---

17. Cardinal, in Hames, *Dark Alchemy*, pp. 82–83.
18. Jan Švankmajer, cited in Jan Uhde, 'The Bare Bones of Horror: Jan Švankmajer's *Kostnice (The Ossuary)*, *Kinoeye*, Vol. 2, Issue 1, 7 Jan 2002 (http://www.kinoeye.org/02/01/uhde01.php) (retrieved 1 August 2008).

The next section will look at how Švankmajer actually inscribes infantile experience in the form of his films, or rather how he seeks to use 'language', the materials of expression, in an infantile way. This will take us from the materiality of the world to the materiality of the body and, as proxy to the latter, the materiality of the signifying apparatus of cinema. It is Švankmajer's bravura use of the film medium that distinguishes him from, say, Menzel, whose concern with materiality and texture does not extend to cinematic technique itself.

Supersaturated Style: Psychic Expression and Inscription

Švankmajer's habitual insistence that he is uninterested in 'art' and his refusal to discuss his work in terms of aesthetic categories have always sat oddly with the extreme formal self-consciousness and technical virtuosity displayed in his films. As an animator, Švankmajer is almost unique for being at least as interested in cinematic technique as in animated technique: the only comparable figures are the Czech Jiří Barta, the Pole Walerian Borowczyk, who in any case acceded successfully to live-action cinema, and those brilliant American-born disciples of Central European animation, the Brothers Quay. Švankmajer's 1960s and 1970s films make particularly impressive use of camera movement, editing, colour, focusing, sound design and music. Petr Král has identified a 'sculpturally supersaturated' quality, a sense of formal overripeness, in films such as *Jabberwocky*. The older Švankmajer seems to disapprove somewhat of the formal flamboyance of his early work, and he has described the development of his career in terms of a process of stylistic purification in which the early trappings of 'Mannerist' excess have been pruned away to let an 'authentic' Surrealism emerge. Here Švankmajer's notions of true Surrealism seem close to the views of such postwar Czech Surrealists as Král himself, for whom Surrealism is supposed to comprise the aesthetically neutral, 'objective' revelation of the world's innate irrationality. Yet once we take a broader perspective, it becomes clear that Švankmajer's preoccupation with the formal properties of art has many precedents both within the Surrealist movement and within avant-garde and modernist art more generally. The idea that the instruments of expression might attain a material presence of their own has long been one of the key distinguishing features of avant-garde painting and literature. In Joyce's novel *Ulysses* (1922), for example, the material properties of the world compete with the material properties of writing itself; the appearance, sound and rhythm of words, even the arrangement of printed text on the page, achieve a corporeality comparable to that of the book's preponderant scatological and erotic description.

Even the most invisible and 'disembodied' aspects of film technique, such as editing, often attain a palpable, physical presence in Švankmajer's films. At the beginning of *Jabberwocky*, brief close-up shots of a hand smacking an

Figure 7.3 Production still from *The Last Trick* (*Poslední trik pana Schwarcewalldea a pana Edgara*, Jan Švankmajer, 1964) ©Czech National Film Archive.

infant's bottom cut into the film's credits, accompanied by a musical 'slap' on the soundtrack: each cut itself seems to comprise a blow. On one level, this heightening of technique can contribute to the theatrical quality of Švankmajer's work (a number of his early films are explicitly staged as 'performances'), thereby supplementing the material realism of his films with a certain (if far from Brechtian) artistic self-reflexivity. Indeed 'realist' techniques are themselves pointedly heightened, or exposed for their deceitfulness: in *A Quiet Week in the House* the *cinéma vérité* style of the live-action sequences is as overbearing, as stylized, as the slow-motion 'dream' effect of the film's animated scenes, and in *The Castle of Otranto* (*Otrantský zámek*, 1973/79) the documentarian pretence of reality cannot guard against an ultimate incursion of Gothic fantasy.

Yet, more importantly, Švankmajer's formal language should also be read in the light of Julia Kristeva's theory of the semiotic, which connects artistic expression with the working of unconscious drives and affects. 'Semiotic' discourse exploits the sensuous properties of a given language or sign-system, and it is through these properties that the subject's flux of desires and his or her psychosomatic 'pulsions' are made manifest. The semiotic is defined in opposition to the 'symbolic', which means language in its propositional, convention-bound, logical form; in terms of verbal signification, the model Kristeva predominantly uses, symbolic discourse requires the adherence to the existing signs and their accepted meanings, to syntactical, grammatical and logical rules. Semiotic language is, quite literally, the language of infancy, as 'semiosis' begins, and achieves its purest form, in that affective, 'meaningless' babble that children make before they have grasped the rules of signification. Whether semiotic discourse comprises a kind of 'signification' is moot: such discourse is opposed to structured argumentation, and the 'meaning' of semiosis is more likely to be *felt* than cognitively understood. Švankmajer has never sought to make cinema approximate what Kristeva considers the pure artistic semiosis of music and dance. His work is never abstract, as in the late experiments of Stan Brakhage, but always emphatically concrete. Furthermore, what interests Švankmajer is the tension and opposition of discourses: the libidinal and affective nature of the semiotic undercuts the methodical, seemingly discursive or 'linguistic' structures by which the films are sometimes framed (the taxonomic groupings of *Historia naturae*, the organization of dialogues into captioned sequences in *Dimensions of Dialogue*, the deceptive oppositions of fantasy and 'real life' in *A Quiet Week in the House* and *The Castle of Otranto*).

It is doubtful that Švankmajer is or ever was acquainted in any way with Kristeva's work, and her key text concerning the 'semiotic', *Revolution in Poetic Language* (*La Révolution du langage poétique*), was not even published in French until 1974. Yet this does not make her ideas any less apposite. Kristeva originally defined her notion of 'semiotic' or 'poetic' language with reference to a tradition of avant-garde literature stretching from Lautréamont (the most important proto-Surrealist) and Stéphane Mallarmé in the eighteenth and nineteenth centuries through to Alfred Jarry and Georges Bataille in the twentieth: as much as Kristeva is coining a theory of linguistic functioning, she is identifying a trend within literature, one that includes Surrealism in its sweep. Moreover, Kristeva's work has particular relevance in the Czech context, as her theory of poetic language was no doubt significantly influenced by the Prague-based Structuralist Roman Jakobson: in a 1974 essay 'The Ethics of Linguistics', Kristeva applauds Jakobson for his insight that poetry is constituted in the struggle between the 'primordial' physicality of 'rhythm' and the laws of signification.[19] Karel Teige himself had surmised, prior to Kristeva, that it is through the sensuous and associative, rather than denotative, qualities of language that the unconscious can be accessed. Kristeva's work could even be seen as the belated culmination of that fusion of psychoanalysis and structuralism that was first established, albeit in an unsystematic fashion, within the Czech avant-garde. Kristeva's 1970s writings should also be linked with the cultural aims of the 'Platform of Prague': theoretically rather than polemically, these writings posit how language might encode desire and become the 'bearer' of psychic 'revelation'.

---

19. Julia Kristeva, 'The Ethics of Linguistics', *Desire in Language*, p. 30.

In a film such as *Jabberwocky*, which takes infantile development as its explicit theme, formal realization is clearly suffused with a keen psychoanalytic awareness. Arguably Švankmajer's greatest film, it is also one of his most deliriously overworked or, in Král's terms, 'supersaturated'. Rhythm is central to *Jabberwocky*: the film develops as an alternation and repetition of different rhythms (including martial and waltz rhythms) at the level of editing, imagery and music (Zdeněk Liška's thrilling score comprises a work of art in its own right). Kristeva relates the presence of rhythm in art to the functioning of 'pulsion' or drive energy, and at a specifically vocal or verbal level she links rhythm with what she calls 'oralization', the tendency towards 'fusion with the mother's body'.[20] Oralization involves the 'erotization [*sic*] of the vocal apparatus', which manifests itself in the musicality of language, in the 'sweet', 'pleasant' qualities of expression.[21] Kristeva argues that, in infantile development, oralization sublimates and restrains the 'violence' of anal 'rejection'. Like her predecessor, the British psychoanalyst Melanie Klein, Kristeva connects 'anality' with sadism. Moreover, the erotic pleasure of rejection disturbs language acquisition. Rejection will later return to disrupt 'linear' expression; it will also make itself manifest in the rhythmic 'expectorations' (or 'spits') of Artaud's writing and in the gesturality of modern painting.[22]

Jabberwocky itself can be seen as offering a counterpoint between those 'oral' and 'anal' qualities, between the sweet and the sadistic. The sublime choral harmonies of Liška's soundtrack, along with Lewis Carroll's mellifluous nonsense verse, contrast with the vigorous sadism of the film's imagery. Within the soundtrack itself those singing and reciting voices are punctuated by a series of visceral musical 'slaps' and 'burps'. Švankmajer himself announces the connection between sadism and anality in that introductory image of a child's bottom being spanked (of course, in a more literal sense these images hint at the role of such chastisements in stimulating masochistic tendencies, but we must remember that Freud describes sadism and masochism as component aspects of the same instinct).[23] Yet some of the film's sadism is of an oral nature, as in the alarming, half-Carrollian-half-Boschian images of a family of dolls cooking and cannibalizing smaller dolls; thus Švankmajer asserts that sadism pertains at the oral as well as the anal stage, and that, as Kristeva writes, '[f]using orality and devouring, refusing, negative orality are ... closely intermingled'.[24] (What are the violent gobbling and spewing heads of *Dimensions of Dialogue* if not images

---

20. Julia Kristeva, *Revolution in Poetic Language*, translated by Margaret Waller (New York; Chichester: Columbia University Press, 1984), p. 153.
21. Ibid.
22. Ibid., p. 152.
23. Sigmund Freud, 'Three Essays on the Theory of Sexuality', in *The Freud Reader*, pp. 239–93.
24. Kristeva, *Revolution in Poetic Language*, p. 154.

Figure 7.4 *Jabberwocky*
(*Žvahlav aneb šatičky slaměného
Huberta*, Jan Švankmajer, 1971)
©Kratký Film.

of 'refusing, negative orality'?) When a stern, paternal figure in a black-and-white portrait sticks out 'his' tongue to eject a series of coloured bricks, Švankmajer provides another image of oral 'negativity' or rejection, although here the oral is also wittily transmuted into the anal: this spitting out of bricks is obviously an image of excretion. At the same time, this conceit mockingly represents the act of speech as the shitting of word-bricks. Considered in these terms, the image has a resonance that takes us back to the early days of the Czech avant-garde: Karel Teige writes, in *The World Which Smells* (*Svět, který voní*, 1930), that '[f]or the poet the word is a substance ... it must be as real as a brick or a piece of marble'.[25] Teige's comment was really another way of expressing Roman Jakobson's notion of 'poeticity', a notion that Jakobson originally conceived in relation to Czech Poetism. For Jakobson, the condition of poeticity 'is present when the word is felt as a word and not a mere representation of the object being named', when the word appears as an 'autonomous' object with a 'weight and value' of its own.[26] One can discern a direct link with Jakobson's ideas in Švankmajer's own approach to the word. In both *Don Juan* and *The Castle of Otranto*, the former a dramatization of a standard of the marionette theatre and the latter freely adapted from Horace Walpole's Gothic novel, the films' images are punctuated by the words of the original texts, set in old typeface. Thus, Švankmajer's attitude towards the verbal is not entirely dismissive: it seems that words are permissible to the extent that they too become material objects. It is, of course, through the material qualities of language that Kristeva's semiosis (or, for Teige, the 'infrared and ultraviolet reality'[27] of the unconscious) emerges. The richly sensuous though strictly meaningless words of Carroll's poem, featured on *Jabberwocky*'s soundtrack and serving less as an explication of the images than as their aural counterpart, also

---

25.   Karel Teige, quoted in Levinger, 'Czech Avant-Garde Art', *The Art Bulletin*, p. 514.
26.   Roman Jakobson, quoted in ibid.
27.   Teige, op. cit.

attest to an essentially avant-garde approach to language. *Jabberwocky*'s word-bricks serve as a self-reflexive allusion to this approach.

Similarly, the living tongue that tears through the portrait, slimy, coarse and fleshy, suggests speech or expression at its most sensual: to speak 'semiotically' means to adopt 'a vulgar tongue',[28] if not actually to 'speak in tongues' (semiosis begins with the infant's glossolalia-like babbling). Here the avant-garde 'revolution' in discourse is linked with the rebellion against the 'paternal'. The father figure represented in the photograph is the object of much violence, his image being ultimately scribbled out. While this obviously has an Oedipal dimension (the heavy scribbling over of the portrait's eyes is an image of castration, and can be read as a displaced allusion to the child's feared castration at the hands of its father), this image also represents the father (or the father function) in his wider role as the one who establishes laws, interdictions, the rules of signification. Thus, the father figure in *Jabberwocky* is also the pedagogue who forces the unseen infantile hero into writing out the exhaustive grammatical exercises, though these exercises are soon set into flight on the wings of paper aeroplanes. Semiotic discourse (present as the emphatically material and sensual bricks and tongue) subverts, literally ruptures, the symbolic order personified by the paternal portrait. Thus the semiotic is not a question of 'representing' bodily or psychic processes but of inscribing or 'imprinting' them in discourse. Tracing the word's Greek etymology, Kristeva links 'semiotic' back to '*semeion*', which means a 'trace', 'engraved mark' or 'imprint'.[29] Švankmajer is concerned with inscription in a wider, though ultimately related, way. The sculptural dimension of Švankmajer's films, his use of such malleable materials as mud and clay, enables the inscription of the 'body' in a much more obvious, visible and concrete sense. Yet it seems that Švankmajer regards this direct physical handling as an opportunity for the inscription of psychic and affective processes as well. This manner of psychic inscription might even be more closely analogous to Kristeva's theoretical conception in the sense that here the process of channelling one's psyche and affects into the artwork is more immediate than it can be at the level of cinematic techniques. This sphere of expression allows for a material, causal relationship between those internal processes and their expression: in a similar way, the infant's spontaneous 'semiotic' outbursts directly ensue from its primary drives.[30] Švankmajer also suggests that the handling of materials can

---

28. Michael O'Pray, 'Jan Švankmajer: A Mannerist Surrealist', in Hames, *Dark Alchemy*, p. 55.

29. Kristeva, 'From One Identity to Another', in *Desire in Language*, p. 133.

30. Bearing this indexical quality of the semiotic in mind, we could suggest that Švankmajer's concern with the camera's capacity for recording three-dimensional reality is consistent with his interest in semiotic expression: the image is also the indexical trace of the reality it depicts.

itself stimulate affective and imaginative processes: after all, we know that touch carries for him an extreme psychic, emotional and erotic potency. This is Švankmajer's own account of the interplay of psychic and material events involved in animating a pool of mud for a sequence in *The Fall of the House of Usher* (*Zánik domu Usherů*, 1980):

> In the first instance [animated mud] stands for the moving swamp of my memory, but it also introduces my tactile experiments into film. I animated this sequence myself and aimed for a particular 'tension' interpretation of [Poe's] poem. It was made more difficult by the fact that the 'gesture' generating the tension had to be constantly slowed down by the animation technique, it couldn't be discharged all at once in one act of release. The slowing down of the tension, on the other hand, produced an intensification of feelings which forcefully manifested themselves, to the extent of cramp in my fingers. The whole process of animation resulted in considerable spiritual exhaustion.[31]

Švankmajer's dialectic between the invisible world of psychic and libidinal forces and the tangible world of objects, materials and gestures reflects the influence of both 'orthodox' Czech Surrealism and, perhaps more importantly, of Czech Informel. Mikuláš Medek, an affiliate of Effenberger and one of the most important exponents of Informel, describes the artwork as resulting from an engagement between psychic and objective worlds, between 'events' and 'things': 'The picture is an objective report about a psychic event. The objectiveness of the report gives to that event the intensity of presence.'[32] An Informel painting comprises a 'field of sensitivity, over which this "event" has rushed', leaving 'behind itself an objective report about its existence in a system of traces and prints'.[33]

Whether considered in these sculptural terms or in the sense of cinematic style, Švankmajer's 'language' of 'traces and prints' can be seen as a way of eluding the semiotic distortions of power: the encoding of desire or affects in form, in the material of the artwork, ensures that self-expression can never be entirely recuperated by the dominant systems of meanings. The 'mark' of desire remains irreducibly and inalienably what it is, even if that mark is more difficult to 'read' than other kinds of sign (including the conventionalized, arbitrary and thus authentically 'linguistic' sign). It is worth noting here that Švankmajer has turned increasingly to art forms that enable physical contact:

---

31. Švankmajer, interviewed by Vratislav Effenberger, 'Švankmajer on *The Fall of the House of Usher*', translated by Gaby Dowdell, *Afterimage* 13, Autumn 1987, p. 33.
32. Mikuláš Medek, 'Text z katalogu výstavy v Teplicích 1963', in Ševčík, Morganová and Dušová, *České umění 1938–1989*, p. 244.
33. Ibid., p. 242.

the tactile reception of a work may comprise a purer, less ideologically mediated form of 'interpretation'. This issue of reception will next be examined in relation to Švankmajer's own 'hermeneutics' of the object. It has already been suggested that objects possess a natural eloquence for Švankmajer, but in what way could objects be said to 'speak'? How does Švankmajer's approach contradict, subvert or coincide with the dominant attitudes to objects?

Fetishes, Toys and Utensils: How Objects Speak

Central to Švankmajer's films is the Surrealist spirit of inquiry. Each of his films, beyond its explicit narrative and themes, could be considered an exploration, or more precisely an excavation, of the 'life' of objects. Švankmajer believes that objects accrue certain 'meanings' throughout their history of use. Subjective experiences are invested in objects, and this process endows objects with their own 'memory':

> I prefer the kind of objects which, in my opinion, have some kind of inner life. I believe in the 'conservation' of certain contents in objects which people touch under conditions of extreme sensitiveness. The 'emotionally' charged objects are then under certain conditions capable of revealing these contents and touching them provides associations and analogies for our own flashes of the unconscious.[34]

This explains Švankmajer's preference for using objects that he has collected, and the older the better, rather than objects he has made himself. He claims he is capable of 'hearing' objects; his creative work thus essentially amounts to the transcription of an object's 'speech' (though not an interpretation, as that would suggest a deciphered, and decipherable, meaning). At the most literal level, the idea that powerful internal experiences are 'conserved' in objects can be related to that process of inscription already discussed. Yet the process of 'listening to' objects should also be seen as a much more intuitive and subjective one, in which the uncovering of an object's 'latent content' and the investment of the artist's own 'associations' and unconscious 'flashes' are closely interwoven, if not indistinguishable. In this sense the 'speech' of an object, far from being unambiguous or identical from moment to moment, can have many different meanings, can resound differently in each listener's imagination. Objects may reveal a residue of past experiences to the extent that their history of use is visible, as with the well-worn toys that we see in *Jabberwocky*. Like the historical Surrealists of Breton's group, Švankmajer is

---

34. 'Interview with Jan Švankmajer', in Hames, *Dark Alchemy*, pp. 110–11.

fond of what Walter Benjamin called 'outmoded' objects, especially in their 'artisanal', pre-modern form. The evocative or 'communicative' quality of the latter is obvious, as such objects bear the 'traces of the practiced hand'.[35] According to both Benjamin and Hal Foster, the outmoded object also has a specific psychoanalytic resonance, evoking a 'maternal memory (or fantasy) of psychic intimacy and bodily unity'.[36]

Thus, Švankmajer's hermetic, almost necromantic account of his involvement with objects is at least partly metaphorical, a way of describing the Surrealist creative process, the interaction between objective and imaginative worlds. Yet in itself that personal mythology of objects makes for a fascinating inversion of the Marxian definition of the commodity. For Marx also, the object, *qua* commodity, is invested with a sign-like or representational power: Marx famously describes the commodity as a 'social hieroglyphic' that represents, albeit in a cryptic and mystifying form, the process of production. What distinguishes the commodity from any other object is that the commodity has a 'value', an exchange value, deriving from the labour that has gone into its production (one form of labour is judged equivalent to, exchangeable with, any other, and that is one of the distorting qualities of the commodity); Marx reminds us that 'to stamp an object of utility with a value, is just as much a social product as language'.[37] Both the Švankmajerian object and the Marxian commodity converge in the sense that each has a 'value' in excess of a mere use-value. Commodities, like Švankmajer's objects, have an almost magical or supernatural aura, something that was originally implied by Marx's term 'commodity fetishism', when the fetish was still primarily associated with the totems of primitive societies. The difference between commodities and Švankmajer's objects consists in how that 'value' is obtained. The commodity derives its value from the sum of 'dead' labour stored up in it. The process of production is thus encoded in the commodity, in the form of an apparently intrinsic value; the commodity 'speaks', in its sibylline fashion, of a realm of social and productive relations. Švankmajer posits a different order of value, whereby objects derive their meaning from the sum of psychological and emotional experiences, whether pleasurable or traumatic, 'conserved' in them. One might suggest that Švankmajer counterposes the Surrealists' 'internal realm' of freedom to Marx's external realm of necessity.[38] In so far as the commodity is always, under either capitalism or state socialism, a token of exploitation, the Švankmajerian object also marks a switch from

---

35. Walter Benjamin, quoted in Foster, *Compulsive Beauty*, p. 163.
36. Ibid.
37. Karl Marx, *Capital: Volume 1: A Critique of Political Economy*, translated by Ben Fowkes (Harmondsworth: Penguin, 1992), p. 167.
38. 'The Prague Platform', in Richardson and Fijałkowski, *Surrealism Against the Current*, p. 59.

alienation to praxis: how would Surrealism supplement the Marxist humanist concept of praxis if not by demanding that an object, even the process of its production, be psychically significant for its creator?

Needless to say, as a fetish, the Švankmajerian object is much closer to Freudian erotic fetishism than to Marxian commodity fetishism. More precisely, the model Švankmajerian object would be the toy, not only because Švankmajer is particularly susceptible to toys but also because, according to Melanie Klein at least, toys are used by young children to express or dramatize their phantasies, drives and wishes. As Klein writes, 'it was by approaching the play of the child in a way similar to Freud's interpretation of dreams that I found I could get access to the child's unconscious'.[39] Toys thus function for the child as a sort of language, though not in any systematized way ('mere generalized translations of symbols are meaningless').[40] It is no surprise that Švankmajer's 'excavation' of the inner life of objects takes its most intense form when he turns to children's toys, as in *Jabberwocky* and *A Quiet Week in the House*, in both of which films toys enact all sorts of libidinal and destructive urges. For Švankmajer, we should approach objects as children, with their greater expressiveness and lack of psychic inhibitions, approach toys: we should create, collect and relate to objects neither as commodities (Švankmajer, like the German Dadaist Kurt Schwitters and the eccentric American Surrealist Joseph Cornell, cultivates something of a 'junk' aesthetic, generally favouring objects that are retrograde, decrepit and 'worthless') nor purely as utilities, but as representatives of our fantasies, gratifying our psychic and affective needs. This is another way in which objects can 'speak', and this time with our own voice rather than that of an imagined other. As in Klein's accounts of children's play, 'representation' here would assume less a communicative than a private, purgative and onanistic function. In Surrealism, a clear precedent for such a new order of object 'relations' can be found in Breton's 'Introduction to the Discourse on the Paucity of Reality', where Breton proposes the fabrication of 'certain objects which are approached only in dreams and which seem no more useful than enjoyable'.[41] Yet such object relations are also augured in those outmoded objects that the Surrealists, including Švankmajer, have always collected, objects whose real usefulness has either grown obsolete or become shrouded in mystery.

While Marx distinguishes between exchange value and use value, it seems that, for Švankmajer, exchange and commodification represent only another

---

39. Melanie Klein, 'The Psycho-analytic Play Technique: Its History and Significance', in *The Selected Melanie Klein*, edited by Juliet Mitchell (New York: The Free Press, 1987), p. 51.
40. Ibid.
41. André Breton, 'Introduction to the Discourse on the Paucity of Reality', translated by Bravig Imbs, in *What is Surrealism? Selected Writings*, edited and introduced by Franklin Rosemont (New York: Pathfinder, 1978), p. 39.

manifestation of the utilitarian mentality. Thus Švankmajer's sensibility is more in accordance with Bataillean theories of 'homogenous' economies than with traditional Marxism. In a society of commodities, the object is instrumentalized in the name of a 'higher' purpose (personal enrichment, economic growth) and that pure relationship of enjoyment, the 'cathexis' of individual to object, is denied or considered the mark of 'immaturity'. Švankmajer has argued that civilization as a whole, whether in its capitalist or Communist forms, is founded on utilitarian principles, and he describes his work as an active subversion of those principles: 'My ambition is to render the audience's utilitarian habits unstable ... The irrationality of the dialogue of objects in my films is ... a rebellion against utilitarianism.'[42] That rebellion can be observed in the alarming mismatches of objects in *Dimensions of Dialogue*, and more generally in the transformation of the most ordinary and omnipresent objects, such as household implements, into things of fantasy, fetish objects and living beings. Strangely enough, however, objects' defiance of their utilitarian role also provides some of the most nightmarish and disturbing images in Švankmajer's films. The domestic objects in *The Flat* and *Picnic with Weissmann*, far from being pliant and manipulable, themselves 'use' and in the latter case destroy the films' human characters for their own sadistic pleasure. As an inversion of the relationship between humans and objects, such films can be seen to illustrate Marx's description of the market system, in which things appear to hold sway over people (an illustration less relevant in the context of Eastern Europe's intensively regulated economies); perhaps more importantly, these representations suggest that the Švankmajerian dystopia is one in which objects become estranged from us, frustrating rather than embodying our desires. That is the condition of an instrumentalist world where the material environment comes to seem ever more hostile to human sensibilities and the imagination (for all that modern consumerism makes its illusory promises of satisfaction), and where we ourselves, indoctrinated by utilitarian thought or inhibited in our imaginative life, grow ever less disposed to seeing beyond the 'rational' uses of objects. As with 'The Platform of Prague', such a condemnation indicts a kind of primal, even environmental, alienation specific neither to capitalism nor to 'really existing socialism'.

Just as Švankmajer's objects defy conventional usage, so does his own creative activity resist the uses to which capitalist and Communist societies have generally put works of art, and cinema especially: as a means of private enrichment and mass pacification under capitalism, as an instrument of political persuasion under Communism (though in practice, Communist regimes were often more economically pragmatic than official ideology would suggest, and Czechoslovakia made its fair share of commercial dross). Švankmajer has always vigorously refused the imposition of such functions on

---

42. 'Interview with Jan Švankmajer', in Hames, *Dark Alchemy*, p. 110.

his work: typically, he made his one explicitly political film, *The Death of Stalinism in Bohemia* (*Konec Stalinismu v Čechách*, 1990, sarcastically subtitled a work of 'agitprop'), at a time when anti-Stalinist satire was redundant in the Czech context, and with the aim not of propagating a certain political line but of psychic purgation, of getting the past system out of *his* system (that said, the film's final moment is a cautionary one, auguring the birth of new Stalins and new totalitarianisms). As regards the pressing of art into ideological service, Švankmajer would surely concur with Lewis Carroll, who once assured his readers: 'I can guarantee that the [*Alice*] books have no religious teaching whatever in them – in fact they do not teach anything at all'.[43] Despite his dependence on large 'mainstream' institutions (including Czechoslovakia's state-owned Krátký Film, British television and US corporate monoliths), Švankmajer has always resisted the incorporation of his work into the mass media machine, the transformation of artwork into 'product': he has retained a degree of creative independence that seems even rarer today than when he began making films. Švankmajer valorizes an amateur, home-made art as the ultimate escape from the demands of the mass media: in *Jabberwocky*, the monstrous Prague radio tower is contrasted with the child's domestic box of tricks, and the protagonists of the 1996 feature *Conspirators of Pleasure* (*Spiklenci slasti*) devise their own ingenious masturbatory 'entertainments'. Of course, during the 1970s and '80s, Czech Surrealist art had no choice but to assume an 'amateur' form, and Švankmajer himself spent the greater part of the former decade producing his artworks beyond the attention of the public. In that sense, a 'pure', uncommodified and unmanipulated culture was created by default, courtesy of the normalisers' repressive cultural policies.

The Language of Childhood

As is evident from many of his films and personal statements, Švankmajer espouses the laudatory view of early childhood expressed in Wordsworth's 'Ode: Intimations of Immortality from Recollections of Early Childhood' (1807): 'Heaven lies about us in our infancy!/Shades of the prison-house begin to close/Upon the growing Boy'.[44] The ending of *Jabberwocky* could even be considered a dramatization of these lines, with its images of constraint, conformity and the imprisoned imagination. Yet Švankmajer would hardly

---

43. Lewis Carroll, quoted in Lancelyn Roger Green, 'The Golden Age of Children's Books', in Sheila Egoff, G.T. Stubbs and L.F. Ashley (eds), *Only Connect* (Toronto; New York: Oxford University Press, 1969), p. 51.
44. William Wordsworth, 'Ode: Intimations of Immortality from Recollections of Early Childhood', in *Complete Poetical Works*, edited by Ernest de Selincourt and Thomas Hutchinson (Oxford: Oxford University Press, 1961), p. 460.

concur that there is anything 'heavenly' about infancy: his own images of childhood seem rather to be drawn from the hellishly cruel iconography of Bosch, Goya or Hans Bellmer. Childhood is neither idealized nor sentimentalized in Švankmajer's work, but is shown to be marked by fear, real or imagined threats and the darkest instincts. Of all the psychoanalytic theorists discussed throughout this study, Švankmajer's vision is most closely aligned with Melanie Klein's account of early childhood experience as a maelstrom of paranoid, persecutory fantasies and sadistic, destructive urges. *Jabberwocky* alone reveals sadism, masochism, cannibalism and parental murder as so many worms in the already rotten apple of the human psyche. Švankmajer's work must therefore be distinguished from those manifestations of countercultural utopianism (such as the Vienna Aktionists) that valorize the return to infancy and to the instinctual freedom that state entails. Švankmajer has affirmed in interviews that Surrealism's ultimate ambition, and implicitly his own, is 'liberation', yet the possibility or advisability of complete instinctual liberation is something severely problematized by the films themselves: as David Sorfa suggests, Thanatos seems to hold greater sway over the instincts and desires in Švankmajer's films than Eros.[45] Švankmajer's most recent film, *Lunacy* (*Šílení*, 2005), makes clear that his 'natural man' is a figure borne from the Marquis de Sade and his treatises on the human disposition to evil, not from the work of Rousseau. Švankmajer is aware of the fact that the unconscious, given its freest reign, tends to lead to the kind of tyranny and violence that Czech Surrealism has always vociferously opposed: the revealed sanctuaries of imaginative freedom in *A Quiet Week in the House* may equally be fascist torture chambers. Švankmajer's work is far removed from the optimistic Sixties libertarianism evident in *Valerie and Her Week of Wonders*, offering no intimation of a future utopia that might reconcile instinctual self-gratification with the right to live in peace.

To that extent Švankmajer's films are representative of the anti-utopian, pessimistic tendencies of postwar Czech Surrealism. However, if his work never implies that we might one day enact our repressed desires and urges in life, it does demonstrate that a certain kind of 'liberation' is offered by self-expression, by art itself. Švankmajer argues that Surrealism has 'tried to return art, which has become representational, aesthetic, commercial, to its level of magic ritual'.[46] In that role, it could be said that what art 'invokes' is not the world of the supernatural but rather that of the unconscious. The reference to ritual is also apposite because it suggests the idea of self-purgation or instinctual release

---

45. David Sorfa, 'The Object of Film in Jan Švankmajer', *KinoKultura*, Special Issue 4: Czech Cinema, November 2006 (http://www.kinokultura.com/specials/4/sorfa. shtml) (retrieved 10 August 2008).

46. Švankmajer, interviewed by Geoff Andrew, 'A Faust Buck', *Time Out*, September 7, 1994.

in a contained, and symbolic, form. As we have seen, 'semiotic' expression involves the literal resurfacing of drives and affects, and their 'concretization' in an external form. In the creation and handling of special objects, desires are not only concretized but may also be gratified: representation and instinctual fulfilment directly coincide. For instance, the life-size mannequins in *Conspirators of Pleasure* enable two of the film's protagonists to vent their sadomasochistic desires harmlessly. Most of the fetish objects of *Conspirators* are also ostentatious Švankmajerian art objects: does fetishism aspire to the condition of art or art to the condition of fetishism? Klein's work shows that this bloodless venting of destructive urges by means of objects already takes place in early childhood: a form of containment is thus operative there too, so that childhood itself cannot quite be considered the idyll of instinctual anarchy it is sometimes portrayed as being.

Yet Švankmajer's preoccupation with infancy goes beyond the hankering after a libidinal paradise lost. What interests Švankmajer perhaps above all is the radical existential alterity of childhood, the idea of childhood as an alternative form of expression and cognition, as a different way of thinking about and relating to the world. This is why Švankmajer calls his childhood his 'alter ego', the implication being that childhood represents a form of consciousness opposed to the logical, 'rational' self. We might align this conception of childhood with the unconscious or the primary process, although what Švankmajer has in mind seems to be something broader, perhaps a distinct mode of being. As already shown, early childhood involves a particular form of discourse (semiosis) and a specific way of using objects (Kleinian play); it also involves the primacy of touch over the other senses and, something that is no doubt related to that, the ascendancy of a more intuitive form of understanding or what Michael Richardson calls an 'embodied knowledge'.[47] As long as childhood is considered in these terms, rather than in those of unchecked fulfilment, the fantasized return to infancy becomes a possibility, though one impeded by existing social and cultural conventions. To the extent that childhood is defined by particular forms of expression or cognition, this recuperation of childhood may be enacted within art itself. It is in this sense that Švankmajer's creative work might be considered synonymous with a kind of 'liberation'; Švankmajer's films may also stimulate 'childish' modes of being, thinking and 'speaking' in the viewer.

So far I have not discussed the central role of 'analogy' in Švankmajer's work, yet the use of the analogical method represents another way in which Švankmajer inscribes that infantile alter ego in the form of his films, this time in terms of cognitive practices. According to Švankmajer, 'analogical' thinking, the process of finding or fostering connections between distinct phenomena,

---

47. Richardson, *Surrealism and Cinema*, p. 126.

Figure 7.5 *Et Cetera* (Jan Švankmajer, 1966) ©Kratký Film, reproduced courtesy of the Czech National Film Archive.

is 'natural to primitive cultures and, of course, to young children'.[48] However, '[o]ur rationalistic civilization is founded on the conceptual principle of identity'. As the child accedes to the 'rationalism of older age', the analogical process is 'suppressed into the unconscious from whence it continues to function by means of symbols or poetic images'.[49] The analogical process has always been integral to Surrealist thought and aesthetics, but it was the postwar Czech Surrealists who consciously formulated the principle of analogy and allotted cardinal importance to it. Analogy can be seen as a playful and fluid means of linking and ordering phenomena prior to the imposition of the stable, supposedly authoritative identifications and differentiations of language and natural science. Many seemingly self-evident categories can themselves be seen as 'analogies' that have been dulled by familiarity; in that sense the natural taxonomies that fascinate Švankmajer so much can unwittingly amount to a form of Surrealist poetry. Yet Švankmajer strives to reassert analogy as an active principle, an aim that is evident in the way he juxtaposes

---

48. Švankmajer, in Effenberger, 'Švankmajer on *The Fall of the House of Usher*', *Afterimage*, p. 33.
49. Ibid.

text and image in, say, *Jabberwocky* or *The Fall of the House of Usher*. In such cases Švankmajer defies that system of 'identities' that makes for conventional narrative, whereby a strict semantic and diegetic coherence is maintained between the various constituent elements, between word and image and between the various sequences. That stimulation of imaginative 'analogies' represents a crucial part of Švankmajer's attempt to circumvent or suppress adult rationality, if only temporarily, and to rekindle the poetry of infancy.

Perhaps the greatest sin of modern industrial society for Švankmajer is that it denies the intensity of childhood experience. At best society restricts that intensity to art, which thereby constitutes a kind of sanctioned, legitimized 'infantilism', yet even there the commercial and political interests imposed on the mass media and the 'art market' ensure that 'authentic' art (as Švankmajer would see it) rarely gets a chance. The situation is no better today than it was when Švankmajer began making films in the 1960s: in fact, whatever Švankmajer's misgivings, the Czech New Wave itself attests that there were greater opportunities at that time for avant-garde experiments within the mainstream, even in the context of an authoritarian Communist state. Švankmajer's films may well seem even more alarming and 'alien' for modern audiences than they did for the Communist authorities who regularly banned them during the 1960s, '70s and '80s. Today Švankmajer and the Surrealists are fighting not a culture of open repression but one of meretricious regression, a culture that is characterized by the overproduction of consumer 'toys', by an insistence on personal gratification and by an abundance of undemanding entertainment. Švankmajer would no doubt consider such decadent infantilism to have as little relation to real childhood experience as digital animation does to Švankmajer's tactile creatures of wood and paint.

Švankmajer's cinema comprises the only significant filmic representation of Czech Surrealism in its contemporary, postwar incarnation. As such, his work defies certain basic principles commonly associated with Surrealism, for instance social and sexual utopianism. Švankmajer's films could thus be distinguished from those New Wave films that appropriate Surrealism in its historical, we might even say stereotypical, form. (This is not true of all the New Wave films: as we have seen, both Menzel and Chytilová are interested in particular strands of post-Surrealism.) On the other hand, Švankmajer's work evidences concerns that had been present in the Czech avant-garde right from the beginning: Švankmajer's preoccupation with sensuality and materiality, while characteristic of later trends such as Informel, also obviously links his work back to Teige, Poetism and Artificialism. Yet, as few other Czech avant-gardists had the opportunity to do, Švankmajer extends these concerns into film, emphasizing and developing the 'bodily' dimension of cinema, considered either as a means of depicting material reality or as a technical apparatus.

If this chapter has deployed a more general and wide-ranging approach, then this is because Švankmajer's oeuvre possesses a greater ideological and aesthetic unity, based on an idiosyncratic application of Surrealist and avant-garde principles, than does that of the other New Wave filmmakers. Partly this unity results from the fact that, by working in the 'ghetto' of animation, Švankmajer generally enjoyed a greater creative freedom than his live-action contemporaries. Despite the bannings of his films that did take place, he never faced the same pressure to conform that marks, and sometimes mars, the later work of Chytilová, Jireš and Menzel. Yet more importantly, the interests, aims and affiliations that Švankmajer developed early on in his career have proved long-lasting, in contrast to the greater eclecticism, perhaps the greater receptivity towards cultural trends and shifts, of the New Wave directors. Švankmajer's engagement with Surrealism has outlived the 1960s, the decade when avant-garde experiment was at its most fashionable. Like only a handful of other figures in world cinema, he has carried the spirit of Sixties' cinema beyond the 1960s and into the demoralized present day. That spirit could be defined in terms of a perceived identity of radical form and subversive content. Švankmajer even trumps such an identity, given that his work is oppositional precisely in its engagement with issues of language and expression.

Conclusion

The Czech culture of the 1960s bit the iron fist that fed it. Throughout the decade writers, philosophers, artists and filmmakers were engaged in an aboveground, state-funded rebellion against the cultural and political establishment. Yet the Czech New Wave, which would become the most internationally celebrated manifestation of this rebellion, was never concerned simply with addressing the past crimes of Stalinism or the present iniquities of neo-Stalinism. The New Wave was interested less in the exposure of lies than in the assertion of neglected truths. It represented an attack on what it saw as a deficient way of looking at the world (and at socialism), and on the translation of that deficiency into aesthetic precepts. The emergence of Surrealist and avant-garde practices was one of the forms that the rebellion took, one of the means of telling 'truths' that had hitherto been concealed. Of course, Surrealism, in its authentic form, has forever been in revolt against existing ideological and social systems, and doubtless, in the absence of any of Breton or Teige's utopian syntheses taking concrete form, it will always remain so. Thus the subversion in question was not only a subversion of Communist, or Stalinist, orthodoxies, notwithstanding the absurd official charges of the 1950s that Surrealism was 'the Trojan horse of western imperialism'.[1] Nonetheless Surrealism's aesthetics and thematics did have a particularly provocative charge within a state socialist context, both because they challenged the Party's monopolistic grip on the interpretation of reality and because they represented something unacceptable to official dogma. Most troublingly of all perhaps, the New Wave's 'avant-garde' films illuminated the benighted, disavowed domain of sexuality, dreams, fantasy and desire, implying in the process that such phenomena comprised an inalienable, if not a central, dimension of human existence.

Such preoccupations comprised part of the challenge to dominant conceptions of identity, a challenge that was for Karel Kosík the primary unifying feature of the 1960s Czech culture. As suggested in the introductory discussion of the 'critical aspects of avant-gardism', one of the key subversive aspects of the avant-

---

1.   Král, *Le surréalisme en Tchécoslovaquie*, p. 62.

garde influence lay in this philosophical, investigative dimension. On occasion, however, that influence meant that filmmakers also exceeded the humanist (or Marxist humanist) framework within which Kosík and others have positioned the Sixties culture. Jiří Menzel's *Closely Observed Trains* and his later film, *Larks on a String*, assert a human nature that seems to persist, stubbornly, through totalitarian systems and their attempts at indoctrination and re-education. Yet Menzel's humanism, like Hrabal's, is perhaps of a more corporeal and rambunctious kind than that envisaged by the Marxist humanists or the philosophers of praxis. Menzel's characters are capable of heroic gestures, and it may even be that such hedonistic, spontaneous types are the ones most concerned with preserving their freedoms. But Menzel's cinema emphasizes the importance of the quotidian, privileging personal and sexual pleasures over the rational, revolutionary agency that concerns Kosík or Sviták. The morbid fantasy life portrayed in Švankmajer's films suggests a self even more intransigent to rational or progressive purposes. That inalienably human realm of dark desires is both alien and nightmarishly inhuman: no wonder it is frequently transposed to the world of objects. It can be argued that Chytilová's *Daisies* transcends any conception of humanism, Marxist or otherwise: identity is depicted here as depthless, inauthentic and collage-like, the self's fragmentations extending beyond the split between conscious and unconscious.

If the ideas produced by the 1960s Czechoslovak cinema sometimes exceed the intellectual context in which they were made, then this has much to do with the fact that these films were seldom conceived as conscious philosophical treatises. In a number of the films discussed here (and in others that there has not been sufficient space to examine, such as Němec's works), the avant-garde influence reveals itself as the downplaying of art's communicative function. The sensuousness of language is prioritized over thematic import, meaning is put in play, and suggestion replaces explication. A tension sometimes ensues between the forthright assertion of particular ideas or perspectives as a means of subversive political intervention, and the blithe offering up of a text to any number of different readings. Meaning coincides with non-meaning, as the polemical need for expression competes with a desire to luxuriate in the plasticity of the image or the concreteness of reality. At the same time, to reiterate what has been suggested in the introduction and emphasized throughout this study, we should not overlook the critical function of the forms of expression themselves. The subversive effect in these films is not only a question of telling subversive truths, but of the manner in which those truths are told and not told. The plurality and indeterminacy of meaning represents an implicit defiance of Stalinist orthodoxy, for which the interpretation of reality is only ever a singular phenomenon.

The New Wave's multiform rebellion was at least in part generational at its source, a reaction by predominantly young filmmakers against the status quo. In that sense we might describe the Czech New Wave as an Oedipal rebellion against political and cultural fathers, an observation that has been made of other contemporaneous New Waves, from the French *Nouvelle Vague* (which famously attacked '*le cinéma du papa*') to Brazil's Cinema Novo.[2] While the Czech movement was undoubtedly a response to the specific conditions of state socialist society, it was also propelled by an international zeitgeist of innovation and iconoclasm and by the new-found empowerment of youth (Susan Hayward reminds us that the term 'new wave' (*nouvelle vague*) was coined by the French newspaper *L'Express* in the late 1950s 'to refer to the new socially active youth class').[3] Some of the Czech and Slovak films of the mid to late 1960s also reflect the entrenchment and politicization of generational conflicts. *Daisies*, *Valerie and Her Week of Wonders* and the Slovak films of Jakubisko and Havetta point to Czechoslovakia's absorption of the youthful counterculture that was then sweeping through the USA and Europe. Chytilová's valorization of the play of identities and desires seems well-attuned to the mentality of the late 1960s; *Closely Observed Trains'* Miloš Hrma, played by pop star Václav Neckář, can be seen as an oblique embodiment of contemporary youthful mores.

The absorption of the counterculture was almost certainly facilitated by the presence of comparable elements within the Czech and Slovak cultures, including native traditions of Surrealism. Conversely, the acceptance of Surrealism and the avant-garde may have been conditioned to some extent by the congruence between the historical avant-gardes and the new values of youth (sexual freedom, imaginative self-expression, altered states of consciousness, etc). The 1960s counterculture would later be described by sociologist Stuart Hall as nothing more than a 'crisis within the dominant [capitalist] culture',[4] though at the time such figures as Marcuse saw in the young hippies, Beats and freaks a fundamental challenge to the values of both capitalist and state socialist systems. The young characters in *Valerie and Her Week of Wonders* hold out the promise, albeit a tenuous one, of a beneficent new order. Jireš here suggests a continuity between the 1960s underground and earlier avant-gardes, and beholds in the new youth culture the prospect of an idealized 'liberation'. Indeed *Valerie* is the New Wave film that best exemplifies the utopian dimension of imaginative art, another of the critical aspects referred to in the introduction.

2. Ella Shohat and Robert Stam, *Unthinking Eurocentricity: Multiculturalism and the Media* (London: Routledge, 1994), p. 248.
3. Susan Hayward, *Key Concepts in Cinema Studies* (London: Routledge, 1996), p. 136.
4. Stuart Hall, quoted in Jonathon Green, *All Dressed Up: The Sixties and the Counterculture* (London: Pimlico, 1999), p. 125.

As we have seen, not all the Czechoslovak filmmakers in this period shared such utopian perspectives (although the use of Surrealist representation for satirical purposes, which has also been explored at length throughout this study, does imply some kind of socially progressive or transformative goal). Švankmajer, like many of the other postwar Czech Surrealists, is anti-utopian and even, up to a point, anti-'liberation', while Pavel Juráček's films offer little suggestion of an ultimate fulfilment that would release us from the eternal quest of desire. Jakubisko's Slovak *Birds, Orphans and Fools* is actually the film that most explicitly evokes the preoccupations of the counterculture, and the one that best reveals the aesthetic affinities of folk traditions, conscious Surrealism and contemporary 'head' culture. However, the attempt at constructing an alternative lifestyle by the film's protagonists culminates in murder and suicide, and the simulation of madness is as much a fatalistic retreat from reality and politics as a form of Surrealist rebellion. Yet even in its inscription of failure, Jakubisko's film, like *Valerie*, attests to the scope of the revolutionary ambitions of the time, in Czechoslovakia and elsewhere. The failure in question transcends that of a democratized or more liberal socialism, even if the aborting of Dubček's reform programme now seems emblematic of the dashed hopes, the lost idealism, of the late 1960s. Disappointment and disillusion haunt other national cinemas after 1968, though in many of these other cases the perceived failures of political radicalism did little, temporarily, to stem aesthetic radicalism. It would probably be fair to say that Normalization, with its repressive enforcement of mediocrity, robbed the Czech and Slovak cinemas of a few of their best and most experimental years. The plethora of original new talents that emerged at the end of the 1960s, along with the undiminished vitality and increased artistic boldness of more established talents, suggests that Czechoslovakia's New Wave still had much life in it, and perhaps greater heights to scale. It is exciting, though frustrating, to imagine a still vital Czechoslovak cinema feeding off and into the New German Cinema, the new Hollywood and other 1970s film movements. Given Czech Surrealism's abiding interest in cinema, it is also conceivable that, in the event of a continued policy of free expression, members of the 'reborn' Surrealist group might have followed Švankmajer's lead and attempted their own films.

Yet rather than speculating on the films that might have been made had the Warsaw Pact armies not intervened, it might be preferable to dwell on the immense achievements of Czech and Slovak cinema during the 1960s (and we should also acknowledge those filmmakers who managed to continue making original works during the Normalization era and beyond, including Švankmajer and Juraj Herz, who made the bravura, Gothic *Morgiana* in 1972). At its most liberal the Communist system enabled cultural accomplishment on a scale that would be impossible for a small nation with a predominantly market-based film industry. (It must also be conceded that the more adventurous international cultural climate of the 1960s created a market for the experimental and the culturally 'exotic', which meant a greater recuperation of costs than would be possible today.) State socialism was not only prohibitive but also in many ways highly productive. It is hard to disagree with Dina Iordanova's argument that censorship has been 'given disproportionate attention' in Western discussion of the Eastern Bloc cinemas.[5] Certainly films were shelved or suppressed in Czechoslovakia during the 1960s, and banned in large numbers during Normalization, yet under an exclusively commercial system many of the New Wave films would never have been made at all.[6] Those experimental, critical and 'dissident' filmmakers existed in a peculiar, hostile yet dependent relationship to authority, being both thwarted and enabled, rebuffed and challenged, artistically limited and galvanized to an ever more ingenious subtlety, by one and the same system. Not only was the state socialism of the day an excellent satirical target, it was also worth taking seriously and attacking on its own terms, for its self-betrayals and its lost promise. Indeed, the re-engagement with the avant-garde was one way of recalling to the Communist establishment its own former, if relative, cultural pluralism and the emancipatory hopes that figures like Teige and Breton had once invested in the Party.

Jean Schuster has described Surrealism as an 'eternal' presence, existing outside the flux of history and the comings and goings of self-defined Surrealist groups.[7] Sadly the existence of film financers sympathetic to avant-garde experimentation is hardly so dependable. Yet even after the New Wave era the Surrealist impulse has sporadically found its way into Czech cinema. We have already discussed Švankmajer's relative success in continuing to apply his Surrealist practices and preoccupations in film during the 1970s and '80s. Another animator of great talent, Jiří Barta, emerged in the late 1970s and manifested some Surrealist tendencies: Barta's 1982 *The Vanished World of Gloves* (*Zaniklý svět rukavic*), an eccentric 'alternative history' of the cinema, can qualify as Surrealist not only in its homages to such cinematic Surrealists as Buñuel and Fellini, but also in its knowing and witty fetishization of the titular item of clothing, a favoured object of the early Surrealists. The 1989 *The Club of the Laid Off* (*Klub odložených*) conflates the quintessentially Surrealist concerns of the outmoded, compulsive repetition and the 'uncanny' humanoid, depicting the routinized half-life of abandoned mannequins.

Since the Velvet Revolution, the presence of the Surrealist, the fantastic and the experimental in Czech cinema has further diminished. The Czech government's reluctance to support film production has recently generated

---

5.   Dina Iordanova, *Cinema of the Other Europe: The Industry and Artistry of East Central European Film* (London: Wallflower, 2003), p. 33.

6.   Ibid., p. 34.

7.   Richardson, *Surrealism and Cinema*, p. 4.

vocal public protest, and lavish funds are certainly no longer forthcoming for 'marginal' projects. Must we then mourn the good old 'bad old days' of Communism? The magic has not entirely disappeared. Švankmajer still remains active, having produced at least one subversive masterpiece in the 1996 *Conspirators of Pleasure*. Original New Waver Jan Němec returned to the Czech Republic after years of exile, and resumed his career with a series of experimental (albeit modest and only intermittently successful) works. Němec explicitly engaged himself with the Czech avant-garde heritage in his films *The Flames of Royal Love* (*V žáru královské lásky*, 1990), based on Ladislav Klima's 'decadent' novel *The Sufferings of Prince Sternenhoch* (*Utrpení knížete Sternenhocha*, 1928), and *Toyen* (2005), an intensely visually experimental film depicting the life of the eponymous Surrealist painter. In the case of younger directors, Petr Zelenka's internationally acclaimed *The Year of the Devil* (*Rok ďábla*, 2002) integrates the marvellous into its deceptive documentary format in a way that evokes the offhand improbabilities of Buñuel, though it would be stretching definitions to describe this film as Surrealist or avant-garde. Martin Šulík's *The Key to Determining Dwarves or the Last Voyage of Lemuel Gulliver* (*Klíč k určování trpaslíků aneb poslední cesta Lemuela Gullivera*, 2002), a dramatized documentary about Pavel Juráček, suggests that there is still an interest in the Absurd and Surrealist traditions of Czech cinema. At the same time, it is hard to escape the feeling that the Czechoslovakia of the 1960s provided a uniquely favourable setting for aesthetic experiment and philosophical adventure, an unrepeatable context in which avant-garde influence enabled not an occasional titillating shock but a challenge, a flash of subversive illumination, a provocation aimed at both authorities and audiences.

Bibliography

Adorno, Theodor. 'Looking Back on Surrealism', in Lawrence S. Rainey (ed.), *Modernism: An Anthology* (Oxford; New York: Blackwell, 2005), pp. 1113–15.

Agger, Ben. 'Marcuse and Habermas on New Science', *Polity*, Vol. 9, No. 2, Winter 1976, pp. 158–81.

Alan, Josef (ed.). *Alternativní kultura: Příběh české společnosti 1945–1989* (Prague: Nakladatelství Lidové noviny, 2001).

Anděl, Jaroslav (ed.). *Czech Modernism 1900–1945* (Houston: Museum of Fine Arts, Houston, 1989).

Anderson, Perry. *The Origins of Postmodernity* (London; New York: Verso, 1989).

Andrew, Geoff. 'A Faust Buck', *Time Out*, September 7, 1994.

Aumont, Jacques, Jean-Louis Comolli, Jean Narboni and Sylvie Pierre. 'Time Overflowing' [interview with Jacques Rivette], in Jim Hillier (ed.), *Cahiers du Cinema: Volume 2: 1960–1968: New Wave, New Cinema, Re-evaluating Hollywood* (London: Routledge and Kegan Paul, 1999), pp. 317–23.

Bakhtin, Mikhail. *Rabelais and His World*, translated by Heléne Iswolsky (Cambridge, MA: M.I.T. Press, 1968).

Barthes, Roland. *The Pleasure of the Text*, translated by Richard Miller (New York: Hill and Wang, 1975).

——— *Image-Music-Text*, translated by Stephen Heath (New York: Hill and Wang, 1977).

——— *Mythologies*, translated by Annette Lavers (London: Vintage, 1993).

Bataille, Georges. *Visions of Excess: Selected Writings 1927–1939*, translated by Allan Stoekl, Carl R. Lovitt and Donald M. Leslie (Minneapolis: University of Minnesota Press, 1985).

——— *The Accursed Share, Volume 1*, translated by Robert Hurley (New York: Zone, 1991).

——— *The Accursed Share, Volumes 2 and 3: The History of Eroticism and Sovereignty*, translated by Robert Hurley (New York: Zone, 1993).

——— *On Nietzsche*, translated by Bruce Boone (New York: Paragon House, 1994).

———— *Eroticism: Death and Sensuality*, translated by Mary Dalwood (London: Marion Boyars, 2006).

Bettelheim, Bruno. *The Uses of Enchantment: The Meaning and Importance of Fairy Tales* (New York: Knopf, 1976).

Blumenfeld, Yorick. *Seesaw: Cultural Life in Eastern Europe* (New York: Harcourt, Brace and World, 1968).

Boček, Jaroslav. *Modern Czechoslovak Film*, translated by Alice Denešová (Brno: Artia, 1965).

———— 'Podobenství Věry Chytilové', in *Film a Doba*, No. 11, 1966, pp. 566–71.

———— *Looking Back on the New Wave* (Prague: Československý Filmexport, 1967).

Bracher, Mark. *Lacan, Discourse and Social Change: A Psychoanalytic Cultural Criticism* (Ithaca: Cornell University Press, 1993).

Bregant, Michal. 'The Devětsil Film Dream', in Rotislav Švácha (ed.), *Devětsil: Czech Avant-Garde Art, Architecture and Design of the 1920s and 30s* (Oxford: Museum of Modern Art, 1990), pp. 70–73.

Bregant, Michal and Martin Čihák. 'Skutečnější než realita: Alternativy v českém filmu', in Josef Alan (ed.), *Alternativní kultura: Příběh české společnosti 1945–1989* (Prague: Nakladatelství Lidové noviny, 2001), pp. 421–41.

Breton, André. *Manifestoes of Surrealism*, translated by Richard Seaver and Helen R. Lane (Ann Arbor: University of Michigan Press, 1969).

———— *What is Surrealism? Selected Writings*, edited and introduced by Franklin Rosemont and translated by Bravig Imbs et al (New York: Pathfinder, 1978).

———— *Nadja*, translated by Mark Polizzotti (Harmondsworth: Penguin, 1999).

Brouk, Bohuslav. 'Afterword', in Vítězslav Nezval and Jindřich Štyrský, *Edition 69*, translated by Jed Slast (Prague: Twisted Spoon, 2004), pp. 109–19.

Brož, Martin. 'O Démantech noci: rozhovor s Janem Němcem', *Film a doba*, No. 7, 1964, pp. 365–66.

Buchar, Robert. *Czech New Wave Filmmakers in Interviews*, (Jefferson; London: McFarland and Company, 2004).

Burian, Jarka M. *Modern Czech Theatre: Reflector and Conscience of a Nation* (Iowa City: University of Iowa Press, 2000).

Bydžovská, Lenka. 'Against the Current: The Story of the Surrealist Group in Czechoslovakia', *Papers of Surrealism*, Issue 1, Winter 2003, pp. 1–10.

Camus, Albert. *The Myth of Sisyphus*, translated by Justin O'Brien (Harmondsworth: Penguin, 2005).

Cardinal, Roger. 'Thinking Through Things: The Presence of Objects in the Early Films of Jan Švankmajer', in Peter Hames (ed.), *Dark Alchemy: The Films of Jan Švankmajer* (Westport: Praeger, 1995), pp. 78–95.

Clark, Katerina. *The Soviet Novel: History as Ritual* (Chicago; London: University of Chicago Press, 1981).

Cohen, Margaret. *Profane Illumination: Walter Benjamin and the Paris of Surrealist Revolution* (Berkeley; Los Angeles: University of California Press, 1993).

Connor, Steven. *Postmodernist Culture: An Introduction to Theories of the Contemporary* (Oxford: Blackwell, 1989).

Cornwell, Neil. *The Absurd in Literature* (Manchester: Manchester University Press, 2006).

Cowie, Peter. *Revolution!: The Explosion of World Cinema in the 60s* (London: Faber, 1994).

DeKoven, Marianne. *Utopia Limited: The Sixties and the Emergence of the Postmodern* (Durham; London: Duke University Press, 2004).

Dewey, Langdon. *Outline of Czechoslovakian Cinema* (London: Informatics, 1971).

Dierna, Guiseppe. 'On Valerie, Nezval, Max Ernst, and Collages: Variations on a Theme', translated by Jed Slast, in Vítězslav Nezval, *Valerie and Her Week of Wonders* (Prague: Twisted Spoon, 2005), translated by David Short, pp. 199–226.

Dluhosch, Eric and Rotislav Švácha (eds). *Karel Teige 1900–1951: L'Enfant Terrible of the Czech Modernist Avant-Garde* (Cambridge, MA: M.I.T. Press, 1999).

Dryje, František. 'The Force of Imagination', translated by Valerie Mason, in Peter Hames (ed.), *Dark Alchemy* (Westport: Praeger, 1995), pp. 119–68.

Dubček, Alexander. *Hope Dies Last: The Autobiography of Alexander Dubček*, translated and edited by Jiří Hochman (New York; Tokyo; London: Kodansha International, 1993).

Dudková, Jana. 'Elo Havetta: *The Gala in the Botanical Garden* (*Slávnosť v botanickej záhrade)*', *KinoKultura*, 2005 (http://www.kinokultura.com/specials/3/slavnost.shtml) (retrieved 1 February 2009).

Durgnat, Raymond. *WR: Mysteries of the Organism* (London: BFI, 1999).
——— *Sexual Alienation in the Cinema* (London: Studio Vista, 1972).

Dvorský, Stanislav. 'Z podzemí do podzemí: Český postsurrealismus čtřicátých let až šedesátých let', in Josef Alan (ed.), *Alternativní kultura: Příběh české společnosti 1945–1989* (Prague: Nakladatelství Lidové noviny, 2001), pp. 77–154.

Eagle, Herbert. 'Dada and Structuralism in Chytilová's *Daisies*', in Ladislav Matejka (ed.), *Cross Currents: A Yearbook of Central European Culture*, Number 10 (New Haven: Yale University Press, 1991), pp. 223–34.

Eagleton, Terry. *Literary Theory: An Introduction* (Oxford: Blackwell, 1995).

―――― 'Bakhtin, Schopenhauer, Kundera', in Ken Hirschkop and David Shepherd (eds), *Bakhtin and Cultural Theory* (Manchester: Manchester University Press, 2001), pp. 229–40.

Eco, Umberto. *The Open Work*, translated by Anna Cancogni (Cambridge, MA: Harvard University Press).

Effenberger, Vratislav. 'Obraz člověka v českém filmu', *Film a doba*, No. 7, 1968, pp. 345–51.

―――― *Realita a poesie: k vývojové dialektice moderního umění* (Prague: Mladá Fronta, 1969).

―――― 'The Raw Cruelty of Life', in Ladislav Matejka (ed.), *Cross Currents 6: A Yearbook of Central European Culture* (Ann Arbor: University of Michigan, 1987), pp. 435–44.

―――― 'Švankmajer on *The Fall of the House of Usher*', translated by Gaby Dowdell, *Afterimage* 13, Autumn 1987, p. 33.

―――― and Jan Svoboda. 'Státem řízený underground', *Film a doba*, No. 5, 1969, p. 278.

Ekiert, Grzegorz. *State Against Society: Political Crises and Their Aftermath in East Central Europe* (Princeton: Princeton University Press, 1996).

Esslin, Martin. *The Theatre of the Absurd* (Harmondsworth: Penguin, 1991).

Fer, Briony, David Batchelor and Paul Wood. *Realism, Rationalism, Surrealism: Art between the Wars* (New Haven; London: Yale University Press, 1993).

Fijałkowski, Krzysztof. 'Invention, Imagination, Interpretation: Collective Activity in the Contemporary Czech and Slovak Surrealist Group', *Papers of Surrealism*, Issue 3, Spring 2005, pp. 1–14.

―――― 'Emila Medková: The Magic of Despair', *Tate Papers*, Autumn 2005 (http://www.tate.org.uk/research/tateresearch/tatepapers/05autumn/fijalkowski.htm) (retrieved 3 August 2008).

Fink, Bruce. *The Lacanian Subject: Between Language and Jouissance* (Princeton: Princeton University Press, 1995).

Forman, Miloš and Jan Novák. *Turnaround: A Memoir* (London: Faber, 1994).

Foster, Hal. *Compulsive Beauty* (Cambridge, MA: M.I.T. Press, 1993).

―――― 'Blinded Insights: On the Modernist Reception of the Art of the Mentally Ill', *October* 97, Summer 2001, pp. 3–30.

Foster, Stephen C. and Rudolf E. Kuenzli (eds). *Dada Spectrum: The Dialectics of Revolt* (Madison: Coda Press, 1979).

Franz Kafka: Liblická konference 1963 (Prague: Nakladatelství Československé akademie věd, 1963).

Freedman, David Noel, Allen C. Myers, Astrid B. Beck (eds). *Eerdmans Dictionary of the Bible* (Grand Rapids, Michigan: William B. Eerdmans Publishing Co, 2000).

French, Alfred. *The Poets of Prague* (London: Oxford University Press, 1969).

—— *Czech Writers and Politics 1945–1969* (New York: Columbia University Press, 1982).

Freud, Sigmund. *The Question of Lay Analysis*, translated by James Strachey (New York; London: Norton, 1989).

—— *The Freud Reader*, edited by Peter Gay (London: Vintage, 1995).

—— *The Uncanny*, translated by David McLintock (New York: Penguin, 2003).

Frucht, Richard C. *Eastern Europe: An Introduction to the People, Lands and Culture* (Santa Barbara, California: ABC-CLIO, 2005).

Fuchik [Fučík], Julius. *Notes From the Gallows* (New York: New Century, 1948).

Fuentes, Carlos. *Myself With Others: Selected Essays* (London: Picador, 1989).

Gardiner, Michael E. *Critiques of Everyday Life* (London; New York: Routledge, 2000).

Garfinkle, Deborah Helen. *Bridging East and West: Czech Surrealism's Interwar Experiment* [doctoral thesis] (University of Texas, 2003).

Geiger, H. Kent. *The Family in Soviet Russia* (Cambridge, MA: Harvard University Press, 1968).

Goetz-Stankiewicz, Marketa. 'Sławomir Mrożek: Two Forms of the Absurd', *Contemporary Literature*, Vol. 12, No. 2. (Spring, 1971), pp. 188–203.

Golan, Galia. *The Czechoslovak Reform Movement: Communism in Crisis 1962–1968* (London: Cambridge University Press, 1971).

Goulding, Daniel J. (ed.). *Post-New Wave Cinema in the Soviet Union and Eastern Europe* (Bloomington: Indiana University Press, 1989).

Graham, Peter. *The New Wave* (London: British Film Institute, 1968).

Green, Jonathon. *All Dressed Up: The Sixties and the Counterculture* (London: Pimlico, 1999).

Green, Lancelyn Roger. 'The Golden Age of Children's Books', in Sheila Egoff, G.T. Stubbs and L.F. Ashley (eds), *Only Connect* (Toronto; New York: Oxford University Press, 1969), pp. 1–16.

Haltof, Marek. *Polish National Cinema* (New York; Oxford: Berghahn Books, 2002).

Hames, Peter (ed.). *Dark Alchemy: The Films of Jan Švankmajer* (Westport: Praeger, 1995).

—— (ed.). *The Cinema of Central Europe* (London: Wallflower Press, 2004).

Hames, Peter. 'Interview with Jan Švankmajer', translated by Karolina Vočadlo, in Peter Hames (ed.). *Dark Alchemy: The Films of Jan Švankmajer* (Westport: Praeger, 1995), pp. 96–118.

—— 'The Film Experiment', in Peter Hames (ed.). *Dark Alchemy: The Films of Jan Švankmajer* (Westport: Praeger, 1995), pp. 7–47.

――― 'The Good Soldier Švejk and After: The Comic Tradition in Czech Film', in Diana Holmes and Alison Smith (eds), *100 Years of European Cinema: Entertainment or Ideology?* (Manchester: Manchester University Press, 2001), pp. 64–76.

――― '*Ostře sledované vlaky/Closely Observed Trains*', in Peter Hames (ed.), *The Cinema of Central Europe* (London: Wallflower Press, 2004), pp. 117–27.

――― *The Czechoslovak New Wave* (London: Wallflower, 2005).

Hammond, Paul (ed.). *The Shadow and its Shadow: Surrealist Writings on the Cinema* (San Francisco: City Lights, 2000).

Hamšik, Dušan. *Writers Against Rulers*, translated by D. Orpington (London: Hutchinson, 1971).

Hanáková, Petra. 'Voices From Another World: Feminine Space and Masculine Intrusion in *Sedmikrásky* and *Vražda Ing. Čerta*', in Anikó Imre (ed.), *East European Cinemas* (London: Routledge, 2005), pp. 63–80.

Hašek, Jaroslav. *The Good Soldier Švejk and His Fortunes in the Great War*, translated by Cecil Parrott (Harmondsworth: Penguin, 2000).

Havlíček, Zbyněk. *Skutečnost snu*, edited by Stanislav Dvorský (Prague: Torst, 2003).

Hayward, Susan. *Key Concepts in Cinema Studies* (London: Routledge, 1996).

Hibbin, Nina. *Screen Series: Eastern Europe* (New York; London: A. Zwemmer; A.S. Barnes, 1969).

Higonnet, Margaret R. *Borderwork: Feminist Engagements with Comparative Literature* (Cornell: Cornell University Press, 1994).

Hillier, Jim (ed.). *Cahiers du Cinéma: Volume 1: The 1950s: Neo-Realism, Hollywood, New Wave* (London: Routledge, 1985).

――― (ed.). *Cahiers du Cinéma: Volume 2: 1960–1968: New Wave, New Cinema, Re-evaluating Hollywood* (London: Routledge and Kegan Paul, 1999).

Hoberman, J. and Jonathan Rosenbaum. *Midnight Movies* (New York: Harper and Row, 1983).

Hoberman, J. *The Red Atlantis: Communist Culture in the Absence of Communism* (Philadelphia: Temple University Press, 1998).

Holý, Ladislav. *The Little Czech and the Great Czech Nation* (Cambridge: Cambridge University Press, 1996).

Horton, Andrew. 'Dreaming a Bad Reality', *Central Europe Review*, Vol. 1, No. 9, 23 August 1999 (http://www.ce-review.org/99/9/kinoeye9horton2.html) (retrieved 3 August 2007).

Hrabal, Bohumil. *The Death of Mr Baltisberger*, translated by Kača Polačková and introduced by Josef Škvorecký [under the pseudonym Daniel S. Miritz] (London: Abacus, 1990).

——— *Closely Observed Trains*, translated by Edith Pargeter (London: Abacus, 2001).

Hutcheon, Linda. *A Poetics of Postmodernism: History, Theory, Fiction* (London; New York, NY: Routledge, 1988).

Iordanova, Dina. *Cinema of the Other Europe: The Industry and Artistry of East Central European Film* (London: Wallflower, 2003).

Jackson, Rosemary. *Fantasy: The Literature of Subversion* (London: Routledge, 1981).

Jakobson, Roman. 'On Realism in Art', in Ladislav Matejka and Krystyna Pomorska (eds), *Readings in Russian Poetics: Formalist and Structuralist Views* (Chicago: Dalkey Archive Press, 2002), pp. 38–46.

Jaroš, Jan. *Juraj Jakubisko* (Prague: Československý filmový ústav, 1989).

Jireš, Jaromil. 'Vlna pravdy ve filmu', in *Film a doba*, No. 8, 1965, pp. 412–13.

Juráček, Pavel. *Postava k podpírání*, edited by Jiří Cieslar (Prague: Havran, 2001).

——— *Deník 1959–1974*, edited by Jan Lukeš (Prague: Národní filmový archiv, 2003).

Kalandra, Záviš. 'The Reality of Dreams', in *Slovo a smysl*, Vol. 2, No. 4, 2005, pp. 329–43.

Kalivoda, Robert. 'Avantgarda a humanistická perspektiva', in *Literární noviny*, Vol. 14, No. 50, 1965, p. 5.

Kaňuch, Martin. '*Vtáčkovia, siroty a blázni/Birds, Orphans and Fools*', in Hames (ed.), *The Cinema of Central Europe*, pp. 163–71.

Kaplan, E. Ann (ed.). *Psychoanalysis and Cinema* (New York: Routledge, 1989).

Klein, Melanie. *The Selected Melanie Klein*, edited by Juliet Mitchell (New York: The Free Press, 1987).

Klimešová, Marie. 'České výtvarné umění druhé poloviny 20. století', in Josef Alan (ed.), *Alternativní Kultura: Příběh české společnosti 1945–1989* (Prague: Nakladatelství Lidové noviny, 2001), pp. 377–420.

Knox, Jim. 'A Report on the 13th Brisbane International Film Festival', *Senses of Cinema*, September 2004 (http://www.sensesofcinema.com/contents/festivals/04/33/biff2004.html) (retrieved 10 November 2007).

Kołakowski, Leszek. *Towards a Marxist Humanism* (New York: Grove Press, 1968).

Kopaněnová, Galina. 'Neznám opravdový čin, který by nebyl riskantní: Rozhovor s Věra Chytilovou', *Film a Doba*, No. 1, 1963, pp. 40–44.

——— 'O jiném filmu: Rozhovor s Janem Švankmajerem, Jiří Lehovcem a Karlem Vachkem', *Film a doba*, No. 7, 1969, pp. 360–70.

Kosík, Karel. *The Crisis of Modernity: Essays and Observations from the 1968 Era* (Lanham: Rowman and Littlefield, 1995).

Král, Petr. *Le surréalisme en Tchécoslovaquie: Choix de textes 1934–1968* (Paris: Gallimard, 1983).

―――― 'Questions to Jan Švankmajer', translated by Jill McGreal, *Afterimage* 13, 1987, p. 22.

―――― *Groteska čili Morálka šlehačkového dortu* (Prague: Narodní filmový archiv, 1998).

Krauss, Rosalind. 'The Photographic Conditions of Surrealism', *October*, Vol. 19, Winter 1981, pp. 3–34.

Kristeva, Julia. *Desire in Language: A Semiotic Approach to Literature and Art*, edited by Léon S. Roudiez and translated by Alice Jardine, Thomas A. Gora and Léon S. Roudiez (Oxford: Blackwell, 1980).

―――― *Revolution in Poetic Language*, translated by Margaret Waller (New York; Chichester: Columbia University Press, 1984).

Krzywińska, Tanya. 'Transgression, transformation and titillation: Jaromil Jireš's *Valerie a týden divů* (*Valerie and Her Week of Wonders*, 1970), *Kinoeye*, Vol. 3, Issue 9, 15 Sept, 2003 (http://www.kinoeye.org/03/09/ krzywinska09.php) (retrieved 12 January 2008).

Kubíček, Tomáš. 'Myšlení o literatuře v prostředí českých literárních časopisů šedesátých let', in *Zlatá šedesátá: Česká literature a společnost v letech tání, kolotání a...zklamání: materiály z konference pořádané Ústavem pro českou literaturu AV ČR 16–18. června 1999* (Prague: Ústav pro českou literaturu, 2000), pp. 125–36.

Kučera, Jan. 'O lidech a smrti', *Film a doba*, No. 9, 1969, pp. 468–75.

Kuenzli, Rudolf E. 'The Semiotics of Dada Poetry', in Stephen C. Foster and Rudolf E. Kuenzli (eds), *Dada Spectrum: The Dialectics of Revolt* (Madison: Coda Press, 1979), pp. 51–70.

―――― (ed.). *Dada and Surrealist Film* (Cambridge, MA: M.I.T. Press, 1996).

Kundera, Milan. 'Appendix: Speeches made at the Fourth Congress of the Czechoslovak Writers' Union June 27–29, 1967', in Dušan Hamšik, *Writers Against Rulers*, translated by D. Orpington (London: Hutchinson, 1971), pp. 167–77.

―――― *The Book of Laughter and Forgetting*, translated by Michael Henry Heim (Harmondsworth: Penguin, 1983).

―――― *The Art of the Novel*, translated by Linda Asher (New York: Harper & Row, 1986).

Kusák, Alexej. 'Ke vzniku konference o Franzi Kafkovi v Liblicích v květnu 1963', in *Zlatá šedesátá: Česká literature a společnost v letech tání, kolotání a...zklamání: materiály z konference pořádané Ústavem pro českou literatura AV ČR 16–18. června 1999* (Prague: Ústav pro českou literaturu, 2000), pp. 103–11.

Kusin, Vladimír. *The Intellectual Origins of the Prague Spring: The Development of Reformist Ideas in Czechoslovakia 1956–1967* (Cambridge: Cambridge University Press, 1971).

Laing, R. D. *The Politics of Experience and The Bird of Paradise* (Harmondsworth: Penguin, 1967).

Levinger, Esther. 'Czech Avant-Garde Art: Poetry for the Five Senses', *The Art Bulletin*, Vol. 81, No. 3. (Sep. , 1999), pp. 513–32.

Lewis, Matthew Gregory. *The Monk* (Oxford: Oxford University Press, 1998).

Liehm, A. [Antonín] J. '*Postava k podpírání*', *Literární noviny*, No. 45, 1964, p. 8.

―――― [Antonín] J. 'Konečně Gogol', *Film a doba*, No. 11, 1967, pp. 591–94.

―――― [Antonín] J. 'Franz Kafka in Eastern Europe', *Telos*, Number 23, Spring 1975, pp. 53–83.

Liehm, Antonín J. (ed.). *The Politics of Culture*, translated by Peter Kussi (New York: Grove Press, 1971).

Liehm, Antonín J. *Closely Watched Films: The Czechoslovak Experience* (White Plains: International Arts and Science, 1974).

Liehm, Mira and Antonín J. Liehm. *The Most Important Art: Eastern European Film After 1945* (Berkeley; Los Angeles; London: University of California Press, 1977).

Lim, Bliss Cua. 'Dolls in Fragments: *Daisies* as Feminist Allegory', *Camera Obscura* Vol. 16, No. 2, 2001, pp. 37–77.

Lomas, David. *The Haunted Self: Surrealism, Psychoanalysis, Subjectivity* (New Haven; London: Yale University Press, 2000).

Lowenstein, Adam. 'Films Without a Face: Shock Horror in the Cinema of Georges Franju', *Cinema Journal*, Vol. 37, No. 4. (Summer, 1998), pp. 37–58.

MacAfee, Noelle. *Julia Kristeva* (London: Routledge, 2004).

Macháček, Miroslav. *Vítězslav Nezval* (Prague: Horizont, 1980).

Machovec, Martin. 'Od avantgardy přes podzemí do undergroundu', in Josef Alan (ed.), *Alternativní Kultura: Příběh české společnosti 1945–1989* (Prague: Nakladatelství Lidové noviny, 2001), pp. 155–200.

Malt, Johanna. *Obscure Objects of Desire: Surrealism, Fetishism, and Politics* (Oxford: Oxford University Press, 2004).

Marcuse, Herbert. *Eros and Civilization: A Philosophical Inquiry into Freud* (Boston: Beacon Press, 1966).

―――― *An Essay on Liberation* (Boston: Beacon Press, 1969).

Marx, Karl. *Capital: Volume 1: A Critique of Political Economy*, translated by Ben Fowkes (Harmondsworth: Penguin, 1992).

Matthews, J. H. *The Imagery of Surrealism* (Syracuse: Syracuse University Press, 1977).

―――― *Surrealism, Insanity, and Poetry* (Syracuse: Syracuse University Press, 1982).

McCabe, Colin. *Godard: Portrait of the Artist at 70* (London: Bloomsbury, 2003).

McHoul, Alec and Wendy Grace. *A Foucault Primer: Discourse, Power and the Subject* (London: UCL Press, 1995).

Medek, Mikuláš. 'Text z katalogu výstavy v Teplicích 1963', in Jiří Ševčík, Pavlína Morganová and Dagmar Dušová (eds), *České umění 1938–1989: programy, kritické texty, dokumenty* (Prague: Academia, 2001), pp. 242–44.

Menzel, Jiří and Bohumil Hrabal. *Closely Observed Trains* (London: Lorrimer, 1971).

Mihalovič, Peter. '*Zběhové a poutníci/Deserters and Pilgrims*' [review], *44ᵗʰ Karlovy Vary International Film Festival* (http://www.kviff.com/en/film-archive-detail/20030192-deserters-and-pilgrims/) (retrieved 5 February 2009).

Miller, Martin A. *Freud and the Bolsheviks: Psychoanalysis in Imperial Russia and the Soviet Union* (New Haven; London: Yale University Press, 1998).

Moullet, Luc. 'Sam Fuller: In Marlowe's Footsteps', in Jim Hillier (ed.), *Cahiers du Cinéma, Volume 1: The 1950s: Neo-Realism, Hollywood, New Wave* (London: Routledge, 1985), 145–55.

Nadeau, Maurice. *Histoire de Surréalisme* (Paris: Éditions du Seuil, 1964).

Nezval, Vítězslav. *Básně noci* (Prague: Odeon, 1966).

——— *Valerie a týden divů* (Prague: Odeon, 1970).

——— *Antilyrik and Other Poems*, translated by Jerome Rothenberg and Miloš Sovak (Los Angeles: Green Integer, 2001).

——— *Pražský chodec* (Prague: Labyrint, 2003).

——— *Valerie and Her Week of Wonders*, translated by David Short, (Prague: Twisted Spoon, 2005).

O'Pray, Michael. 'Surrealism, Fantasy and the Grotesque: The Cinema of Jan Švankmajer', in James Donald (ed.), *Fantasy and the Cinema* (London: BFI Publishing, 1989), pp. 253–68.

——— 'Jan Švankmajer: A Mannerist Surrealist', in Peter Hames (ed.), *Dark Alchemy: The Films of Jan Švankmajer* (Westport: Praeger, 1995), pp. 48–77.

Paul, David W. *The Cultural Limits of Revolutionary Politics: Change and Continuity in Socialist Czechoslovakia* (New York: Columbia University Press, 1979).

——— (ed.). *Politics, Art and Commitment in the East European Cinema* (London: Macmillan, 1983).

Pegrum, Mark A. *Challenging Modernity: Dada Between Modern and Postmodern* (Oxford, New York: Berghahn, 2000).

Petro, Patrice. 'From Lukács to Kracauer and Beyond: Social Film Histories and the German Cinema', *Cinema Journal*, Vol. 22, No. 3. (Spring, 1983), pp. 47–70.

Petro, Peter. 'Slovak Surrealist Poetry: The Movement and its Rediscovery', *Canadian Slavonic Papers* (Volume 20, No. 2, June 1978), pp. 237–44.

––––––– 'Slovak Surrealism as a Parable of Modern Uprootedness', *Cross Currents* (Ann Arbor: University of Michigan, 1982), pp. 219–32.

––––––– 'Dominik Tatarka: An Introduction to a Rebel', *Cross Currents 6* (Ann Arbor: University of Michigan, 1987), pp. 281–83.

Petrović, Gajo. *Marx in the Mid-Twentieth Century* (New York: Anchor, 1967)

'The Platform of Prague', in *Surrealism Against the Current*, edited and translated by Michael Richardson and Krzysztof Fijałkowski (London: Pluto Press, 2001), pp. 58–65.

Polizzotti, Mark. *Revolution of the Mind: The Life of Andre Breton* (London: Bloomsbury, 1996).

Pošová, Kateřina. *Jiří Menzel* (Prague: Český filmový ústav, 1992).

Přádná, Stanislava, Zdena Škapová and Jiří Cieslar. *Démanty všednosti: Český a slovenský film 60. let: Kapitoly o nové vlně* (Prague: Pražská scéna, 2002).

Reed, Susan E. and David Crowley. *Style and Socialism: Modernity and Material Culture in Post-War Eastern Europe* (Oxford; New York: Berg, 2000).

Reich, Wilhelm. *The Mass Psychology of Fascism* (New York: Farrar, Straus and Giroux, 1970).

Richardson, Michael. *Surrealism and Cinema* (Oxford; New York: Berg, 2006).

Rivette, Jacques. '"Time Overflowing": Rivette in interview with Jacques Aumont, Jean-Louis Comolli, Jean Narboni and Sylvie Pierre', in Jim Hillier (ed.), *Cahiers du Cinema: Volume 2: 1960–1968: New Wave, New Cinema, Re-evaluating Hollywood* (London: Routledge and Kegan Paul, 1999), pp. 317–23.

Roud, Richard. *Jean-Luc Godard* (London: Thames and Hudson, 1970).

Satterwhite, James H. *Varieties of Marxist Humanism: Philosophical Revision in Postwar Eastern Europe* (Pittsburgh; London: University of Pittsburgh Press, 1992).

Schopflin, George. *Politics in Eastern Europe, 1945–1992* (Oxford: Blackwell, 1993).

Schulz, Bruno. *The Fictions of Bruno Schulz: The Street of Crocodiles and Sanatorium Under the Sign of the Hourglass*, translated by Celina Wieniewska (London: Picador, 1988).

Sedláček, Jakub. 'Zbyněk Havlíček – podoby surrealistické metafory', *Slovo a smysl*, Vol. 1, No. 2, 2004, pp. 91–103.

Seifert, Jaroslav. *The Poetry of Jaroslav Seifert* (North Haven, CT: Catbird, 1998), edited by George Gibian and translated by Ewald Osers and George Gibian.

Selden, Raman and Peter Widdowson. *A Reader's Guide to Contemporary Literary Theory* (Hemel Hempstead: Harvester Wheatsheaf, 1993).

Ševčík, Jiří, Pavlína Morganová and Dagmar Dušová (eds). *České umění 1938–1989: programy, kritické texty, dokumenty* (Prague: Academia, 2001).

Shklovsky, Victor. 'Art as Technique', in *Russian Formalist Criticism: Four Essays*, translated and edited by Lee T. Lemon and Marion J. Reis (Lincoln: University of Nebraska Press, 1965), pp. 3–24.

Shohat, Ella and Robert Stam. *Unthinking Eurocentricity: Multiculturalism and the Media* (London: Routledge, 1994).

Silverman, Kaja. *The Subject of Semiotics* (New York: Oxford University Press, 1984).

Šimečka, Milan. *The Restoration of Order: The Normalization of Czechoslovakia* (New York: Verso, 1984).

Škapová, Zdena. '*Sedmikrásky/Daisies*', in Peter Hames (ed.), *The Cinema of Central Europe* (London: Wallflower Press, 2004), pp. 129–37.

Škvorecký, Josef. *All the Bright Young Men and Women: A Personal History of the Czech Cinema*, translated by Michael Schonberg (Toronto: Peter Martin Associates, 1971).

——— *Jiří Menzel and the History of the Closely Watched Trains* (New York: Columbia University Press, 1982).

——— *Talkin' Moscow Blues* (London: Faber, 1988).

Šmejkal, František. 'From Lyrical Metaphors to Symbols of Fate: Czech Surrealism of the 1930s', in Jaroslav Anděl (ed.), *Czech Modernism 1900–1945* (Houston: Museum of Fine Arts, Houston, 1989), pp. 65–86.

Sontag, Susan. *On Photography* (New York: Farrar, Straus and Giroux, 1973).

Sorfa, David. 'Architorture: Jan Švankmajer and Surrealist Film', in Mark Shiel and Tony Fitzmaurice (eds), *Screening the City* (London: Verso, 2003).

——— 'The Object of Film in Jan Švankmajer', *KinoKultura*, Special Issue 4: Czech Cinema, November 2006 (http://www.kinokultura.com/specials/4/sorfa.shtml) (retrieved 10 August 2008).

Soviet Writers' Congress 1934: The Debate on Socialist Realism and Modernism in the Soviet Union (London: Lawrence and Wishart, 1977).

'Spisovatelé komunisté komunistickým dělníkům', in Štěpán Vlašín (ed.), *Avantgarda: Svazek 3: Generační diskuse* (Prague: Svoboda, 1970), pp. 47–53.

Srp, Karel. *Karel Teige*, translated by Karolina Vočadlo (Prague: Torst, 2001).

Stam, Robert, Robert Burgoyne and Sandy Flitterman-Lewis. *New Vocabularies in Film Semiotics: Structuralism, Post-Structuralism and Beyond* (London; New York: Routledge, 1992).

Steiner, Eugen. *The Slovak Dilemma* (Cambridge: Cambridge University Press, 1973).

Steiner, Peter. *The Deserts of Bohemia: Czech Fiction and its Social Context* (Ithaca; London: Cornell University Press, 2000).

Stojanović, Svetozar. *Between Ideals and Reality: A Critique of Socialism and Its Future* (New York; London; Toronto: Oxford University Press, 1973).

Štoll, Ladislav. 'Skutečnosti tváří v tvář', in Jiří Ševčík, Pavlína Morganová and Dagmar Dušová (eds), *České umění 1938–1989: programy, kritické texty, dokumenty* (Prague: Academia, 2001), pp. 138–40.

Suleiman, Susan Rubin. *Subversive Intent: Gender, Politics and the Avant-Garde* (Cambridge, MA: Harvard University Press, 1992).

Švácha, Rotislav (ed.). *Devětsil: Czech Avant-Garde Art, Architecture and Design of the 1920s and 30s* (Oxford: Museum of Modern Art, 1990).

Sviták, Ivan. 'Groteskní lyrika Jana Němce', *Film a doba*, No. 5, 1968, pp. 250–55.

———— *Man and His World: A Marxian View*, translated by Jarmila Veltruský (New York: Delta, 1970).

———— *The Czechoslovak Experiment 1968–1969* (New York; London: Columbia University Press, 1971).

———— *'The Politics of Culture'* by Antonín J. Liehm and Peter Kussi' [book review], *The American Political Science Review*, Vol. 67, No. 3. (Sep. , 1973), pp. 1073–74.

Svoboda, Jan. 'Stylistická kritika a situace filmového myšlení v Československu', *Film a doba*, No. 3, 1967, pp. 123–24.

Teige, Karel. 'Báseň, svět, člověk', in *Zvěrokruh*, no. 1, November 1930, pp. 9–15.

———— 'Deset let Surrealismu', in *Surrealismus v diskusi, Knihovna Levé fronty*, Vol. 8 (Prague: Levá fronta, 1934), pp. 7–56.

———— 'Poetism', translated by Alexandra Büchler, in Eric Dluhosch and Rotislav Švácha (eds), *Karel Teige 1900–1951: L'Enfant Terrible of the Czech Modernist Avant-Garde* (Cambridge, MA: M.I.T. Press, 1999), pp. 66–71.

———— *Svět, který se směje* (Prague: Akropolis, 2004).

———— *Svět, který voní* (Prague: Akropolis, 2004).

Tertz, Abram [Andrei Sinyavsky]. *The Trial Begins and On Socialist Realism*, translated by Max Hayward and George Dennis (London: Harvill Press, 1960).

Turner, Adrian. *'Daisies'*, in John Pym (ed.), *The Time Out Film Guide* (Harmondsworth: Penguin, 2000), p. 243.

'U.D.S.' [manifesto], in Josef Alan (ed.), *Alternativní Kultura: Příběh české společnosti 1945–1989* (Prague: Nakladatelství Lidové noviny, 2001), pp. 529–31.

Uhde, Jan. 'The Bare Bones of Horror: Jan Švankmajer's *Kostnice* (*The Ossuary*), *Kinoeye*, Vol. 2, Issue 1, 7 January 2002 (http://www.kinoeye.org/02/01/uhde01.php) (retrieved 1 August 2008).

Vagaday, Jozef. 'O autentickom filme a o veciach okolo hovorí Štefan Uher: Rozhovor s Štefanem Uherem', *Film a doba*, No. 6, 1963, pp. 288–91.

Veltruský, Jiří. 'Jan Mukařovský's Structural Poetics and Esthetics', *Poetics Today*, Vol. 2, No. 1b. (Winter, 1980–1981), pp. 117–57.

Walsh, Martin. '*Rome Open City; The Rise to Power of Louis XIV*: Re-evaluating Rossellini', *Jump Cut*, No. 15, 1977, pp. 13–15.

Wells, Paul. 'Animated Anxiety: Jan Švankmajer, Surrealism and the "Agit-Scare"', *Kinoeye*, Vol. 2, Issue 16, 21 October 2002 (http://www.kinoeye. org/02/16/wells16.php) (retrieved 20 September 2008).

Whyte, Alistair. *New Cinema in Eastern Europe* (London: Studio Vista, 1971).

Williams, Kieran. *The Prague Spring and its Aftermath: Czechoslovak Politics 1968–1970* (Cambridge: Cambridge University Press, 1997).

Wilson, David. '*Valerie and Her Week of Wonders*', *Monthly Film Bulletin*, Vol. 38, No. 448, May 1971, p. 104–5.

Wood, Robin. 'Narrative Pleasure: Two Films of Jacques Rivette', *Film Quarterly*, Vol. 35, No. 1, Autumn 1981, pp. 2–12.

Wordsworth, William. *Complete Poetical Works*, edited by Ernest de Selincourt and Thomas Hutchinson (Oxford: Oxford University Press, 1961).

Žalman, Jan. *Films and Filmmakers in Czechoslovakia* (Prague: Orbis, 1968).

Zandová [Zand], Gertraude. *Totální realismus a trapná poezie: Česká neoficiální literatura 1948–1953*, translated by Zuzana Adamová (Brno: Host, 2002).

'Zásadní stanovisko k projevu "sedmi"', in Štěpán Vlašín (ed.), *Avantgarda: Svazek 3: Generační diskuse* (Prague: Svoboda, 1970), p. 54–55.

Zeman, Z.A.B. *Prague Spring: A Report on Czechoslovakia 1968* (Harmondsworth: Penguin, 1969).

Zetkin, Clara. 'My Recollections of Lenin', in V.I. Lenin, *On the Emancipation of Women* (Moscow: Progress Publishers, 1972), pp. 95–123.

Žižek, Slavoj. *The Sublime Object of Ideology* (London: Verso, 1989).

—— *For They Know Not What They Do: Enjoyment as a Political Factor* (London: Verso, 1991).

—— *Enjoy Your Symptom!: Jacques Lacan in Hollywood and Out* (London; New York: Routledge, 1992).

—— 'Move the Underground!' (http://www.lacan.com/zizunder.htm) (retrieved 20 January 2008).

Zlatá šedesátá: Česká literatura a společnost v letech tání, kolotání a...zklamání: materiály z konference pořádané Ústavem pro českou literaturu AV ČR 16–18. června 1999 (Prague: Ústav pro českou literaturu, 2000).

Index